W9-DCV-129

SECOND EDITION

Intermediate Perl

Randal L. Schwartz, brian d foy, and Tom Phoenix

O'REILLY®

Beijing · Cambridge · Farnham · Köln · Sebastopol · Tokyo

Intermediate Perl, Second Edition

by Randal L. Schwartz, brian d foy, and Tom Phoenix

Copyright © 2012 Randal Schwartz, brian d foy, Tom Phoenix. All rights reserved.
Printed in the United States of America.

Published by O'Reilly Media, Inc., 1005 Gravenstein Highway North, Sebastopol, CA 95472.

O'Reilly books may be purchased for educational, business, or sales promotional use. Online editions are also available for most titles (*http://my.safaribooksonline.com*). For more information, contact our corporate/institutional sales department: 800-998-9938 or *corporate@oreilly.com*.

Editors: Simon St. Laurent and Shawn Wallace		**Indexer:** Lucie Haskins	
Production Editor: Kristen Borg		**Cover Designer:** Karen Montgomery	
Copyeditor: Absolute Service, Inc.		**Interior Designer:** David Futato	
Proofreader: Absolute Service, Inc.		**Illustrator:** Rebecca Demarest	

March 2006:	First Edition.
August 2012:	Second Edition.

Revision History for the Second Edition:

2012-07-20	First release
2013-06-07	Second release

See *http://oreilly.com/catalog/errata.csp?isbn=9781449393090* for release details.

Nutshell Handbook, the Nutshell Handbook logo, and the O'Reilly logo are registered trademarks of O'Reilly Media, Inc. *Intermediate Perl*, the image of an alpaca, and related trade dress are trademarks of O'Reilly Media, Inc.

Many of the designations used by manufacturers and sellers to distinguish their products are claimed as trademarks. Where those designations appear in this book, and O'Reilly Media, Inc., was aware of a trademark claim, the designations have been printed in caps or initial caps.

While every precaution has been taken in the preparation of this book, the publisher and authors assume no responsibility for errors or omissions, or for damages resulting from the use of the information contained herein.

ISBN: 978-1-449-39309-0

[LSI]

1370446347

Table of Contents

Foreword

Perl's object-oriented mechanism is classic prestidigitation. It takes a collection of Perl's existing non-OO features such as packages, references, hashes, arrays, subroutines, and modules, and then–with nothing up its sleeve–manages to conjure up fully functional objects, classes, and methods. Seemingly out of nowhere.

That's a great trick. It means you can build on your existing Perl knowledge and ease your way into OO Perl development, without first needing to conquer a mountain of new syntax or navigate an ocean of new techniques. It also means you can progressively fine-tune OO Perl to meet your own needs, by selecting from the existing constructs the one that best suits your task.

But there's a problem. Since Perl co-opts packages, references, hashes, arrays, subroutines, and modules as the basis of its OO mechanism, to use OO Perl you already need to understand packages, references, hashes, arrays, subroutines, and modules.

And there's the rub. The learning curve hasn't been eliminated; it's merely been pushed back half a dozen steps.

So then: how are you going to learn everything you need to know about non-OO Perl so you can start to learn everything you need to know about OO Perl?

This book is the answer. In the following pages, Randal draws on two decades of using Perl, and four decades of watching *Gilligan's Island* and *Mr. Ed*, to explain each of the components of Perl that collectively underpin its OO features. And, better still, he then goes on to show exactly how to combine those components to create useful classes and objects.

So if you still feel like Gilligan when it comes to Perl's objects, references, and modules, this book is just what the Professor ordered.

And that's straight from the horse's mouth.

—Damian Conway, May 2003

Preface

Almost 20 years ago (nearly an eternity in Internet time), Randal Schwartz wrote the first edition of *Learning Perl*. In the intervening years, Perl itself has grown substantially from a "cool" scripting language used primarily by Unix system administrators to a robust object-oriented programming language that runs on practically every computing platform known to mankind, and maybe some that aren't.

Throughout its six editions, *Learning Perl* remained about the same size, around 300 pages, and continued to cover much of the same material to remain compact and accessible to the beginning programmer. But there is much more to learn about Perl.

Randal called the first edition of this book *Learning Perl Objects, References, and Modules*, and we renamed its update *Intermediate Perl*, but we like to think of it as just *Learning More Perl*. This is the book that picks up where *Learning Perl* leaves off. We show how to use Perl to write larger programs.

As in *Learning Perl*, we designed each chapter to be small enough to read in just an hour or so. Each chapter ends with a series of exercises to help you practice what you've just learned, and the answers are provided in the appendix for your reference. And, like *Learning Perl*, we've developed the material in this book for use in a teaching environment.

Unless we note otherwise, everything in this book applies equally well to Perl on any platform, whether that is Unix, Linux, Windows ActivePerl from ActiveState, Strawberry Perl, or any other modern implementation of Perl. To use this book you just need to be comfortable with the material in *Learning Perl* and have the ambition to go further.

After you finish this book, you will have seen most of the core Perl language concepts that you'll need. The next book in the series is *Mastering Perl*, which focuses on applying what you already know to writing effective and robust Perl applications as well as managing the Perl software development life cycle.

At any point in your Perl career, you should also have *Programming Perl*, the (mostly) definitive bible of the language.

Structure of This Book

There are three major sections of this book. The first section deals with references, which are the keys to complex data structures as well as to object-oriented programming. The second section introduces objects and how Perl implements object-oriented programming. The third and last section deals with Perl's module structure, testing, and the community infrastructure for distributing our work.

You should read this book from front to back, stopping to do the exercises. Each chapter builds on preceding chapters, and we'll assume that you know the material from those chapters as we show new topics.

Chapter 1, Introduction
> An introduction to the material.

Chapter 2, Using Modules
> Use Perl's core modules as well as modules from other people. We're going to show you how to create your own modules later in the book, but until we do you can still use modules you already have.

Chapter 3, Intermediate Foundations
> Pick up some intermediate Perl skills you'll need for the rest of the book.

Chapter 4, Introduction to References
> Introduce a level of redirection to allow the same code to operate on different sets of data.

Chapter 5, References and Scoping
> Learn how Perl manages to keep track of pointers to data, and read an introduction to anonymous data structures and autovivification.

Chapter 6, Manipulating Complex Data Structures
> Create, access, and print arbitrarily deep and nested data structures including arrays of arrays and hashes of hashes.

Chapter 7, Subroutine References
> Capture behavior as an anonymous subroutine that you create dynamically and execute later.

Chapter 8, Filehandle References
> Store filehandles in scalar variables that you can easily pass around your program or store in data structures.

Chapter 9, Regular Expression References
> Compile regular expressions without immediately applying them, and use them as building blocks for larger patterns.

Chapter 10, Practical Reference Tricks
> Sorting complex operations, the *Schwartzian Transform*, and working with recursively defined data.

Chapter 11, Building Larger Programs
　Build larger programs by separating code into separate files and namespaces.

Chapter 12, Creating Your Own Perl Distribution
　Create a Perl distribution as your first step toward object-oriented programming.

Chapter 13, Introduction to Objects
　Work with classes, method calls, inheritance, and overriding.

Chapter 14, Introduction to Testing
　Start to test your modules so you find problems with the code as you create it.

Chapter 15, Objects with Data
　Add per instance data, including constructors, getters, and setters.

Chapter 16, Some Advanced Object Topics
　Use multiple inheritance, automatic methods, and references to filehandles.

Chapter 17, Exporter
　How use works, how we can decide what to export, and how we can create our own import routines.

Chapter 18, Object Destruction
　Add behavior to an object that is going away, including object persistence.

Chapter 19, Introduction to Moose
　Moose is an object framework available on CPAN.

Chapter 20, Advanced Testing
　Test complex aspects of code and metacode things such as documentation and test coverage.

Chapter 21, Contributing to CPAN
　Share your work with the world by uploading it to CPAN.

Appendix, Exercise Answers
　Where to go to get answers.

Conventions Used in This Book

The following typographic conventions are used in this book:

`Constant width`
　Used for function names, module names, filenames, environment variables, code snippets, and other literal text

Italics
　Used for emphasis and for new terms where they are defined

Using Code Examples

This book is here to help you get your job done. In general, you may use the code in this book in your programs and documentation. You do not need to contact us for permission unless you're reproducing a significant portion of the code. For example, writing a program that uses several chunks of code from this book does not require permission. Selling or distributing a CD-ROM of examples from O'Reilly books does require permission. Answering a question by citing this book and quoting example code does not require permission. Incorporating a significant amount of example code from this book into your product's documentation does require permission.

We appreciate, but do not require, attribution. An attribution usually includes the title, author, publisher, and ISBN. For example: "*Intermediate Perl* by Randal L. Schwartz, brian d foy, and Tom Phoenix. Copyright 2012 Randal L. Schwartz, brian d foy, and Tom Phoenix, 978-1-449-39309-0."

If you feel your use of code examples falls outside fair use or the permission given above, feel free to contact us at *permissions@oreilly.com*.

Safari® Books Online

Safari Books Online (*www.safaribooksonline.com*) is an on-demand digital library that delivers expert content in both book and video form from the world's leading authors in technology and business.

Technology professionals, software developers, web designers, and business and creative professionals use Safari Books Online as their primary resource for research, problem solving, learning, and certification training.

Safari Books Online offers a range of product mixes and pricing programs for organizations, government agencies, and individuals. Subscribers have access to thousands of books, training videos, and prepublication manuscripts in one fully searchable database from publishers like O'Reilly Media, Prentice Hall Professional, Addison-Wesley Professional, Microsoft Press, Sams, Que, Peachpit Press, Focal Press, Cisco Press, John Wiley & Sons, Syngress, Morgan Kaufmann, IBM Redbooks, Packt, Adobe Press, FT Press, Apress, Manning, New Riders, McGraw-Hill, Jones & Bartlett, Course Technology, and dozens more. For more information about Safari Books Online, please visit us online.

How to Contact Us

Please address comments and questions concerning this book to the publisher:

O'Reilly Media, Inc.
1005 Gravenstein Highway North
Sebastopol, CA 95472

800-998-9938 (in the United States or Canada)
707-829-0515 (international or local)
707-829-0104 (fax)

We have a web page for this book where we list errata, examples, and any additional information. You can access this page at:

http://oreil.ly/int-perl-2e

To comment or ask technical questions about this book, send an email to:

bookquestions@oreilly.com

For more information about our books, courses, conferences, and news, see our website at *http://www.oreilly.com.*

Find us on Facebook: *http://facebook.com/oreilly*

Follow us on Twitter: *http://twitter.com/oreillymedia*

Watch us on YouTube: *http://www.youtube.com/oreillymedia*

Acknowledgments

From Randal. In the preface of the first edition of *Learning Perl*, I acknowledged the Beaverton McMenamin's Cedar Hills Pub[1] just down the street from my house for the "rent-free booth-office space" while I wrote most of the draft on my Powerbook 140. Well, like wearing your lucky socks every day when your favorite team is in the playoffs, I wrote nearly all of this book (including these words) at the same brewpub, in hopes that the light of success of the first book will shine on me twice. (As I update this preface for the second edition, I can see that my lucky socks do indeed work!)

This McM's has the same great local microbrew beer and greasy sandwiches, but they've gotten rid of my favorite pizza bread, replacing it with new items like marionberry cobbler (a local treat) and spicy jambalaya. (And they added two booths, and put in some pool tables.) Also, instead of the Powerbook 140, I'm using a Titanium Powerbook, with 1,000 times more disk space, 500 times more memory, and a 200-times-faster CPU running a real Unix-based operating system (OS X) instead of the limited MacOS. I also uploaded all of the draft sections (including this one) over my 144K cell-phone modem and emailed them directly to the reviewers, instead of having to wait to rush home to my 9600-baud external modem and phone line. How times have changed!

So, thanks once again to the staff of the McMenamin's Cedar Hills Pub for the booth space and the hospitality.

---

1. *http://www.mcmenamins.com/*

Like the previous editions of *Learning Perl*, I also owe much of what I'm saying here and how I'm saying it to the students of Stonehenge Consulting Services who have given me immediate and precise feedback (by their glazed eyes and awkwardly constructed questions) when I was exceeding the "huh?" factor threshold. With that feedback over many dozens of presentations, I was able to keep refining and refactoring the materials that paved the way for this book.

Speaking of which, those materials started as a half-day "What's new in Perl 5?" summary commissioned by Margie Levine of Silicon Graphics, in addition to my frequently presented onsite four-day Llama course (targeted primarily for Perl Version 4 at the time). Eventually, I got the idea to beef up those notes into a full course and enlisted fellow Stonehenge presenter Joseph Hall for the task. (He's the one that selected the universe from which the examples are drawn.) Joseph developed a two-day course for Stonehenge in parallel with his excellent *Effective Perl Programming* book (Addison-Wesley Professional), which we then used as the course textbook (until now).

Other Stonehenge instructors have also dabbled a bit in the "Packages, References, Objects, and Modules" course over the years, including Chip Salzenberg and Tad McClellan. But the bulk of the recent changes have been the responsibility of my senior trainer Tom Phoenix, who has been "Stonehenge employee of the month" so often that I may have to finally give up my preferred parking space.

Tom Phoenix contributed most exercises in this book and a timely set of review notes during my writing process, including entire paragraphs for me to just insert in place of the drivel I had written. We work well as a team, both in the classroom and in our joint writing efforts. It is for this effort that we've acknowledged Tom as a coauthor, but I'll take direct blame for any parts of the book you end up hating; none of that could have possibly been Tom's fault.

And last but not least, a special thanks to brian d foy, who shepherded this book into its second revision, and wrote most of the changes between the previous edition and this edition.

A book is nothing without a subject and a distribution channel, and for that I must acknowledge longtime associates Larry Wall and Tim O'Reilly. Thanks guys, for creating an industry that has paid for my essentials, discretionary purchases, and dreams for nearly 20 years.

And, as always, a special thanks to Lyle and Jack for teaching me nearly everything I know about writing and convincing me that I was much more than a programmer who might learn to write; I was also a writer who happened to know how to program. Thank you.

And to you, the reader of this book, for whom I toiled away the countless hours while sipping a cold microbrew and scarfing down a piece of incredible cheesecake, trying to avoid spilling on my laptop keyboard: thank you for reading what I've written. I sincerely hope I've contributed (in at least a small way) to your Perl proficiency. If you ever meet me on the street, please say hi.[2] I'd like that. Thank you.

From brian. I have to thank Randal first, since I learned Perl from the first edition of *Learning Perl*, and learned the rest teaching the Llama and Alpaca courses for Stonehenge Consulting. Teaching is often the best way to learn.

The most thanks has to go to the Perl community, the wonderfully rich and diverse group of people who have made it a pleasure to work with the language and make the tools, websites, and modules that make Perl so useful. Many people have contributed indirectly to this book through my other work and discussions with them. There are too many to list, but if you've ever done anything with Perl with me, there's probably a little of you in this book.

From Tom. First of all, thanks to the entire team at O'Reilly for helping us to bring this book to fruition.

Thanks to my Stonehenge coworkers and the students I've worked with over the years, and the people I've assisted on Usenet. Your ideas and suggestions have greatly improved this material.

Especially deep thanks to my coauthor Randal for giving me freedom to explore teaching this material in varied ways.

To my wife Jenna Padbury, thanks for being a cat person, and everything thereafter.

From all of us. Thanks to our reviewers for providing comments on the draft of this book. Tom Christiansen did an amazing job not only correcting every technical problem he found, but also improving our writing quite a bit. This book is much better for it. David Golden, a fellow PAUSE admin and CPAN toolchain hacker, helped quite a bit in straightening out the details of the module release process. Several of the Moose crowd, including Stevan Little, Curtis "Ovid" Poe, and Jesse Luehrs, kindly helped with that chapter. Sawyer X, the current maintainer of `Module::Starter`, helped tremendously as we developed those parts of the book.

Thanks also to our many students who have let us know what parts of the course material have needed improvement over the years. It's because of you that we're all so proud of it today.

Thanks to the many Perl Mongers who have made us feel at home as we've visited your cities. Let's do it again sometime.

And finally, our sincerest thanks to our friend Larry Wall, for having the wisdom to share his really cool and powerful toys with the rest of the world so that we can all get our work done just a little bit faster, easier, and with more fun.

---

2. And yes, you can ask a Perl question at the same time. I don't mind.

CHAPTER 1
Introduction

Welcome to the next step in your understanding of Perl. You're probably here either because you want to learn to write programs that are more than 100 lines long or because your boss has told you to do so.

Our *Learning Perl* book was great because it introduced the use of Perl for short and medium programs (which is most of the programming done in Perl, we've observed). But, to keep "the Llama book" from being big and intimidating, we deliberately and carefully left a lot of information out.

In the pages that follow, you can get "the rest of the story" in the same style as our friendly Llama book. It covers what you need to write programs that are 100 to 10,000 (or even longer) lines long.

For example, you'll learn how to work with multiple programmers on the same project by writing reusable Perl modules that you can wrap in distributions usable by the common Perl tools. This is great, because unless you work 35 hours each day, you'll need some help with larger tasks. You'll also need to ensure that your code all fits with the other code as you develop it for the final application.

This book will also show you how to deal with larger and more complex data structures, such as what we might casually call a "hash of hashes" or an "array of arrays of hashes of arrays." Once you know a little about references, you're on your way to arbitrarily complex data structures, which can make your life much easier.

Then there's the buzzworthy notion of object-oriented programming, which allows parts of your code (or hopefully code from others) to be reused with minor or major variations within the same program. The book will cover that as well, even if you've never seen objects before.

An important aspect of working in teams is having a release cycle and a process for unit and integration testing. You'll learn the basics of packaging your code as a distribution and providing unit tests for that distribution, both for development and for verifying that your code works in your target environment.

And, just as was promised and delivered in *Learning Perl*, we'll entertain you along the way by interesting examples and bad puns. We've sent Fred and Barney and Betty and Wilma home, though. A new cast of characters will take the starring roles.

What Should You Know Already?

We'll presume that you've already read *Learning Perl*, using at least the fifth edition, or at least pretend you have, and that you've played enough with Perl to already have those basics down. For example, you won't see an explanation in this book that shows how to access the elements of an array or return a value from a subroutine.

Make sure you know the following things, all of which we covered in *Learning Perl*:

- How to run a Perl program on your system
- The three basic Perl variable types: scalars, arrays, and hashes
- Control structures such as `while`, `if`, `for`, and `foreach`
- Subroutines
- Basic regular expressions
- List operators such as `grep`, `map`, `sort`, and `print`
- File manipulation such as `open`, file reading, and `-X` (file tests)

You might pick up deeper insight into these topics in this book, but we're going to presume you know the basics.

The final parts of this book deal with distributions and contributing to CPAN. To do that, you should apply for a PAUSE account now so it's ready to use when you get there. Request an account at *https://pause.perl.org/pause/query?ACTION=request_id*.

strict and warnings

We introduced the `strict` and `warnings` pragmas in *Learning Perl*, and we expect that you'll use them for all of your code. However, for most of the code that you'll see in this book, assume that we've already turned on `strict` and `warnings` so we don't distract from the examples with repeated boilerplate code, just like we leave off the shebang line and the usual documentation bits. When we present full examples, we'll include these pragmas as well.

You might want to do what we do. Instead of starting a program from scratch, we open a template that has the usual bits of code in it. Until you develop your own template, complete with standard documentation and your favorite way of doing things, you can start with this simple one that you can assume is around all of our code examples:

```
#!/usr/local/bin/perl
use strict;
use warnings;

__END__
```

Perl v5.14

This book is current up to at least Perl v5.14, released in 2011. Usually, the details of the language are stable within the version. Some of the modules we use might have updates, especially since many *dual-lived* modules that come with Perl also show up separately on CPAN. Since we generally present the basic ideas of Perl and usually only brief overviews of modules, you should always check the modules' documentation for any updates.

 As we finish writing in the middle of 2012, Perl v5.16 is going to be released about a week after we turn this book in to the publisher, and we may have snuck some of those features in the book.

Some of the newer features require us to explicitly state that we want to use them so that they don't disturb programs targeting earlier versions of Perl. The easiest way to enable these features is to tell Perl which version we require. The number 5.014 has to have three digits after the decimal point (in case there is ever a Perl 5.140):

```
use 5.014;

say "Hello World!";
```

You can also write this with the v notation and its multiple parts:

```
use v5.14.2;
```

With the double-dotted form, we could leave off the v:

```
use 5.14.2;
```

But, that leaves us the temptation to leave it off in all cases.

Whenever we write some code that requires a feature from a specific version of *perl*, we'll insert that use v5.14 line (or whatever the appropriate version is) using the first version that made that feature available. If we can, we'll also show a version of the code that can work with earlier versions of Perl. We consider Perl v5.8, first released in 2002, to be the earliest version that anyone should use, so code samples that don't specify a version assume Perl v5.8. In general, we strive to write code that works for as many people and as many versions of Perl as possible, but we also want you to be as up-to-date as you wish to be.

To learn more about some of the basics of Perl v5.14, you might want to check out *Learning Perl, Sixth Edition*.

A Note on Versions

In this book, we write the Perl version as v5.*M.N*, with the leading *v*. So far, we've also prefixed the version with "Perl," but that's going to get tedious as we mention version differences. Instead, we'll leave off the Perl for this point on. When we say "v5.14.2," we're talking about Perl 5.14.2. That's the current *maintenance* version as we write this book, although v5.16 is right around the corner.

The number after the v5 can be either odd or even, and these distinguish between the experimental and maintenance versions. The maintenance version, such as v5.14, is for normal users and production use. The experimental version, such as v5.15, is where the Perl 5 Porters add new features, reimplement or optimize code, and make other unstable changes. When they are ready, they graduate the experimental version to a maintenance version by bumping that second number to the next higher even number.

The third number, the 2 in v5.14.2 for instance, is a *point release*. When we say v5.14, our point should apply to all point releases in that version. Sometimes, we need to denote a particular version; from *Learning Perl*, you might remember that between v5.10.0 and v5.10.1, smart matching fixed a serious design bug and changed behavior.

This book is strictly about v5. There's another thing, sometimes called Perl v6, but that's related to v5 tangentially. It's designed as a new language specification and is also designed by Larry Wall, but it's not an upgrade to v5 (even if, in 2000, we thought it might be). We know that's confusing, and so do the v6 people, which is why the implementations of the v6 specification have been given different names, such as Rakudo and Niecza.

What About All Those Footnotes?

Like *Learning Perl*, this book relegates some of the more esoteric items out of the way for the first reading and places those items in footnotes.[1] You should skip those the first time through and pick them up on a rereading. You will not find anything in a footnote that you'll need to understand any of the material we present later.

What's With the Exercises?

It's critical that you do the exercises. Hands-on training gets the job done better. The best way to provide this training is with a series of exercises after every half hour to hour of presentation. If you're a speed reader, the end of the chapter may come a bit sooner than a half hour. Slow down, take a breather, and do the exercises!

Each exercise has a "minutes to complete" rating. We intend for this rating to hit the midpoint of the bell curve, but don't feel bad if you take more or less time. Sometimes

---

1. Like this.

it's just a matter of how many times you've faced similar programming tasks in your studies or jobs. Use the numbers merely as a guideline.

Every exercise has its answer in the Appendix. Again, try not to peek; you'll ruin the value of the exercise.

How to Get Help

As the book authors, we're always glad to help when we can, but we're already inundated with more email than we can manage. There are several online resources where you can get help, either from us directly, or from many of the other helpful people in the Perl community.

Stack Overflow (http://www.stackoverflow.com/)
> Stack Overflow is a no-pay question-and-answer site for all sorts of programming questions, and there are many clueful Perlers who regularly answer your questions. You're likely to get excellent answers within an hour and for free. You might even get an answer from one of the authors.

Perlmonks (http://www.perlmonks.org/)
> Perlmonks is an online Perl community where you can ask questions, post your thoughts on Perl, and interact with other Perlers. If you have a question regarding something about Perl, people have probably already discussed it at Perlmonks. You can search the archives or start a new thread.

learn@perl.org and http://learn.perl.org/
> The *learn@perl.org* mailing list is specifically designed as a safe place for Perl neophytes to ask questions without fear that you are bothering anyone. It's just waiting for your questions, no matter how basic you think they are.

module-authors@perl.org
> If your question is specifically about writing and distributing modules, there's a special mailing list for that: *module-authors@perl.org*.

comp.lang.perl.misc
> If Usenet is more of your thing, you can ask questions on *comp.lang.perl.misc*. Several longtime Perl users monitor the group, and sometimes they are even helpful.

What If I'm a Perl Course Instructor?

If you're a Perl instructor who has decided to use this as your textbook, you should know that each set of exercises is short enough for most students to complete the whole set in 45 minutes to an hour, with a little time left over for a break. Some chapters' exercises should be quicker, and some may take longer. That's because once all those little numbers in square brackets were written, we discovered that we don't know how to add.

So let's get started. Class begins after you turn the page...

Exercises

At the end of each chapter, we've included exercises like these. Before each exercise, we show the time we think it will take most people to complete the exercise. If you take longer, that's just fine, at least until we figure out how to make ebooks with timers.

You can find the answers to this exercises in "Answers for Chapter 1" on page 311.

1. [5 minutes] Get a PAUSE account by requesting it from *http://pause.perl.org/*. You'll need this for the last chapter in the book, and we want it waiting for you.

2. [5 minutes] Visit this book's website, *http://www.intermediateperl.com/*. You should be especially interested in the Download section, which has files useful for the exercises. Download the archive so you have it even if you don't have Internet access later.

CHAPTER 2

Using Modules

The killer feature of Perl is the Comprehensive Perl Archive Network, which we just call CPAN. Perl already comes with many modules, but there are many more third-party modules available from CPAN. If we have a problem to solve or a task to complete with Perl, there's probably a module on CPAN that will help us. An effective Perl programmer is the one who uses CPAN wisely. We covered this briefly in *Learning Perl*, but we'll cover it again here. It's that important.

 We can explore CPAN through its master site (*http://www.cpan.org/*) or one of its search interfaces, CPAN Search (*http://search.cpan.org/*) and MetaCPAN (*https://www.metacpan.org/*).

Modules are the building blocks for our programs. They can provide reusable subroutines, variables, and even object-oriented classes. On our way to building our own modules, we'll show some of those you might be interested in. We'll also look at the basics of using modules that others have already written.

As we noted in *Learning Perl*, we don't have to understand everything about modules and how they work on the inside to use them (although by the end of this book you should know much more about that). By following the examples in the module documentation, we can still get quite a bit done. To jump-start our Perl, we'll start to use Perl modules right away even though we explain their mechanics and special syntax later.

The Standard Distribution

Perl comes with many of the popular modules already. Indeed, most of the over 66 MB of the v5.14 distribution is from modules. In October 1996, v5.3.7 had 98 modules. Today, in the beginning of 2012, v5.14.2 has 652. Indeed, this is one of the advantages of Perl: it already comes with a lot of stuff that we need to make useful and complex programs without doing extra work ourselves.

Use `Module::CoreList` to see the modules that came with any version of Perl. That's what we did to get those numbers, after all.

Throughout this book, we'll try to identify which modules come with *perl* (and, usually, which version of *perl* first included them). We'll call these "core modules" or note that they're in "the standard distribution." If we have *perl*, we should have these modules. Since we're using v5.14 as we write this, we'll assume that's the current version of Perl when we consider what's in core.

As we develop our code, we may want to consider whether we wish to use only core modules so that we can be sure that anyone with *perl* will have that module as long as they have at least the same version as us. We'll avoid that debate here, mostly because we love CPAN too much to do without it. We'll also show how to figure out which modules come with which version of Perl in a moment.

Exploring CPAN

CPAN is arguably the most attractive feature of Perl, and it got that way by the hard work of some dedicated volunteers providing tools and services to make it easy for people to release quality software and easy for users to evaluate and install the modules. Although this isn't a comprehensive list of useful CPAN tools, it includes the services we most often use. Starting with this list, we'll quickly find the other useful services, too.

CPAN Search (http://search.cpan.org/)
    The most popular and well-known CPAN search service is Graham Barr's CPAN Search. We can browse or search for modules, and each distribution page has links to the important facts and information about that distribution, including information from third parties such as test results, bug reports, and so on.

MetaCPAN (https://www.metacpan.org/)
    MetaCPAN is the next generation discovery interface for CPAN. It does just about everything that CPAN Search does, but adds an API so we can write our own applications on top of their data.

CPAN Testers (http://cpantesters.org/)
    Every module that an author uploads to CPAN is automatically tested. An army of testers downloads the current releases and tests them on their platforms. They send their results back to the central CPAN Testers database, which collates all of the reports. As a module author, we have a free testing service. As a module user, we can check test reports to judge a distribution's quality or to see if it is likely to work with our setup.

CPANdeps (http://deps.cpantesters.org/)

David Cantrell went a bit further than CPAN Testers by combining information about module dependencies with test reports. Instead of relying solely on a distribution's own tests, we can see the likelihood of installation problems by noting the test results from the entire dependency chain. One of the frustrating tasks with any software installation is a failure in the middle of the process, and CPANdeps can help us head off those problems. As part of the service, David also maintains the C5.6PAN and C5.8PAN, which are specialized versions of CPAN with only the latest version of each module that works on v5.6 and v5.8, respectively.

CPAN RT (http://rt.cpan.org/)

RT is the issue tracker from Best Practical, and they've kindly set up a service for CPAN authors. Every module of CPAN automatically gets an issue queue in RT, and for many modules, RT is the main issue queue. Some authors may have other bug-tracking preferences, but RT is a good place to start.

Using Modules

Almost every Perl module comes with documentation, and even though we might not know how all the behind-the-scenes magic works, we really don't have to worry about that stuff if we know how to use the interface. That's why the interface is there, after all: to hide the details.

 We can also use the *http://perldoc.perl.org/* website to read the documentation for several versions of Perl, in either HTML or PDF formats.

On our local machine, we can read the module documentation with the `perldoc` command.[1] We give it the module name we're interested in, and it prints its documentation:

```
% perldoc File::Basename

NAME
    File::Basename - Parse file paths into directory, filename and suffix.

SYNOPSIS
    use File::Basename;

    ($name,$path,$suffix) = fileparse($fullname,@suffixlist);
    $name = fileparse($fullname,@suffixlist);

    $basename = basename($fullname,@suffixlist);
    $dirname  = dirname($fullname);
```

---

1. On Unix, the man command works, too.

```
DESCRIPTION
       These routines allow you to parse file paths into their directory,
       filename and suffix.
```

We've included only the top portion of the documentation to show the most important section (at least, the most important when we're starting). Module documentation typically follows the old Unix manpage format, which starts with a NAME and SYN-OPSIS section.

The synopsis gives us examples of the module's use, and if we can suspend understanding for a bit and follow the example, we can use the module. That is to say, it may be that we're not yet familiar with some of the Perl techniques and syntax in the synopsis, but we can generally just follow the example and make everything work.

Now, since Perl is a mix of procedural, functional, object-oriented, and other sorts of language types, Perl modules come in variety of different interfaces. We'll employ these modules in slightly different fashions, but as long as we can check the documentation, we shouldn't have a problem.

Functional Interfaces

To load a module, we use the Perl built-in use. We're not going to go into all of the details here, but we'll get to those in Chapter 11 and Chapter 17. At the moment, we just want to use the module. We start with File::Basename, that same module from the core distribution. To load it into our script, we say:

```
use File::Basename;
```

When we do this, File::Basename introduces three subroutines, fileparse, basename, and dirname, into our script (using the stuff we show in Chapter 17). From this point forward, we can use the subroutines just as if we had defined them directly in the same file:

```
my $basename = basename( $some_full_path );
my $dirname  = dirname(  $some_full_path );
```

These routines pick out the filename and the directory parts of a pathname. For example, if we were running on Windows and $some_full_path were D:\Projects\Island Rescue\plan7.rtf, then $basename would be plan7.rtf and the $dirname would be D:\Projects\Island Rescue. If we were running on a Unix-like system and $some _full_path were /home/Gilligan/Projects/Island Rescue/plan7.rtf, then $basename would be plan7.rtf and the $dirname would be /home/Gilligan/Projects/Island Rescue.

The File::Basename module knows what sort of system it's on, and thus its functions figure out how to correctly parse the strings for the different delimiters we might encounter.

However, suppose we already had a `dirname` subroutine. We've now overwritten it with the definition provided by `File::Basename`! If we had turned on warnings, we would have seen a message stating that, but otherwise, Perl really doesn't care.

Selecting What to Import

Fortunately, we can tell the `use` operation to limit its actions by specifying a list of subroutine names following the module name, called the *import list*:

```
use File::Basename ('fileparse', 'basename');
```

Now the module gives us only those two subroutines and leaves our own `dirname` alone. But this is awkward to type, so more often we'll see this written with the quotewords operator:

```
use File::Basename qw( fileparse basename );
```

Even if there's only one item, we tend to write it with a `qw( )` list for consistency and maintenance; often, we'll go back to say "give me another one from here," and it's simpler if it's already a `qw( )` list.

We've protected the local `dirname` routine, but what if we still want the functionality provided by `File::Basename`'s `dirname`? No problem. We just spell it out with its full package specification:

```
my $dirname = File::Basename::dirname($some_path);
```

The list of names following `use` doesn't change which subroutines are defined in the module's package (in this case, `File::Basename`). We can always use the full name regardless of the import list, as in:

```
my $basename = File::Basename::basename($some_path);
```

 We don't need the ampersand in front of any of these subroutine invocations because the subroutine name is already known to the compiler following `use`.

In an extreme (but extremely useful) case, we can specify an empty list for the import list, as in:

```
use File::Basename ();              # no import
my $base = File::Basename::basename($some_path);
```

An empty list is different from an absent list. An empty list says "don't give me anything," while an absent list says "give me the defaults." If the module's author has done their job well, the default will probably be exactly what we want.

Object-Oriented Interfaces

Contrast the subroutines imported by File::Basename with what another core module has by looking at File::Spec. The File::Spec module is designed to support common file specification operations. (A file specification is usually a file or directory name, but it may be a name of a file that doesn't exist—in which case, it's not really a filename, is it?)

 We can use File::Spec::Functions if we want a functional interface.

Unlike the File::Basename module, the File::Spec module has a primarily object-oriented interface. We load the module with use, as we did before:

```
use File::Spec;
```

However, since this module has an object-oriented interface, it doesn't import any subroutines. Instead, the interface tells us to access the functionality of the module using its class methods. The catfile method joins a list of strings with the appropriate directory separator:

```
my $filespec = File::Spec->catfile( $homedir{gilligan},
    'web_docs', 'photos', 'USS_Minnow.gif' );
```

This calls the class method catfile of the File::Spec class, which builds a path appropriate for the local operating system and returns a single string.[2] This is similar in syntax to the nearly two dozen other operations provided by File::Spec.

The File::Spec module provides several other methods for dealing with file paths in a portable manner. We can read more about portability issues in the *perlport* documentation.

A More Typical Object-Oriented Module: Math::BigInt

So as not to get dismayed about how "un-OO" the File::Spec module seems since it doesn't create objects, we look at yet another core module, Math::BigInt, which can handle integers beyond Perl's native reach.

---

2. That string might be something like */home/gilligan/web_docs/photos/USS_Minnow.gif* on a Unix system. On a Windows system, it would typically use backslashes as directory separators. This module lets us write portable code easily, at least where file specs are concerned.

Perl is limited by the architecture it's on. It's one of the few places where the hardware shows through.

Instead of using numbers as literals, `Math::BigInt` turns them into numbers:

```
use Math::BigInt;

my $value = Math::BigInt->new(2);  # start with 2

$value->bpow(1000);                # take 2**1000

print $value->bstr, "\n";          # print it out
```

As before, this module imports nothing. Its entire interface uses class methods, such as new, against the class name to create instances, and then calls instance methods, such as bpow and bstr, against those instances.

Fancier Output with Modules

One of Perl's strengths is its reporting capabilities. We might think that is limited to just text, but with the right module, we can create just about any format. For instance, with Spreadsheet::WriteExcel, we can be the star of our office as we make not only useful, but nicely formatted Excel documents.

As we may already know from using the Excel application directly, we start with a workbook and put our stuff in worksheets. Starting with the code directly from the documentation, we easily create our first worksheet:

```
use Spreadsheet::WriteExcel;

# Create a new Excel workbook
my $workbook = Spreadsheet::WriteExcel->new('perl.xls');

# Add a worksheet
my $worksheet = $workbook->add_worksheet();
```

From there, we can insert information. Like Excel, the module can track rows and columns as letters for the rows and a number for the column. To put something in the first cell, we use the write method by following the example in the documentation:

```
$worksheet->write( 'A1', 'Hello Excel!' );
```

Inside our program, however, it's easier to track both rows and columns as numbers, so Spreadsheet::WriteExcel does that, too. The write method is smart enough to recognize which cell description we are using, although we have to remember that the module counts from zero, so the first row is 0 and the first column is 0:

```
$worksheet->write( 0, 0, 'Hello Excel' ); # in Excel's A1 cell
```

This lets us to do quite a bit already, but we can do even more by making our worksheet look a little prettier. First we have to create a format:

```
my $red_background = $workbook->add_format(
    color    => 'white',
    bg_color => 'red',
    bold     => 1,
    );

my $bold = $workbook->add_format(
    bold     => 1,
    );
```

Once we have a format, we can use it with our calls to `write` by supplying it as the last argument:

```
$worksheet->write( 0, 0, 'Colored cell', $red_background );
$worksheet->write( 0, 1, 'bold cell', $bold );
```

Besides `write`, there are several methods that handle specific types of data. If we wanted to insert the string 01234 exactly like that, we don't want Excel to ignore the leading 0. Without giving Excel a hint, however, it does its best to guess what the data is. We tell Excel that it is a string by using `write_string`:

```
my $product_code = '01234';
$worksheet->write_string( 0, 2, $product_code );
```

There are several other specializations of the `write` method, so check out the module documentation to see what else we can put into a cell.

Besides data, we can also create formulas. We could use the `write_formula` method, but our string starts with an = (just as it would in the GUI):

```
$worksheet->write( 'A2', 37 );
$worksheet->write( 'B2', 42 );
$worksheet->write( 'C2', '= A2 + B2');
```

There's a lot more to this module, and we should be able to quickly figure out its other features by checking its documentation. We'll also show some more examples as we go through the chapters on references.

What's in Core?

Core, or *the Standard Library* or *Distribution* or *Version*, is the set of modules and add-ons that comes with the standard distribution (the one we'd download from CPAN). When people talk about "core," they are most often talking about the set of modules that we can count on any particular Perl having, usually so we can be sure that someone using our program doesn't need to install extra modules.

This has become a bit fuzzy, though. Some distributions, such as Strawberry Perl (*http://strawberryperl.com/*) or ActivePerl (*http://www.activestate.com/activeperl*), include extra modules. Some vendor versions, such as OS X, add modules to the Perl packages they distribute with their operating system, or even change some of the standard modules. Those situations aren't that annoying. Annoyance comes from the vendors that remove parts from the standard distribution or break up the standard distribution into multiple vendor packages so we have to work to get what we should already have.[3]

The `Module::CoreList` module is really just a data structure and interface that pulls together the historical information about the modules that came with the versions of v5 and give us a programmatic way to access them. It's a mix of variables and object-like interfaces.

We can see which version of a module came with a particular version of Perl, which we specify with five digits after the decimal place (three for the minor version and two for the patch level):

```
use Module::CoreList;

print $Module::CoreList::version{5.01400}{CPAN}; # 1.9600
```

Sometimes we want to know it the other way around: which version of Perl first put a module into the standard library? `Module::Build` is the Perl build system, which we'll show in Chapter 12. `Module::CoreList` has been part of the Standard Library since v5.8.9:

```
use Module::CoreList;

print Module::CoreList->first_release('Module::Build'); # 5.009004
```

If we want to check a module's first release, we don't need to write a program since one already comes with `Module::CoreList`. We run the `corelist` program:

```
% corelist Module::Build
```

```
Module::Build was first released with perl v5.9.4
```

If we have a recent version of Perl, we should also already have `Module::CoreList`, which we know by using the module to find out about itself:

```
% corelist Module::CoreList
```

```
Module::CoreList was first released with perl v5.8.9
```

The Comprehensive Perl Archive Network

CPAN is the result of many volunteers working together, many of whom were originally operating their own little (or big) Perl FTP sites back before that Web thing came along. They coordinated their efforts on the *perl-packrats* mailing list in late 1993 and decided that disks were getting cheap enough that the same information should be replicated on all sites rather than having specialization on each site. The idea took about a year

---

3. According to *perl*'s license, these vendors aren't allowed to call these modified versions "perl," but they do anyway.

to ferment, and Jarkko Hietaniemi established the Finnish FTP site as the CPAN mothership from which all other mirrors drew their daily or hourly updates.

Part of the work involved rearranging and organizing the separate archives. Places were established for Perl binaries for non-Unix architectures, scripts, and Perl's source code itself. However, the modules portion has come to be the largest and most interesting part of the CPAN.

The modules in CPAN are organized as a symbolic-link tree in hierarchical functional categories, pointing to author directories where the actual files are located. The modules area also contains indices that are generally in easy-to-parse-with-Perl formats, such as the `Data::Dumper` output for the detailed module index. These indices are all derived automatically from databases at the master server using other Perl programs. Often, the mirroring of the CPAN from one server to another is done with a now-ancient Perl program called *mirror.pl*.

From its small start of a few mirror machines, CPAN has now grown to over 200 public archives in all corners of the Net, all churning away updating at least daily, sometimes as frequently as hourly. No matter where we are in the world, we can find a nearby CPAN mirror from which to pull the latest goodies.

One of the CPAN search and aggregation sites, such as *https://www.metacpan.org/* or *http://search.cpan.org/*, will probably become our favorite way to interact with the module repository. From these websites, we can search for modules, look at their documentation, browse through their distributions, inspect their CPAN Testers reports, and many other things.

Installing Modules from CPAN

Installing a simple module from CPAN can be straightforward. We can use the `cpan` program that comes with Perl. We tell it which modules to install. If we want to install the `Perl::Critic` module, which can review code automatically, we give `cpan` that module name:

```
% cpan Perl::Critic
```

The first time we run this, we might have to go through the configuration steps to initialize `CPAN.pm`, but after that it should get directly to work. The program downloads the module and starts to build it. If the module depends on other modules, `cpan` will automatically fetch and then build those as well.

If we start `cpan` with no arguments, we start the interactive shell from `CPAN.pm`. From the shell prompt, we can issue commands. We can install `Perl::Tidy`, the module that can clean up the formatting of Perl code:

```
% cpan
cpan> install Perl::Tidy
```

To read about the other features of `cpan`, we can read its documentation with `perldoc`:

```
% perldoc cpan
```

CPANPLUS became core with v5.10, and it provides another programmatic interface to CPAN. It works much like CPAN.pm, but also has some extra features we won't show here. CPANPLUS has the cpanp command, and we use the -i switch with it to install modules:

```
% cpanp -i Perl::Tidy
```

Like cpan, we can start an interactive shell and then install the module we need. We install the module that allows us to programmatically create Excel spreadsheets:

```
% cpanp
CPAN Terminal> i Spreadsheet::WriteExcel
```

To read about the other features of cpanp, we can read its documentation with *perldoc*:

```
% perldoc cpanp
```

CPANminus

There's another handy tool, *cpanm* (for *cpanminus*), although it doesn't come with Perl (yet). It's designed as a zero-conf, lightweight CPAN client that handles most of what people want to do. We can download the single file from *http://xrl.us/cpanm* and follow its easy instructions to get started.

Once we have *cpanm*, we tell it which modules to install:

```
% cpanm DBI WWW::Mechanize
```

Installing Modules Manually

We could also do the work ourselves that cpan does for us, which can at least be educational if we have never tried it before. If we understand what the tools are doing, we'll have an easier time tracking down problems as we run into them.

We download the module distribution archive, unpack it, and change into its directory. We use wget here, but which download tool we use doesn't matter. We have to find the exact URL to use, which we can get from one of the CPAN sites:

```
% wget http://www.cpan.org/.../HTTP-Cookies-Safari-1.10.tar.gz
% tar -xzf HTTP-Cookies-Safari-1.10.tar.gz
% cd HTTP-Cookies-Safari-1.10
```

From there, we go one of two ways (which we'll explain in detail in Chapter 12). If we find a file named *Makefile.PL*, we run this series of commands to build, test, and finally install the source:

```
% perl Makefile.PL
% make
% make test
% make install
```

If we don't have permission to install modules in the system-wide directories, we can tell *perl* to install them under another path by using the `INSTALL_BASE` argument:

 Perl's default library directories are set by whoever configured and installed *perl*, even if that meant they accepted the default settings. We can see them with *perl –V*.

```
% perl Makefile.PL INSTALL_BASE=/Users/home/Ginger
```

To make *perl* look in that directory for modules, we can set the `PERL5LIB` environment variable. Perl adds those directories to its module directory search list. Here's how we'd do that for the Bourne shell:

```
% export PERL5LIB=/Users/home/Ginger/lib
```

We can also use the `lib` pragma to add to the module search path, although this is not as friendly since not only we have to change the code but also because it might not be the same directory on other machines where we want to run the code:

```
#!/usr/bin/perl
use lib qw(/Users/home/Ginger/lib);
```

Backing up for a minute, if we found a *Build.PL* file instead of a *Makefile.PL*, the process is the same. These distributions use `Module::Build` to build and install code:

```
% perl Build.PL
% perl Build
% perl Build test
% perl Build install
```

To install into our private directories using `Module::Build`, we add the `--install_base` parameter. We tell Perl how to find modules the same way we did before:

```
% perl Build.PL --install_base /Users/home/Ginger
```

Sometimes we find both *Makefile.PL* and *Build.PL* in a distribution. What do we do then? We can use either one.

Setting the Path at the Right Time

Perl finds modules by looking through the directories in the special Perl array, `@INC`. When our *perl* was compiled, a default list of directories was chosen for the module search path. We can see these in the output we get from running *perl* with the `-V` command-line switch:

```
% perl -V
```

We can also write a Perl one-liner to print them:

```
% perl -le "print for @INC"
```

The use statement executes at compile time, so it looks at the module search path, @INC, at compile time. That can break our program in hard-to-understand ways unless we take @INC into consideration. We need to make our @INC modifications before we try to load modules.

For example, suppose we have our own directory under */home/gilligan/lib*, and we installed our own `Navigation::SeatOfPants` module in */home/gilligan/lib/Navigation/SeatOfPants.pm*. When we load our module, Perl won't find it:

```
use Navigation::SeatOfPants;    # where is it?
```

Perl complains to us that it can't find the module in @INC and shows us all of the directories it has in that array:

```
Can't locate Navigation/SeatofPants.pm in @INC (@INC contains: ...)
```

We might think that we should just add our module directory to @INC before we call the use. However, even adding:

```
unshift @INC, '/Users/gilligan/lib';    # broken
use Navigation::SeatOfPants;
```

doesn't work. Why? Because the `unshift` happens at runtime, long after the use was attempted at compile time. The two statements are lexically adjacent but not temporally adjacent. Just because we wrote them next to each other doesn't mean they execute in that order. We want to change @INC before the use executes. One way to fix this is to add a `BEGIN` block around the `unshift`:

```
BEGIN { unshift @INC, '/Users/gilligan/lib'; }
use Navigation::SeatOfPants;
```

Now the `BEGIN` block compiles and executes at compile time, setting up the proper path for the following use.

However, this is noisy and prone to require far more explanation than we might be comfortable with, especially for the maintenance programmer who has to edit our code later. We replace all that clutter with that simple pragma we used before:

```
use lib '/Users/gilligan/lib';
use Navigation::SeatOfPants;
```

Here, the `lib` pragma takes one or more arguments and adds them at the beginning of the @INC array, just like `unshift` did before. It works because it executes at compile time, not at runtime. Hence, it's ready in time for the use immediately following.

 use `lib` also unshifts an architecture-dependent library below the requested library, making it more valuable than the explicit counterpart presented earlier.

Because a use `lib` pragma will pretty much always have a site-dependent pathname, it is traditional and we encourage you to put it near the top of the file. This makes it easier to find and to update when we need to move the file to a new system or when the lib directory's name changes. (We can eliminate use lib entirely if we can install our modules in a standard @INC location, but that's not always practical.)

Think of use lib as not "use this library," but rather "use this path to find my libraries (and modules)." Too often, we see code written like:

```
use lib '/Users/gilligan/lib/Navigation/SeatOfPants.pm'; # WRONG
```

and then the programmer wonders why it didn't pull in the definitions. The use lib indeed runs at compile time, so this also doesn't work:

```
my $LIB_DIR = '/Users/gilligan/lib';
...
use lib $LIB_DIR;     # BROKEN
use Navigation::SeatOfPants;
```

Perl establishes the declaration of the $LIB_DIR variable at compile time (so we won't get an error with use strict, although the actual use lib should complain), but the actual assignment of the */Users/gilligan/lib/* value doesn't happen until runtime. Oops, too late again!

At this point, we need to put something inside a BEGIN block or perhaps rely on yet another compile-time operation: setting a constant with use constant:

```
use constant LIB_DIR => '/Users/gilligan/lib';
...
use lib LIB_DIR;
use Navigation::SeatOfPants;
```

There. Fixed again. That is, until we need the library to depend on the result of a calculation. This should handle about 99 percent of our needs.

We don't always have to know the path ahead of time either. In the previous examples, we've hardcoded the paths. If we don't know what those will be because we're passing code around to several machines, the FindBin module, which comes with Perl, can help. It finds the full path to the script directory so we can use it to build paths:

```
use FindBin qw($Bin);
```

Now, in $Bin is the path to the directory that holds our script. If we have our libraries in the same directory, our next line can be:

```
use lib $Bin;
```

If we have the libraries in a directory close to the script directory, we put the right path components together to make it work:

```
use lib "$Bin/lib";    # in a subdirectory
```

```
use lib "$Bin/../lib"; # up one, then down into lib
```

So, if we know the relative path from the script directory, we don't have to hardcode the whole path. This makes the script more portable.

Some of these techniques will matter more to us when we start writing our own modules in Chapter 12.

Setting the Path Outside the Program

The use lib has a big drawback. We have to put the library path in the source. We might have our local modules installed in one place, but our coworkers have them in another. We don't want to change the source every time we get it from a teammate, and we don't want to list everyone's locations in the source. Perl offers a couple of ways that we can extend the module search path without bothering the source.

Extending @INC with PERL5LIB

The Skipper must edit each program that uses his private libraries to include those lines from the previous section. If that seems like too much editing, he can instead set the PERL5LIB environment variable to the directory name. For example, in the C shell, he'd use the line:

```
setenv PERL5LIB /home/skipper/perl-lib
```

In Bourne-style shells, he'd use something like:

```
export PERL5LIB=/home/skipper/perl-lib
```

The Skipper can set PERL5LIB once and forget about it. However, unless Gilligan has the same PERL5LIB environment variable, his program will fail! While PERL5LIB is useful for personal use, we can't rely on it for programs we intend to share with others. (And we can't make our entire team of programmers add a common PERL5LIB variable. Believe us, we've tried.)

The PERL5LIB variable can include multiple directories separated by colons on Unix-like systems and semicolons on Windows-like systems (other than that, we're on our own). Perl inserts all specified directories at the beginning of @INC. On Unix using a *bash*-like shell, that would be:

```
% export PERL5LIB=/home/skipper/perl-lib:/usr/local/lib/perl5
```

On Windows, that would be:

```
C:\.. set PERL5LIB="C:/lib/skipper;C:/lib/perl5"
```

While a sysadmin might add a setting of PERL5LIB to a system-wide startup script, most people frown on that. The purpose of PERL5LIB is to enable nonadministrators to extend Perl to recognize additional directories. If a system administrator wants additional directories, he merely needs to recompile and reinstall Perl.

Extending @INC on the Command Line

If Gilligan recognizes that one of the Skipper's programs is missing the proper directive, Gilligan can either add the proper PERL5LIB variable or invoke *perl* directly with one or more -I options. For example, to invoke the Skipper's get_us_home program, the command line might be something like:

```
% perl -I/home/skipper/perl-lib /home/skipper/bin/get_us_home
```

Obviously, it's easier for Gilligan if the program itself defines the extra libraries. But sometimes adding a -I fixes things right up. This works even if Gilligan can't edit the Skipper's program. He still has to be able to read it, but Gilligan can use this technique to try a new version of his library with the Skipper's program, for example.

 Extending @INC with either PERL5LIB or -I also automatically adds the version- and architecture-specific subdirectories of the specified directories. Adding these directories automatically simplifies the task of installing Perl modules that include architecture- or version-sensitive components, such as compiled C code.

local::lib

By default, the CPAN tools install new modules into the same directories where *perl* is, but we probably don't have permission to create files there, or we might have to invoke some sort of administrator privilege to do so. This is a common problem with Perl neophytes because they don't realize how easy it is to install Perl modules anywhere they like. Once we know how to do that, we can install and use any module we like without bugging a sysadmin to do it for us.

The local::lib module, which we'll have to get from CPAN since it doesn't come with *perl* (yet), sets various environment variables that affect where CPAN clients install modules and where Perl programs will look for those modules. We can see what they set by loading the module on the command line using the -M switch, but without any other arguments. In that case, local::lib prints out its settings using the Bourne shell commands we can stick right in one of our login files:

```
% perl -Mlocal::lib
export PERL_LOCAL_LIB_ROOT="/Users/Ginger/perl5";
export PERL_MB_OPT="--install_base /Users/Ginger/perl5";
export PERL_MM_OPT="INSTALL_BASE=/Users/Ginger/perl5";
export PERL5LIB="...";
export PATH="/Users/Ginger/perl5/bin:$PATH";
```

 local::lib outputs Bourne shell commands even if we are using a different shell. We have to convert those commands ourselves.

The trick is installing `local::lib` so we can start using it. We can bootstrap `local::lib` by downloading and installing the module by hand:

```
% perl Makefile.PL --bootstrap
% make install
```

 We need a recent version of `CPAN.pm` or the `App::Cpan` module to use *cpan*'s -I switch. The `local::lib` feature was added for Perl v5.14.

Once we have `local::lib`, we can use it with the CPAN tools. The *cpan* client supports `local::lib` if we use the -I switch to install modules:

```
% cpan -I Set::CrossProduct
```

The *cpanm* tool is a bit smarter. If we've already set the same environment variables `local::lib` would set for us, it uses them. If not, it checks the default module directories for write permissions. If we don't have write permissions, it automatically uses `local::lib` for us. If we want to be sure to use `local::lib` explicitly, we can do that:

```
% cpanm --local-lib HTML::Parser
```

If we are using `local::lib`, we load that module in our program so our program knows where to find our installed modules:

```
# inside our Perl program
use local::lib;
```

We've shown `local::lib` using the default settings, but it has a way to work with any path that we want to use. On the command line, we can give an import list to the module we load with -M:

```
% perl -Mlocal::lib='~/perlstuff'
export PERL_LOCAL_LIB_ROOT="/Users/Ginger/perlstuff";
export PERL_MB_OPT="--install_base /Users/Ginger/perlstuff";
export PERL_MM_OPT="INSTALL_BASE=/Users/Ginger/perlstuff";
export PERL5LIB="/Users/Ginger/perlstuff/lib/perl5/darwin-2level:
    /Users/Ginger/perlstuff/lib/perl5";
export PATH="/Users/Ginger/perlstuff/bin:$PATH";
```

Exercises

You can find the answers to these exercises in "Answers for Chapter 2" on page 312.

1. [25 minutes] Read the list of files in the current directory and convert the names to their full path specification. Don't use the shell or an external program to get the current directory. The `File::Spec` and `Cwd` modules, both of which come with Perl, should help. Print each path with four spaces before it and a newline after it.

2. [20 minutes] Install the `local::lib` module and use it when you install `Module::CoreList` (or another module if you like). Write a program that reports the name and first release date for all the modules in Perl v5.14.2. Read the documentation for `local::lib` to see if it has special installation instructions.

3. [35 minutes] Parse the International Standard Book Number from the back of this book (9781449393090). Install the `Business::ISBN` module from CPAN and use it to extract the group code and the publisher code from the number.

## CHAPTER 3

Intermediate Foundations

Before we get started on the meat of the book, we want to introduce some intermediate-level Perl idioms that we use throughout the book. These are the things that typically set apart the beginning and intermediate Perl programmers. We'll also introduce the first cast of characters that we'll use in the examples throughout the book.

List Operators

A list is an ordered collection of scalars. Lists are the values themselves, and sometimes we store lists in arrays, the container that holds an ordered list. List operators do something with multiple elements, and most don't care if they use a literal list, the return values from a subroutine, or an array variable.

We already know several list operators in Perl, but we may not have thought of them as working with lists. The most common list operator is print. We give it one or more arguments, and it puts them together for us:

```
print 'Two castaways are ', 'Gilligan', ' and ', 'Skipper', "\n";
```

There are several other list operators that we already showed in *Learning Perl*. The sort operator puts its input list in order. In their theme song, the castaways don't come in alphabetical order, but sort can fix that for us:

```
my @castaways = sort qw(Gilligan Skipper Ginger Professor Mary-Ann);
```

The reverse operator returns a list in the opposite order:

```
my @castaways = reverse qw(Gilligan Skipper Ginger Professor Mary-Ann);
```

We can even use these operators "in place" by having the same array on both the righthand and lefthand sides of the assignment. Perl figures out the righthand side first, knows the result, and then assigns that back to the original variable name:

```
my @castaways = qw(Gilligan Skipper Ginger Professor);
push @castaways, 'Mary-Ann';

@castaways = reverse @castaways;
```

Perl has many other operators that work with lists, and once you get used to them you'll find yourself typing less and expressing your intent more clearly.

List Filtering with grep

The grep operator takes a "testing expression" and a list of values. It takes each item from the list in turn and places it into the $_ variable. It then evaluates the testing expression in scalar context. If the expression evaluates to a true value, grep passes $_ on to the output list:

```
my @lunch_choices = grep is_edible($_), @gilligans_possessions ;
```

In list context, the grep operator returns a list of all such selected items. In scalar context, grep returns the number of selected items:

```
my @results = grep EXPR, @input_list;
my $count   = grep EXPR, @input_list;
```

Here, *EXPR* stands in for any scalar expression that should refer to $_ (explicitly or implicitly). For example, to find all the numbers greater than 10, in our grep expression we check if $_ is greater than 10:

```
my @input_numbers = (1, 2, 4, 8, 16, 32, 64);
my @bigger_than_10 = grep $_ > 10, @input_numbers;
```

The result is 16, 32, and 64. This uses an explicit reference to $_. Here's an example of an implicit reference to $_ from the pattern match operator:

```
my @end_in_4 = grep /4$/, @input_numbers;
```

And now we get 4 and 64.

While the grep is running, it shadows any existing value in $_, which is to say that grep borrows the use of this variable, but restores the original value when it's done. The variable $_ isn't a mere copy of the data item, though; it is an alias for the actual data element, similar to the control variable in a foreach loop.

If the testing expression is complex, we can hide it in a subroutine:

```
my @odd_digit_sum = grep digit_sum_is_odd($_), @input_numbers;

sub digit_sum_is_odd {
  my $input = shift;
  my @digits = split //, $input;  # Assume no nondigit characters
  my $sum;
  $sum += $_ for @digits;
  return $sum % 2;
}
```

Now we get back the list of 1, 16, and 32. These numbers have a digit sum with a remainder of "1" in the last line of the subroutine, which counts as true.

The syntax comes in two forms, though: we just showed the expression form, and now here's the block form. Rather than define an explicit subroutine that we'd use for only a single test, we can put the body of a subroutine directly in line in the grep operator, using the block forms. In the block form of grep, there's no comma between the block and the input list:

```
my @results = grep {
  block;
  of;
  code;
} @input_list;

my $count = grep {
  block;
  of;
  code;
} @input_list;
```

This is a little quirk of Perl syntax. That block of code is really an anonymous subroutine, just like the ones that we showed with sort in *Learning Perl* and that we'll talk about in Chapter 7.

Like the expression form, grep temporarily places each element of the input list into $_. Next, it evaluates the entire block of code. The last evaluated expression in the block is the testing expression, and like all testing expressions, it's evaluated in scalar context. Because it's a full block, we can introduce variables that are scoped to the block. We rewrite that last example to use the block form:

```
my @odd_digit_sum = grep {
  my $input = $_;
  my @digits = split //, $input;    # Assume no nondigit characters
  my $sum;
  $sum += $_ for @digits;
  $sum % 2;
} @input_numbers;
```

Note the two changes: the input value comes in via $_ rather than an argument list, and we removed the keyword return. We would have been wrong to keep the return because we're no longer in a separate subroutine: just a block of code. We can optimize a few things out of that routine since we don't need the intermediate variables:

```
my @odd_digit_sum = grep {
  my $sum;
  $sum += $_ for split //;
  $sum % 2;
} @input_numbers;
```

A return in the grep would have exited the subroutine that contains this entire section of code. And yes, some of us have been bitten by that mistake in real, live coding on the first draft.

We can do whatever we like in that `grep` block. Suppose we have a list of URLs in `@links` and we want to know which ones are no longer good. We can send that list of links through the `grep`, check them with `HTTP::SimpleLinkChecker` (available on CPAN), and pass through only the links that don't have an error:

```
use HTTP::SimpleLinkChecker qw(check_link);

my @good_links = grep {
  check_link( $_ );
  ! $HTTP::SimpleLinkChecker::ERROR;
} @links;
```

We can crank up the explicitness if it helps us and our coworkers understand and maintain the code. That's the main thing that matters.

Transforming Lists with map

The `map` operator transforms one list into another. It has a syntax identical to the `grep` operator's and shares a lot of the same operational steps. For example, it temporarily places items from a list into `$_` one at a time, and the syntax allows both the expression block forms.

Our `map` expression is for transformation instead of testing. The `map` operator evaluates our expression in list context, not scalar context like `grep`. Each evaluation of the expression gives a portion of the list that becomes the final list. The end result is the concatenation of all individual results. In scalar context, `map` returns the number of elements returned in list context. But `map` should rarely, if ever, be used in anything but list context.

We start with a simple example:

```
my @input_numbers = (1, 2, 4, 8, 16, 32, 64);
my @result = map $_ + 100, @input_numbers;
```

For each of the seven items `map` places into `$_`, we get a single item to add to the output list: the number that is 100 greater than the input number, so the value of `@result` is 101, 102, 104, 108, 116, 132, and 164.

But we're not limited to having only one output per input. We can see what happens when each input produces two output items:

```
my @result = map { $_, 3 * $_ } @input_numbers;
```

Now there are two items for each input item: 1, 3, 2, 6, 4, 12, 8, 24, 16, 48, 32, 96, 64, and 192. We can store those pairs in a hash, if we need a hash showing what number is three times a small power of two:

```
my %hash = @result;
```

Or, without using the intermediate list from the `map`:

```
my %hash = map { $_, 3 * $_ } @input_numbers;
```

That was fine for making a meaningful value for each hash key, but sometimes we don't care about the value because we want to use the hash as an easier way to check that an element is in a list. In that case, we can give the keys any value just to have the key in the hash. Using 1 is a good value to use:

```
my %hash = map { $_, 1 } @castaways;

my $person = 'Gilligan';

if( $hash{$person} ) {
  print "$person is a castaway.\n";
}
```

That map is pretty versatile; we can produce any number of output items for each input item. And we don't always need to produce the same number of output items. We see what happens when we break apart the digits:

```
my @result = map { split // } @input_numbers;
```

The inline block of code splits each number into its individual digits. For 1, 2, 4, and 8, we get a single result. For 16, 32, and 64, we get two results per number. When map concatenates the results lists, we end up with 1, 2, 4, 8, 1, 6, 3, 2, 6, and 4.

If a particular invocation results in an empty list, map concatenates that empty result into the larger list, contributing nothing to the list. We can use this feature to select and reject items. For example, suppose we want to split the digits of only the numbers ending in 4:

```
my @result = map {
  my @digits = split //, $_;
  if ($digits[-1] == 4) {
    @digits;
  } else {
    ( );
  }
} @input_numbers;
```

If the last digit is 4, we return the digits themselves by evaluating @digits, which is in list context. If the last digit is not 4, we return an empty list, effectively removing results for that particular item. Thus, we can always use a map in place of a grep, but not vice versa.

Everything we can do with map and grep, we can also do with explicit foreach loops. But then again, we can also code in assembler or by toggling bits into a front panel. The point is that the proper application of grep and map can help reduce the complexity of the program, allowing us to concentrate on high-level issues rather than details.

Trapping Errors with eval

Many lines of ordinary code have the potential to terminate a program prematurely if something goes wrong:

```
my $average = $total / $count;  # divide by zero?
print "okay\n" unless /$match/; # illegal pattern?

open MINNOW, '>', 'ship.txt'
  or die "Can't create 'ship.txt': $!";  # user-defined die?

implement($_) foreach @rescue_scheme;  # die inside sub?
```

Just because something has gone wrong with one part of our code, that doesn't mean that we want everything to crash. Perl uses the `eval` operator as its error-trapping mechanism:

```
eval { $average = $total / $count } ;
```

 The `eval` is Perl's primitive exception mechanism. See *Mastering Perl* for a deeper treatment of handling errors in Perl, including some modules that have more fancy exception frameworks.

If an error happens while running code inside an `eval` block, the block stops executing. But even though the code inside the block is finished, Perl continues running the code right after the `eval`. It's most common after an `eval` to immediately check `$@`, which will either be empty (meaning that there was no error) or the dying words Perl had from the code that failed, perhaps something like `"divide by zero"` or a longer error message:

```
eval { $average = $total / $count } ;
print "Continuing after error: $@" if $@;

eval { rescue_scheme_42() } ;
print "Continuing after error: $@" if $@;
```

The semicolon is needed after the `eval` block because `eval` is a term (not a control structure, such as `if` or `while`).

The block is a true block and may include lexical variables ("my" variables) and any other arbitrary statements. As a function, `eval` has a return value much like a subroutine's (the last expression evaluated, or a value returned early by the `return` keyword). If the code in the block fails, it returns no value; this gives `undef` in scalar context, or an empty list in list context. Thus, another way to calculate an average safely looks like this:

```
my $average = eval { $total / $count };
```

Now `$average` is either the quotient or `undef`, depending on whether the operation completed successfully or not.

Perl even supports nested `eval` blocks. The power of an `eval` block to trap errors extends for as long as it's executing, so it catches errors deep within nested subroutine calls. `eval` can't trap the most serious of errors, though: the ones in which *perl* itself stops running. These include things such as an uncaught signal, running out of memory, and other catastrophes. `eval` doesn't catch syntax errors, either; because *perl* compiles the eval block with the rest of the code, it catches syntax errors at compile time, not at run time. It doesn't catch warnings either (although Perl does provide a way to intercept warning messages; see $SIG{__WARN__} in *perlvar*).

For simple operations, a straight eval is fine. For reasons we won't go into, correctly handling complex situations can be tricky. Fortunately for us, v5.14 fixed some of these problems, or we can use the the Try::Tiny module (available on CPAN):

```
use Try::Tiny;
my $average = try { $total / $count } catch { "NaN" };
```

Many of these weird edge cases were fixed in v5.14.

Dynamic Code with eval

There's also a second form of eval whose parameter is a string expression instead of a block. It compiles and executes code from a string at runtime. While this is useful and supported, it is also dangerous if any untrustworthy data has gotten into the string. With a few notable exceptions, we recommend you avoid eval on a string. We'll use it a bit later, and it might show up in other people's code, so we'll show how it works anyway:

```
eval '$sum = 2 + 2';
print "The sum is $sum\n";
```

Perl executes that code in the lexical context of the code around it, meaning that it's as if we had typed that eval-ed code right there. The result of the eval is the last evaluated expression, so we really don't need the entire statement inside the eval:

```
#!/usr/bin/perl

foreach my $operator ( qw(+ - * /) ) {
  my $result = eval "2 $operator 2";
  print "2 $operator 2 is $result\n";
}
```

 Before an eval does its work, Perl interpolates the double-quoted string first. If we intend a variable to be in the eval-ed code, we must ensure it doesn't interpolate.

Here, we go through the operators +, -, *, and /, and use each of those inside our eval code. In the string we give to eval, we interpolate the value of $operator into the string. The eval executes the code that the string represents and returns the last evaluated expression, which we assign to $result.

If eval can't properly compile and run the Perl code we hand it, it sets $@ just like in its block form. In this example, we trap any divide-by-zero errors, but we don't divide by anything (another sort of error):

```
print 'The quotient is ', eval '5 /', "\n";
warn $@ if $@;
```

The eval catches the syntax error and puts the message in $@, which we check immediately after calling eval:

```
The quotient is
syntax error at (eval 1) line 2, at EOF
```

If you didn't catch our warning before, we'll say it again: be careful with this form of eval. If we can find another way to do what we need, we should try that first. We'll use eval later, in Chapter 11, to load code from an external file, but then we'll also show a much better way to do that, too.

The do Block

The do block is one powerful but overlooked feature of Perl. It provides a way to group statements as a single expression that we can use in another expression. It's almost like an inline subroutine. As with subroutines, the result of do is the last evaluated expression.

First, consider a bit of code to assign one of three possible values to a variable. We declare $bowler as a lexical variable, and we use an if-elsif-else structure to choose which value to assign. We end up typing the variable name four times to get a single assignment:

```
my $bowler;
if( ...some condition... ) {
  $bowler = 'Mary-Ann';
}
elsif( ... some condition ... ) {
  $bowler = 'Ginger';
}
else {
  $bowler = 'The Professor';
}
```

However, with do, we only have to use the variable name once. We can assign to it at the same time that we declare it because we can combine everything else in the do as if it were a single expression:

```
my $bowler = do {
  if( ... some condition ... )     { 'Mary-Ann' }
  elsif( ... some condition ... ) { 'Ginger' }
  else                            { 'The Professor' }
};
```

The do is also handy for creating a scope around an operation. We might want to slurp all of a file's contents into a variable. One Perl idiom for doing that uses do to provide a scope for $/, the input record separator, and a localized version of @ARGV so we can use the <> to handle all of the filehandle details for us:

```
my $file_contents = do {
  local $/;
  local @ARGV = ( $filename );
  <>
};
```

Like eval, do has a string argument form. Given a string instead of a block of code, do attempts to load a file with that name, compile that file, and execute its code right there:

```
do $filename;
```

The do finds the file and reads it, then hands off the contents to the string form of eval to execute it. If there's an error, do doesn't care; our program will just keep going. Not only that, but do goes through its entire process, even if it has loaded the file already. For these reasons, virtually no one uses do. There's a better way.

In the previous chapter, we showed use as a way to load modules, and we said that happened at compile time. There's another way to load modules. The built-in require also loads modules, but does it at run time:

```
require List::Util;
```

A use is really a require in a BEGIN block and a call to the class's import:

```
BEGIN {   # what use is really doing
  require List::Util;
  List::Util->import(...);
}
```

We had to give use a module name, but we can give require a filename just like we could with do:

```
require $filename;
```

In either case, the require remembers which files it has already loaded so it won't do the work to reload the same file.

We'll show more of this in Chapter 12.

Exercises

You can find the answers to these exercises in "Answers for Chapter 3" on page 314.

1. [15 minutes] Write a program that takes a list of filenames on the command line and uses grep to select the ones whose size is less than 1,000 bytes. Use map to transform the strings in this list, putting four space characters in front of each and a newline character after. Print the resulting list.

2. [25 minutes] Write a program that asks the user to enter a pattern (regular expression). Read this as data from standard input; don't get it from the command line arguments. Report a list of files in some hardcoded directory (such as "/etc" or 'C:\\Windows') whose names match the pattern. Repeat this until the user enters an empty string instead of a pattern. The user should not type the slashes traditionally used to delimit pattern matches in Perl; the input pattern is delimited by the trailing newline. Ensure that a faulty pattern, such as one with unbalanced parentheses, doesn't crash the program.

## CHAPTER 4

Introduction to References

References are the basis for complex data structures, object-oriented programming, and fancy subroutine handling. They're the magic that was added between Perl versions 4 and 5 to make it all possible.

A Perl scalar variable holds a single value. An array holds an ordered list of scalars. A hash holds an unordered collection of scalars as values, keyed by strings. Although a scalar can be an arbitrary string, which lets us encode complex data in an array or hash, none of the three data types are well suited to complex data interrelationships. This is a job for the reference. We look at the importance of references by starting with an example.

Doing the Same Task on Many Arrays

Before the *Minnow* can leave on an excursion (for example, a three-hour tour), we should check every passenger and crew member to ensure they have all the required trip items in their possession. For maritime safety, every person aboard the *Minnow* needs to have a life preserver, some sunscreen, a water bottle, and a rain jacket. We can write a bit of code to check for the Skipper's supplies:

```
my @required = qw(preserver sunscreen water_bottle jacket);
my %skipper  = map { $_, 1 }
  qw(blue_shirt hat jacket preserver sunscreen);

foreach my $item (@required) {
  unless ( $skipper{$item} ) { # not found in list?
    print "Skipper is missing $item.\n";
  }
}
```

Notice that we created a hash from the list of the Skipper's items. That's a common and useful operation. Since we want to check if a particular item is in the Skipper's list, the easiest way is to make all the items keys of a hash then check the hash with exists. Here, we've given every key a true value, so we don't use exists. Instead of typing out the hash completely, we use the map to create it from the list of items.

If we want to check on Gilligan and the Professor, we might write the following code:

```perl
my %gilligan = map { $_, 1 } qw(red_shirt hat lucky_socks water_bottle);
foreach my $item (@required) {
  unless ( $gilligan{$item} ) { # not found in list?
    print "Gilligan is missing $item.\n";
  }
}

my %professor = map { $_, 1 }
  qw(sunscreen water_bottle slide_rule batteries radio);
for my $item (@required) {
  unless ( $professor{$item} ) { # not found in list?
    print "The Professor is missing $item.\n";
  }
}
```

When we program like this, we start to realize a lot of repeated code here and think that we should refactor that into a common subroutine that we can reuse:

```perl
sub check_required_items {
  my $who = shift;
  my %whos_items = map { $_, 1 } @_; # the rest are the person's items

  my @required = qw(preserver sunscreen water_bottle jacket);

  for my $item (@required) {
    unless ( $whos_items{$item} ) { # not found in list?
      print "$who is missing $item.\n";
    }
  }
}

my @gilligan = qw(red_shirt hat lucky_socks water_bottle);
check_required_items('gilligan', @gilligan);
```

Perl gives the subroutine five items in its argument list, the @_ array, initially: the name gilligan and the four items belonging to Gilligan. After the shift, @_ only has the items.

> Perl subroutines are covered in *perlsub*, as well as in Chapter 4 in *Learning Perl*.

So far, so good. We can check the Skipper and the Professor with a bit more code:

```perl
my @skipper   = qw(blue_shirt hat jacket preserver sunscreen);
my @professor = qw(sunscreen water_bottle slide_rule batteries radio);
check_required_items('skipper', @skipper);
check_required_items('professor', @professor);
```

And for the other passengers, we repeat as needed. Although this code meets the initial requirements, we've got two problems to deal with:

- To create @_, Perl copies the entire contents of the array we want to check. This is fine for a few items, but if the array is large, it seems a bit wasteful to copy the data just to pass it into a subroutine.
- Suppose we want to modify the original array to force the provisions list to include the mandatory items. Because we have a copy in the subroutine ("pass by value"), any changes we make to @_ aren't reflected automatically in the corresponding provisions array.

 Assigning new scalars to elements of @_ after the shift modifies the corresponding variable being passed, but that still wouldn't let us extend the array with additional mandatory provisions.

To solve either or both of these problems, we need pass by reference rather than pass by value. And that's just what the doctor (or Professor) ordered.

PeGS: Perl Graphical Structures

Before we get started with references, however, we want to introduce Perl Graphical Structures, or PeGS. These are graphical representations of Perl data structures developed by Joseph Hall. With a pretty picture, some of these illustrate the data layout better than simple text.

Most PeGS diagrams have two parts: the name of the variable and the data it references. The name portion is at the top of the diagram as a box with a pointy right side (see Figure 4-1). The variable name is inside the box.

Figure 4-1. A partial PeGS diagram showing the identifier portion

For a scalar, we have a single box under the name to hold its single value (see Figure 4-2).

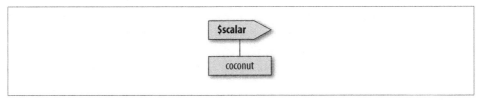

Figure 4-2. The PeGS diagram for a scalar

For an array (Figure 4-3), which can have multiple values, we do a bit more. The data portion starts with a filled-in, solid bar at the top to denote that it is a collection (to distinguish the single element array from a scalar).

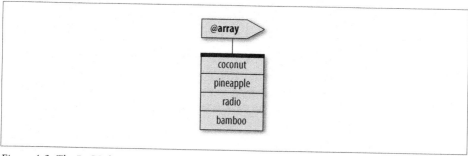

Figure 4-3. The PeGS diagram for an array

The hash is even more fancy. Like the array, the data portion starts with a black bar, but under that it has two parts. On the left are the keys, in pointy-sided boxes pointing at the box on their right, which shows the corresponding value (see Figure 4-4).

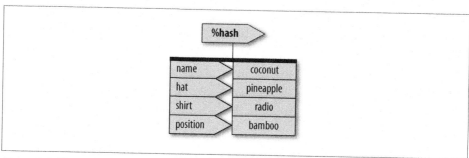

Figure 4-4. The PeGS diagram for a hash

We'll draw some of our complex data structures using these diagrams, and as we go further along we'll introduce some other features of PeGS.

Taking a Reference to an Array

Among its many other meanings, the backslash (\) character is also the "take a reference to" operator. When we use it in front of an array name, for example, \@skipper, the result is a *reference* to that array. A reference to the array is like a pointer:[1] it points at the array, but is not the array itself. (See Figure 4-5.)

---

1. We're not talking about pointers in the C sense, but in the dog sense. Think of an English pointer showing where the duck is, not a memory address.

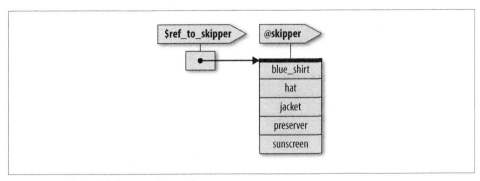

Figure 4-5. The PeGS diagram for a reference

A reference fits wherever a scalar fits. It can go into an element of an array or a hash, or into a plain scalar variable, like this:

```
my $ref_to_skipper = \@skipper;
```

In the PeGS notation, the reference is just a scalar, so its diagram looks like a scalar. However, in the data portion, it points to the data it references. Notice that the arrow from the reference to the data points specifically to the data, not the name of the variable that also references the data. That's going to be important very soon.

We can copy the reference to another reference, and both references point to the same data (see Figure 4-6):

```
my $second_ref_to_skipper = $reference_to_skipper;
```

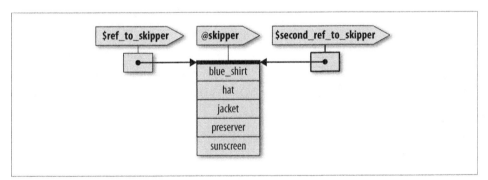

Figure 4-6. @skipper with one other reference pointing to the same data

We can even do it again (see Figure 4-7):

```
my $third_ref_to_skipper = \@skipper;
```

We can interchange all three references. We can even say they're identical, because they are the same thing. When we compare reference with ==, we get back true if they point to the same data address:

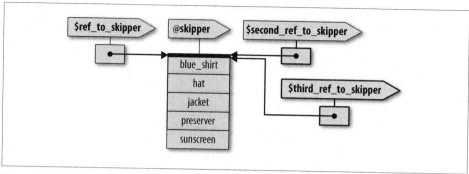

Figure 4-7. @skipper with two other references pointing to the same data

```
if ($reference_to_skipper == $second_reference_to_skipper) {
  print "They are identical references.\n";
}
```

This equality compares the numeric forms of the two references. The numeric form of the reference is the unique memory address of the @skipper internal data structure, which is unchanging during the life of the data. If we look at the string form instead, with eq or print, we get a string form of the reference:

```
ARRAY(0x1a2b3c)
```

This string is unique for this array because it includes the hexadecimal (base 16) representation of the array's memory address. The debugging string also notes that this is an array reference. If we ever see something like this in our output, it almost certainly means we have a bug; users of our program have little interest in hex dumps of storage addresses!

Also, the references need to point to the same data in Perl's memory, not two different data that just happen to have the same values.

Because we can copy a reference, and passing an argument to a subroutine is really just aliasing, we can use this code to pass a reference to the array into the subroutine:

```
my @skipper = qw(blue_shirt hat jacket preserver sunscreen);
check_required_items("The Skipper", \@skipper);

sub check_required_items {
  my $who = shift;
  my $items = shift;
  my @required = qw(preserver sunscreen water_bottle jacket);
  ...
}
```

Now $items in the subroutine is a reference to the array of @skipper. But how do we get from a reference back into the original array? We *dereference* the reference.

Dereferencing the Array Reference

If we look at @skipper, we'll see that it consists of two parts: the @ symbol and the name of the array. Similarly, the syntax $skipper[1] consists of the name of the array in the middle and some syntax around the outside to get at the second element of the array (index value 1 is the second element because index values start at 0).

Here's the trick: we can place any reference to an array in curly braces in place of the name of an array, ending up with a method to access the original array. That is, wherever we write skipper to name the array, we use the reference inside curly braces: { $items }. For example, both of these lines refer to the entire array:

```
@  skipper
@{ $items }
```

whereas both of these refer to the second item of the array:[2]

```
$  skipper [1]
${ $items }[1]
```

By using the reference form, we've decoupled the code and the method of array access from the actual array. We see how that changes the rest of this subroutine:

```
sub check_required_items {
  my $who   = shift;
  my $items = shift;

  my %whos_items = map { $_, 1 } @{$items};

  my @required = qw(preserver sunscreen water_bottle jacket);
  for my $item (@required) {
    unless ( $whos_items{$item} ) { # not found in list?
      print "$who is missing $item.\n";
    }
  }
}
```

All we did was replace @_ (the copy of the provisions list) with @{$items}, a dereferencing of the reference to the original provisions array. Now we can call the subroutine a few times as before:

```
my @skipper = qw(blue_shirt hat jacket preserver sunscreen);
check_required_items('The Skipper', \@skipper);

my @professor = qw(sunscreen water_bottle slide_rule batteries radio);
check_required_items('Professor', \@professor);

my @gilligan = qw(red_shirt hat lucky_socks water_bottle);
check_required_items('Gilligan', \@gilligan);
```

2. We added whitespace in these two displays to make the similar parts line up. This whitespace is legal in a program, even though most programs won't use it.

In each case, $items points to a different array, so the same code applies to different arrays each time we invoke it. This is one of the most important uses of references: decoupling the code from the data structure on which it operates so we can reuse the code more readily.

Passing the array by reference fixes the first of the two problems we mentioned earlier. Now, instead of copying the entire provision list into the @_ array, we get a single element, which is a reference to that provisions array.

Could we have eliminated the two shifts at the beginning of the subroutine? Sure, but we sacrifice clarity:

```
sub check_required_items {
  my %whos_items = map {$_, 1} @{$_[1]};

  my @required = qw(preserver sunscreen water_bottle jacket);
  for my $item (@required) {
    unless ( $whos_items{$item} ) { # not found in list?
      print "$_[0] is missing $item.\n";
    }
  }
}
```

We still have two elements in @_. The first element is the passenger or crew member name, which we use in the error message. The second element is a reference to the correct provisions array, which we use in the grep expression.

Getting Our Braces Off

Most of the time, the array reference we want to dereference is a simple scalar variable, such as @{$items} or ${$items}[1]. In those cases, we can drop the curly braces, unambiguously forming @$items or $$items[1].

However, we cannot drop the braces if the value within the braces is not a bareword identifier with one or more leading $s. For example, for @{$_[1]} from that last subroutine rewrite, we can't remove the braces. That's a single element access to an array, not a scalar variable, so it has more than the identifier and $s. We could drop the braces from @{$items} and @{$$items} though.

This rule also means that it's easy to see where the "missing" braces need to go. When we see $$items[1], a pretty noisy piece of syntax, we can tell that the curly braces must belong around the simple scalar variable, $items. Therefore, $items must be a reference to an array.

Thus, an easier-on-the-eyes version of that subroutine might be:

```
sub check_required_items {
  my( $who, $items ) = @_;
  my %whos_items = map {$_, 1} @$items;

  my @required = qw(preserver sunscreen water_bottle jacket);
```

```
    for my $item (@required) {
      unless ( $whos_items{$item} ) { # not found in list?
        print "$who is missing $item.\n";
      }
    }
  }
```

The difference here is that we removed the braces around @$items.

Modifying the Array

We solved the excessive copying problem with an array reference. Now we modify the original array.

For every missing provision, we push that provision onto an array, forcing the passenger to consider the item:

```
sub check_required_items {
  my $who   = shift;
  my $items = shift;

  my %whose_items = map { $_, 1 } @$items;

  my @required = qw(preserver sunscreen water_bottle jacket);
  my @missing = (  );

  for my $item (@required) {
    unless ( $whose_items{$item} ) { # not found in list?
      print "$who is missing $item.\n";
      push @missing, $item;
    }
  }

  if (@missing) {
    print "Adding @missing to @$items for $who.\n";
    push @$items, @missing;
  }
}
```

Note the addition of the @missing array. If we find any items missing during the scan, we push them into @missing. If there's anything there at the end of the scan, we add it to the original provision list.

The key is in the last line of that subroutine. We're dereferencing the $items array reference, accessing the original array, and adding the elements from @missing. Without passing by reference, we'd modify only a local copy of the data, which has no effect on the original array.

Also, @$items (and its more generic form @{$items}) works within a double-quoted string and interpolates like a normal, named array. We can't include any whitespace between the @ and the character immediately following, although we can include arbitrary whitespace within the curly braces as if it were normal Perl code.

Nested Data Structures

In this next example, the array @_ contains two elements, one of which is an array reference. What if we take a reference to an array that also contains a reference to an array? We end up with a complex data structure, which can be quite useful.

For example, we can iterate over the data for the Skipper, Gilligan, and the Professor by first building a larger data structure holding the entire list of provision lists:

```
my @skipper = qw(blue_shirt hat jacket preserver sunscreen);
my @skipper_with_name = ('Skipper' => \@skipper);

my @professor = qw(sunscreen water_bottle slide_rule batteries radio);
my @professor_with_name = ('Professor' => \@professor);

my @gilligan = qw(red_shirt hat lucky_socks water_bottle);
my @gilligan_with_name = ('Gilligan' => \@gilligan);
```

At this point, @skipper_with_name has two elements, the second of which is an array reference similar to what we passed to the subroutine. Now we group them all:

```
my @all_with_names = (
  \@skipper_with_name,
  \@professor_with_name,
  \@gilligan_with_name,
);
```

We have three elements in @all_with_names, each of which is a reference to an array with two elements: the name and its corresponding initial provisions. A picture of that is in Figure 4-8.

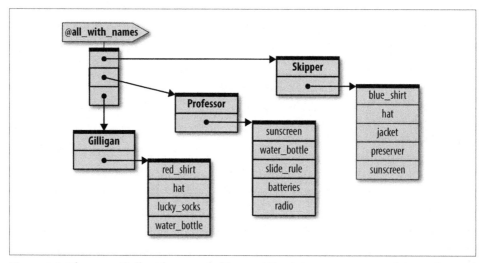

Figure 4-8. The array @all_with_names holds a multilevel data structure containing strings and references to arrays

---

Therefore, $all_with_names[2] is the array reference for the Gilligan's data. If we dereference it as @{$all_with_names[2]}, we get a two-element array, "Gilligan," and another array reference.

How do we access that array reference? Using our rules again, it's ${$all_with_names[2]}[1]. In other words, taking $all_with_names[2], we dereference it in an expression that would be something like $DUMMY[1] as an ordinary array, so we'll place {$all_with_names[2]} in place of DUMMY.

How do we call the existing check_required_items with this data structure? The following code is easy enough:

```
for my $person (@all_with_names) {
    my $who = $$person[0];
    my $provisions_reference = $$person[1];
    check_required_items($who, $provisions_reference);
}
```

This requires no changes to our subroutine. The control variable $person goes through each of $all_with_names[0], $all_with_names[1], and $all_with_names[2], as the loop progresses. When we dereference $$person[0], we get "Skipper," "Professor," and "Gilligan," respectively. $$person[1] is the corresponding array reference of provisions for that person.

We can shorten this as well since the entire dereferenced array matches the argument list precisely:

```
for my $person (@all_with_names) {
    check_required_items(@$person);
}
```

or even:

```
check_required_items(@$_) for @all_with_names;
```

Various levels of optimization can lead to obfuscation. We should consider where our heads will be a month from now when we have to reread our own code. If that's not enough, we should consider the new person who takes over our job after we have left.[3]

Simplifying Nested Element References with Arrows

Look at the curly-brace dereferencing again. As in our earlier example, the array reference for Gilligan's provision list is ${$all_with_names[2]}[1]. Now, what if we want to know Gilligan's first provision? We need to dereference *this* item one more level, so it's yet another layer of braces: ${${$all_with_names[2]}[1]}[0]. That's a really noisy piece of syntax. Can we shorten that? Yes!

---

3. O'Reilly Media, Inc., has a great book to help us be nice to the next guy. *Perl Best Practices*, by Damian Conway, has 256 tips on writing more readable and maintainable Perl code.

Everywhere we write `${DUMMY}[$y]`, we can write `DUMMY->[$y]` instead. In other words, we can dereference an array reference, picking out a particular element of that array by following the expression defining the array reference with an arrow and a square-bracketed subscript.

For this example, this means we can pick out the array reference for Gilligan with a simple `$all_with_names[2]->[1]`, and Gilligan's first provision with `$all_with_names[2]->[1]->[0]`. Wow, that's definitely easier on the eyes.

If *that* wasn't already simple enough, there's one more rule: if the arrow ends up between "subscripty kinds of things," such as square brackets, we can also drop the arrow because multiple subscripts imply a dereference already. `$all_with_names[2]->[1]->[0]` becomes `$all_with_names[2][1][0]`. Now it's looking even easier on the eyes.

The arrow has to be *between* nonsubscripty things. Why wouldn't it be between subscripty things? Well, imagine a reference to the array `@all_with_names`:

```
my $root = \@all_with_names;
```

Now how do we get to Gilligan's first item? We line up the subscripts:

```
$root -> [2] -> [1] -> [0]
```

More simply, using the "drop arrow" rule, we can use:

```
$root -> [2][1][0]
```

We cannot drop the first arrow, however, because that would mean an array `@root`'s third element, an entirely unrelated data structure. We compare this to the full curly-brace form again:

```
${${${$root}[2]}[1]}[0]
```

It looks much better with the arrow. Note, however, that no shortcut gets the entire array from an array reference. If we want all of Gilligan's provisions, we say:

```
@{$root->[2][1]}
```

Reading this from the inside out, we can think of it like this:

1. Take `$root`.
2. Dereference it as an array reference, taking the third element of that array (index number 2): `$root->[2]`
3. Dereference that as an array reference, taking the second element of that array (index number 1): `$root->[2][1]`
4. Dereference that as an array reference, taking the entire array: `@{$root->[2][1]}`

The last step doesn't have a shortcut arrow form. Oh well.

References to Hashes

Just as we can take a reference to an array, we can also take a reference to a hash. Once again, we use the backslash as the "take a reference to" operator and store the result in a scalar (see Figure 4-9):

```
my %gilligan_info = (
    name     => 'Gilligan',
    hat      => 'White',
    shirt    => 'Red',
    position => 'First Mate',
);
my $hash_ref = \%gilligan_info;
```

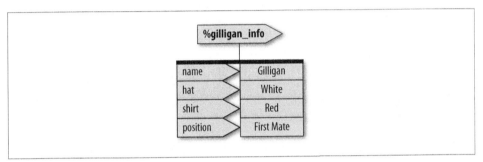

Figure 4-9. The PeGS for the %gilligan_info hash

We can dereference a hash reference to get back to the original data. The strategy is the same as dereferencing an array reference. We write the hash syntax as we would have without references and then replace the name of the hash with a pair of curly braces surrounding the thing holding the reference. For example, to pick a particular value for a given key, we do this:

```
my $name = $ gilligan_info { 'name' };
my $name = $ { $hash_ref } { 'name' };
```

Here, the curly braces have two different meanings. The first pair denotes the expression returning a reference while the second pair delimits the expression for the hash key.

To apply an operation on the entire hash, we proceed similarly:

```
my @keys = keys % gilligan_info;
my @keys = keys % { $hash_ref };
```

As with array references, we can use shortcuts to replace the complex curly-braced forms under some circumstances. For example, if the only thing inside the curly braces is a simple scalar variable (as shown in these examples so far), we can drop the curly braces:

```
my $name = $$hash_ref{'name'};
my @keys = keys %$hash_ref;
```

Like an array reference, when referring to a specific hash element, we can use an arrow form (see Figure 4-10):

```perl
my $name = $hash_ref->{'name'};
```

Because a hash reference fits wherever a scalar fits, we can create an array of hash references:

```perl
my %gilligan_info = (
  name     => 'Gilligan',
  hat      => 'White',
  shirt    => 'Red',
  position => 'First Mate',
);
my %skipper_info = (
  name     => 'Skipper',
  hat      => 'Black',
  shirt    => 'Blue',
  position => 'Captain',
);
my @crew = (\%gilligan_info, \%skipper_info);
```

Thus, $crew[0] is a hash reference to the information about Gilligan. We can get to Gilligan's name via any one of:

```perl
${ $crew[0] } { 'name' }
my $ref = $crew[0]; $$ref{'name'}
$crew[0]->{'name'}
$crew[0]{'name'}
```

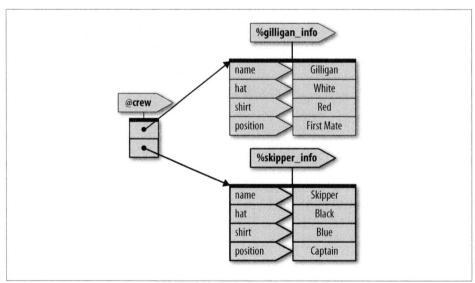

Figure 4-10. Crew roster PeGS

With those last two, we can still drop the arrow between "subscripty kinds of things," even though one is an array bracket and one is a hash brace.

We print a crew roster:

```
my %gilligan_info = (
   name     => 'Gilligan',
   hat      => 'White',
   shirt    => 'Red',
   position => 'First Mate',
);
my %skipper_info = (
   name     => 'Skipper',
   hat      => 'Black',
   shirt    => 'Blue',
   position => 'Captain',
);
my @crew = (\%gilligan_info, \%skipper_info);

my $format = "%-15s %-7s %-7s %-15s\n";
printf $format, qw(Name Shirt Hat Position);
foreach my $crewmember (@crew) {
  printf $format,
    $crewmember->{'name'},
    $crewmember->{'shirt'},
    $crewmember->{'hat'},
    $crewmember->{'position'};
}
```

That last part looks repetitive. We can shorten it with a hash slice. Again, if the original syntax is:

```
@ gilligan_info { qw(name position) }
```

the hash slice notation from a reference looks like:

```
@ { $hash_ref } { qw(name position) }
```

 For a review of hash slices, see *Learning Perl*, Chapter 17. These are also documented in *perldata*.

We can drop the first brace pair because the only thing within is a simple scalar value, yielding:

```
@ $hash_ref { qw(name position) }
```

Thus, we can replace that final loop with:

```
for my $crewmember (@crew) {
  printf $format, @$crewmember{qw(name shirt hat position)};
}
```

There is no shortcut form with an arrow (->) for array slices or hash slices.

A hash reference prints as a string that looks like HASH(0x1a2b3c), showing the hexadecimal memory address of the hash. That's not useful to an end user and only barely more usable to the programmer, except as an indication of the lack of appropriate dereferencing.

Checking Reference Types

Once we start using references and passing them around, we have to ensure that we know which sort of reference we have. If we try to use the reference as a type that it is not, our program will blow up:

```
show_hash( \@array );

sub show_hash {
  my $hash_ref = shift;

  foreach my $key ( keys %$hash_ref ) {
    ...
  }
}
```

The show_hash subroutine expects a hash and trusts that we pass it one. However, since we passed it an array reference, our program blows up:

```
Not a HASH reference at line ...
```

If we want to be careful, we should check the argument to show_hash to ensure that it's actually a hash reference. There are a couple ways that we could do this. The easy way uses ref, which returns the reference type. We compare the return value from ref to what we expected:

```
use Carp qw(croak);

sub show_hash {
  my $hash_ref = shift;
  my $ref_type = ref $hash_ref;
  croak "I expected a hash reference!"
    unless $ref_type eq 'HASH';

  foreach my $key ( keys %$hash_ref ) {
    ...
  }
}
```

That looks odd to us, though, because we had to hardcode the literal string HASH. We never like to do that. We can, however, get rid of the literal string with a double use of ref. We call ref a second time with a trivial version of the reference type that we expect:

```
croak "I expected a hash reference!"
  unless $ref_type eq ref {};
```

Alternatively, we can use the constant module to store the hash reference string:

```
use constant HASH => ref {};
```

```
croak "I expected a hash reference!"
  unless $ref_type eq HASH;
```

Using a constant looks a lot like a literal string, but it has an important difference: the constant will fail if we use the wrong name because it is not defined, but a wrong literal string will never fail because Perl has no way to know that we used the wrong string.

Our use of ref has another problem, which we can't fully explain until we talk about objects. Since ref returns a string that gives the reference type, if we have an object that can act like a hash reference, our technique fails because the strings won't be the same. The Scalar::Util module, which comes with Perl, gets around that with its reftype function that does the same thing:

```
use Carp qw(croak);
use Scalar::Util qw(reftype);

sub show_hash {
  my $hash_ref = shift;
  my $ref_type = reftype $hash_ref;  # works with objects
  croak "I expected a hash reference!"
    unless $ref_type eq ref {};

  foreach my $key ( keys %$hash_ref ) {
    ...
  }
}
```

However, objects are interfaces, so things that are not based on hash references can still *act* like hashes. In that case, ref doesn't return the string HASH necessarily.

Instead of asking "What are you?" we should ask "What can you do?" We really only want to know if the argument to show_hash can act like a hash reference so it doesn't blow up. We don't specifically care that it is exactly a hash reference.

In that case, we might use an eval in which we try to do something hash-like. If the eval fails and returns false, we didn't have a hash:

```
croak "I expected a hash reference!"
  unless eval { keys %$hash_ref; 1 };
```

If we expect to check this often, we should probably wrap the check in its own subroutine:

```
sub is_hash_ref {
  my $hash_ref = shift;

  return eval { keys %$ref_type; 1 };
}

croak "I expected a hash reference!"
  unless is_hash_ref( $ref_type );
```

Exercises

You can find the answers to these exercises in "Answers for Chapter 4" on page 315.

1. [5 minutes] How many different things do these expressions refer to? Draw a PeGS structure for each of these:

   ```
   $ginger->[2][1]
   ${$ginger[2]}[1]
   $ginger->[2]->[1]
   ${$ginger->[2]}[1]
   ```

2. [30 minutes] Using the final version of check_required_items, write a subroutine check_items_for_all that takes as its only parameter a reference to a hash whose keys are the people aboard the *Minnow* and whose corresponding values are array references of the things they intend to bring on board.

   For example, the hash reference might be constructed like so:

   ```
   my @gilligan  = (... gilligan items  ...);
   my @skipper   = (... skipper items   ...);
   my @professor = (... professor items ...);

   my %all = (
     Gilligan  => \@gilligan,
     Skipper   => \@skipper,
     Professor => \@professor,
   );

   check_items_for_all(\%all);
   ```

   The newly constructed subroutine should call check_required_items for each person in the hash, updating their provisions list to include the required items.

   Some starting code is in the Downloads section on *http://www.intermediateperl.com/*.

3. [20 minutes] Modify the crew roster program to add a location field for each castaway. At the start, set each person's location to "The Island." After you've added that field to each person's hash, change the Howells' locations to "The Island Country Club." Make a report of everyone's location, like this:

   ```
   Gilligan at The Island
   Skipper at The Island
   Mr. Howell at The Island Country Club
   Mrs. Howell at The Island Country Club
   ```

   Some starting code is in the Downloads section on *http://www.intermediateperl.com/*.

## CHAPTER 5

References and Scoping

We can copy and pass around references like any other scalar. At any given time, Perl knows the number of references to a particular data item. Perl can also create references to *anonymous data structures* that do not have explicit names and create references automatically as needed to fulfill certain kinds of operations. We'll show you how to copy references and how it affects scoping and memory usage.

More than One Reference to Data

Chapter 4 explored how to take a reference to an array `@skipper` and place it into a new scalar variable:

```
my @skipper = qw(blue_shirt hat jacket preserver sunscreen);
my $ref_to_skipper = \@skipper;
```

We can then copy the reference or take additional references, and they'll all refer to the same thing and are interchangeable:

```
my $second_ref_to_skipper = $reference_to_skipper;
my $third_ref_to_skipper  = \@skipper;
```

At this point, we have four different ways to access the data contained in `@skipper`:

```
@skipper
@$ref_to_skipper
@$second_ref_to_skipper
@$third_ref_to_skipper
```

Perl tracks how many ways it can access the data through a mechanism called *reference counting*. The original name counts as one, and each additional reference that we create (including copies of references) also counts as one. The total number of references to the array of provisions is now four.

We can add and remove references as we wish, and as long as the reference count doesn't hit zero, Perl maintains the array in memory, and it is still accessible via any of the other access paths. For example, we might have a temporary reference:

```
check_provisions_list(\@skipper)
```

When this subroutine executes, Perl creates a fifth reference to the data and copies it into @_ for the subroutine. The subroutine is free to create additional copies of that reference, which Perl detects as needed. Typically, when the subroutine returns, Perl discards all such references automatically, and we're back to four references again.

We can kill off each reference by using the variable for something other than a reference to the value of @skipper. For example, we can assign undef to the variable:

```
$ref_to_skipper = undef;
```

Or, maybe we let the variable go out of scope:

```
my @skipper = ...;

{ # bare block
...
my $ref = \@skipper;
...
...
} # $ref goes out of scope at this point
```

In particular, a reference held in a subroutine's private (lexical) variable goes away at the end of the subroutine.

Whether we change the value or the variable itself goes away, Perl notes it as an appropriate reduction in the number of references to the data.

Perl recycles the memory for the array only when all references (including the name of the array) go away. Here, Perl only reclaims memory when @skipper and all the references we created to it disappear.

Such memory is available to Perl for other data later in this program invocation, and generally Perl doesn't give it back to the operating system.

What If That Was the Name?

Typically, all references to a variable are gone before the variable itself. But what if one of the references outlives the variable name? For example, consider this code:

```
my $ref;

{
  my @skipper = qw(blue_shirt hat jacket preserver sunscreen); # ref count is 1
  $ref       = \@skipper;                                      # ref count is 2

  print "$ref->[2]\n"; # prints jacket\n
}

print "$ref->[2]\n"; # still prints jacket\n                   # ref count is 1
```

Immediately after we declare the @skipper array, we have one reference to the five-element list. After $ref is initialized, we'll have two, down to the end of the block. When the block ends, the @skipper name disappears. However, this was only one of the two ways to access the data! Thus, the five-element list is still in memory, and $ref still points to that data.

At this point, the five-element list is in an *anonymous array*, which is a fancy term for an array without a name.

Until the value of $ref changes, or $ref itself disappears, we can still use all the dereferencing strategies we used prior to when the name of the array disappeared. It's still a fully functional array that we can shrink or grow just as we do any other Perl array:

```
push @$ref, 'sextant'; # add a new provision
print "$ref->[-1]\n"; # prints sextant\n
```

We can even increase the reference count at this point:

```
my $copy_of_ref = $ref;
```

or equivalently:

```
my $copy_of_ref = \@$ref;
```

The data stays alive until we destroy the last reference:

```
$ref = undef; # not yet...
$copy_of_ref = undef; # poof!
```

Reference Counting and Nested Data Structures

The data remains alive until we destroy the last reference, even if that reference lives within a larger active data structure. Suppose an array element is itself a reference. Recall the example from Chapter 4:

```
my @skipper = qw(blue_shirt hat jacket preserver sunscreen);
my @skipper_with_name  = ('The Skipper' => \@skipper);

my @professor = qw(sunscreen water_bottle slide_rule batteries radio);
my @professor_with_name = ('The Professor' => \@professor);

my @gilligan = qw(red_shirt hat lucky_socks water_bottle);
my @gilligan_with_name  = ('Gilligan' => \@gilligan);

my @all_with_names = (
  \@skipper_with_name,
  \@professor_with_name,
  \@gilligan_with_name,
);
```

Imagine for a moment that the intermediate variables are all part of a subroutine:

```
my @all_with_names;

sub initialize_provisions_list {
```

```
    my @skipper = qw(blue_shirt hat jacket preserver sunscreen);
    my @skipper_with_name = ('The Skipper' => \@skipper);

    my @professor = qw(sunscreen water_bottle slide_rule batteries radio);
    my @professor_with_name = ('The Professor' => \@professor);

    my @gilligan = qw(red_shirt hat lucky_socks water_bottle);
    my @gilligan_with_name = ('Gilligan' => \@gilligan);

    @all_with_names = ( # set global
      \@skipper_with_name,
      \@professor_with_name,
      \@gilligan_with_name,
    );
  }

  initialize_provisions_list();
```

We set the value of @all_with_names to contain three references. Inside the subroutine, we have named arrays with references to arrays first placed into other named arrays. Eventually, the values end up in the global @all_with_names. However, as the subroutine returns, the names for the six arrays disappear. Each array has had one other reference taken to it, making the reference count temporarily two, and then back to one as the name disappears. Because the reference count is not yet zero, the data continues to live on, although it is now referenced only by elements of @all_with_names.

Rather than assign the global variable, we can rewrite this without @all_with_names and return the list directly:

```
  sub get_provisions_list {
    my @skipper = qw(blue_shirt hat jacket preserver sunscreen);
    my @skipper_with_name = ('The Skipper', \@skipper);

    my @professor = qw(sunscreen water_bottle slide_rule batteries radio);
    my @professor_with_name = ('The Professor', \@professor);

    my @gilligan = qw(red_shirt hat lucky_socks water_bottle);
    my @gilligan_with_name = ('Gilligan', \@gilligan);

    return (
      \@skipper_with_name,
      \@professor_with_name,
      \@gilligan_with_name,
    );
  }

  my @all_with_names = get_provisions_list( );
```

Here, we create the value that we'll eventually store in @all_with_names as the last expression evaluated in the subroutine. The subroutine returns a three-element list. As long as the named arrays within the subroutine have had at least one reference taken of them, and it is still part of the return value, the data remains alive. If we alter or discard the references in @all_with_names, Perl reduces the reference count for the corresponding arrays. If that means the reference count has become zero (as in this example), Perl also eliminates the arrays themselves. Because the arrays inside @all_with_names also contain a reference (such as the reference to @skipper), Perl reduces that reference count by one. Again, that reduces the reference count to zero, freeing that memory as well, in a cascading effect.

Removing the top of a tree of data generally removes all the data contained within. The exception is when we make additional copies of the references of the nested data. For example, if we copy Gilligan's provisions:

```
my $gilligan_stuff = $all_with_names[2][1];
```

then when we remove @all_with_names, we still have one live reference to what was formerly @gilligan, and the data from there downward remains alive.

The bottom line is this: Perl does the right thing. If we still have a reference to data, we still have the data.

When Reference Counting Goes Bad

Reference counting as a way to manage memory has been around for a long time. A really long time. The downside of reference counting is that it breaks when the data structure is not a *directed graph*—that is, when some parts of the structure point back in to other parts in a looping way. For example, suppose each of two data structures contains a reference to the other (see Figure 5-1):

```
my @data1 = qw(one won);
my @data2 = qw(two too to);

push @data2, \@data1;
push @data1, \@data2;
```

At this point, we have two names for the data in @data1: @data1 itself and @{$data2[3]}, and two names for the data in @data2: @data2 itself and @{$data1[2]}. We've created a loop. We can access won with an infinite number of names, such as $data1[2][3][2][3][2][3][1].

What happens when these two array names go out of scope? Well, the reference count for the two arrays goes down from two to one, but not zero! And because it's not zero, Perl thinks there might still be a way to get to the data, even though there isn't! Thus, we've created a *memory leak*. A memory leak in a program causes the program to consume more and more memory over time. Ugh.

At this point, you're right to think that example is contrived. We would never make a looped data structure in a real program! Actually, programmers often make these loops as part of doubly linked lists, linked rings, or many other data structures, or even by accident. The key is that Perl programmers rarely do so because the most important reasons to use those data structures don't apply in Perl. Most of that deals with managing memory and connecting discontiguous memory blocks, which Perl does for us.

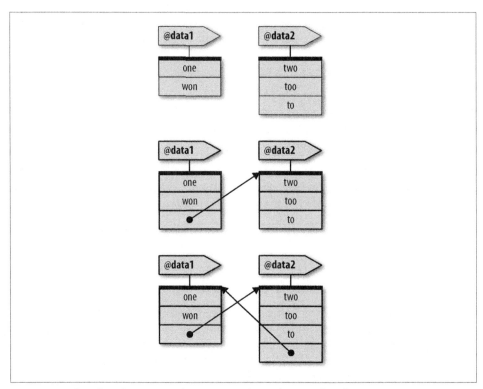

Figure 5-1. When the references in a data structure form a loop, Perl's reference-counting system may not be able to recognize and recycle the no-longer-needed memory space

If you've used other languages, you may have noticed programming tasks that are much easier in Perl. For example, it's easy to sort a list of items or to add or remove items, even in the middle of the list. Those tasks are difficult in some other languages, and using a looped data structure is a common way to get around the language's limitations. Why mention it here? Well, even Perl programmers sometimes copy an algorithm from another programming language. There's nothing inherently wrong with doing this, although it would be better to decide why the original author used a "loopy" data structure and then recode the algorithm to use Perl's strengths. Perhaps you should use a hash instead or perhaps the data should go into an array that will be sorted later.

Some future version of Perl might come up with a different method for *garbage collection* in addition to or instead of referencing counting.[1] Until then, we must be careful not to create circular references, or if we do, break the circle before the variables go out of scope. For example, the following code doesn't leak:

```
{
    my @data1 = qw(one won);
    my @data2 = qw(two too to);
```

---

1. We might be able to find these problems with `Test::MemoryCycle`.

```
    push @data2, \@data1;
    push @data1, \@data2;
    ... use @data1, @data2 ...
    # at the end:
    @data1 = ( );
    @data2 = ( );
}
```

We eliminated the reference to @data2 from within @data1, and vice versa. Now the data have only one reference each, which all go to zero references at the end of the block. We can clear out either one and not the other, and it still works nicely. Chapter 18 shows how to create weak references, which can help with many of these problems.

Creating an Anonymous Array Directly

In the get_provisions_list routine earlier, we created a half dozen array names that we used only so that we could take a reference to them immediately afterward. When the subroutine exited, the array names all went away, but the references remained.

While creating temporarily named arrays would work in the simplest cases, creating such names becomes more complicated as the data structures become more detailed. We'd have to keep thinking of names of arrays just so we can forget them shortly thereafter.

We can reduce the namespace clutter by narrowing down the scope of the various array names. Rather than declaring them within the scope of the subroutine, we can create a temporary block:

```
my @skipper_with_name;
{
  my @skipper = qw(blue_shirt hat jacket preserver sunscreen);
  @skipper_with_name = ('The Skipper', \@skipper);
}
```

At this point, the second element of @skipper_with_name is a reference to the array formerly known as @skipper. However, that name is no longer relevant.

This is a lot of typing to say "the second element should be a reference to an array containing these elements." We can create such a value directly using the *anonymous array constructor*, which is yet another use for square brackets:

```
my $ref_to_skipper_provisions =
  [ qw(blue_shirt hat jacket preserver sunscreen) ];
```

The square brackets take the value within (evaluated in list context); establish a new, anonymous array initialized to those values; and (here's the important part) return a reference to that array. It's as if we had said:

```
my $ref_to_skipper_provisions;
{
  my @temporary_name =
  qw(blue_shirt hat jacket preserver sunscreen);
```

```
    $ref_to_skipper_provisions = \@temporary_name;
}
```

We don't need to come up with a temporary name, and we don't need the extra noise of the temporary block. The result of a square-bracketed anonymous array constructor is an array reference, which fits wherever a scalar variable fits.

Now we can use it to construct the larger list:

```
my $ref_to_skipper_provisions =
  [ qw(blue_shirt hat jacket preserver sunscreen) ];
my @skipper_with_name = ('The Skipper', $ref_to_skipper_provisions);
```

We didn't actually need that scalar temporary, either. We can put a scalar reference to an array as part of a larger list:

```
my @skipper_with_name = (
  'The Skipper',
  [ qw(blue_shirt hat jacket preserver sunscreen) ]
);
```

We've declared @skipper_with_name, the first element of which is the Skipper's name string, while the second is an array reference, obtained by placing the five provisions into an array and taking a reference to it. So @skipper_with_name is only two elements long, just as before.

Don't confuse the square brackets with the parentheses here. They each have their distinct purpose. If we replace the square brackets with parentheses, we end up with a six-element list. If we replace the outer parentheses (on the first and last lines) with square brackets, we construct an anonymous array that's two elements long and then take the reference to that array as the only element of the ultimate @skipper_with_name array.[2] So, in summary, if we have this syntax:

```
my $fruits;
{
  my @secret_variable = ('pineapple', 'papaya', 'mango');
  $fruits = \@secret_variable;
}
```

we can replace it with:

```
my $fruits = ['pineapple', 'papaya', 'mango'];
```

Does this work for more complicated structures? Yes! Any time we need an element of a list to be a reference to an array, we can create that reference with an anonymous array constructor. We can also nest them in our provisions list:

```
sub get_provisions_list {
  return (
    ['The Skipper',   [qw(blue_shirt hat jacket preserver sunscreen)       ] ],
    ['The Professor', [qw(sunscreen water_bottle slide_rule batteries radio) ] ],
```

---

2. In classrooms, we've seen that too much indirection (or not enough indirection) tends to contribute to the most common mistakes made when working with references.

```
        ['Gilligan',      [qw(red_shirt hat lucky_socks water_bottle)          ] ],
    );
}

    my @all_with_names = get_provisions_list( );
```

Walking through this from the outside in, we have a return value of three elements. Each element is an array reference, pointing to an anonymous two-element array. The first element of each array is a name string, while the second element is a reference to an anonymous array of varying lengths naming the provisions—all without having to come up with temporary names for any of the intermediate layers.

To the caller of this subroutine, the return value is identical to the previous version. However, from a maintenance point of view, the reduced clutter of not having all the intermediate names saves screen and brain space.

We can show a reference to an empty anonymous array using an empty anonymous array constructor. For example, if we add one "Mrs. Howell" to that travel list, as someone who has packed rather light, we'd insert:

```
['Mrs. Howell',
  [ ]    # anonymous empty array reference
],
```

This is a single element of the larger list. This item is a reference to an array with two elements, the first of which is the name string, and the second is a reference to an empty anonymous array. The array is empty because Mrs. Howell hasn't packed anything for this trip.

Creating an Anonymous Hash

Similar to creating an anonymous array, we can also create an anonymous hash. Consider the crew roster from Chapter 4:

```
my %gilligan_info = (
    name     => 'Gilligan',
    hat      => 'White',
    shirt    => 'Red',
    position => 'First Mate',
);

my %skipper_info = (
    name     => 'Skipper',
    hat      => 'Black',
    shirt    => 'Blue',
    position => 'Captain',
);

    my @crew = (\%gilligan_info, \%skipper_info);
```

The variables %gilligan_info and %skipper_info are temporaries we needed to create the hashes for the final data structure. We can construct the reference directly with the *anonymous hash constructor*, which is yet another meaning for curly braces. We can define the reference variable then assign to it, using two steps:

```
my $ref_to_gilligan_info;

{
  my %gilligan_info = (
    name     => 'Gilligan',
    hat      => 'White',
    shirt    => 'Red',
    position => 'First Mate',
  );
  $ref_to_gilligan_info = \%gilligan_info;
}
```

We can replace that with a single step:

```
my $ref_to_gilligan_info = {
  name     => 'Gilligan',
  hat      => 'White',
  shirt    => 'Red',
  position => 'First Mate',
};
```

The value between the opening and closing curly braces is an eight-element list. The eight-element list becomes a four-element anonymous hash (four key-value pairs). Perl takes a reference to this hash and returns as a single scalar value, which we assign to the scalar variable. Thus, we can rewrite the roster creation as:

```
my $ref_to_gilligan_info = {
  name     => 'Gilligan',
  hat      => 'White',
  shirt    => 'Red',
  position => 'First Mate',
};

my $ref_to_skipper_info = {
  name     => 'Skipper',
  hat      => 'Black',
  shirt    => 'Blue',
  position => 'Captain',
};

my @crew = ($ref_to_gilligan_info, $ref_to_skipper_info);
```

As before, we can now avoid the temporary variables and insert the values directly into the top-level list:

```
my @crew = (
  {
    name     => 'Gilligan',
    hat      => 'White',
    shirt    => 'Red',
    position => 'First Mate',
  },
```

```
{
  name     => 'Skipper',
  hat      => 'Black',
  shirt    => 'Blue',
  position => 'Captain',
},
);
```

Note that we use trailing commas on the lists when the element is not immediately next to the closing brace, bracket, or parenthesis. This is a nice style element to adopt because it allows for easy maintenance. We can add or rearrange lines quickly, or comment out lines without destroying the integrity of our list.

Now @crew is identical to the value it had before, but we no longer need to invent names for the intermediate data structures. As before, the @crew variable contains two elements, each of which is a reference to a hash containing keyword-based information about a particular crew member.

The anonymous hash constructor always evaluates its contents in list context and then constructs a hash from key-value pairs, just as if we had assigned that list to a named hash. Perl returns a reference to that hash as a single value that fits wherever a scalar fits.

Now, a word from our parser: because blocks and anonymous hash constructors both use curly braces in roughly the same places in the syntax tree, the compiler has to guess which of the two we mean. If the compiler ever decides incorrectly, we might need to provide a hint to get what we want. To show the compiler that we want an anonymous hash constructor, put a plus sign before the opening curly brace: +{ ... }. To get a block of code, put a semicolon (representing an empty statement) at the beginning of the block: {; ... }.

Autovivification

We look again at the provisions list. Suppose we were reading the data from a file, in this format:

```
The Skipper
  blue_shirt
  hat
  jacket
  preserver
  sunscreen
Professor
  sunscreen
  water_bottle
  slide_rule
Gilligan
  red_shirt
  hat
  lucky_socks
  water_bottle
```

We indent provisions with some whitespace, following a nonindented line with the person's name. We construct a hash of provisions. The keys of the hash will be the person's name, and the value will be an array reference to an array containing a list of provisions.

Initially, we might gather the data using a simple loop:

```
my %provisions;
my $person;

while (<>) {
  if (/^(\S.*)/) { # a person's name (no leading whitespace)
    $person = $1;
    $provisions{$person} = [  ] unless $provisions{$person};
  } elsif (/^\s+(\S.*)/) { # a provision
    die 'No person yet!' unless defined $person;
    push @{ $provisions{$person} }, $1;
  } else {
    die "I don't understand: $_";
  }
}
```

First, we declare the variables for the resulting hash of provisions and the current person. For each line that we read, we determine if it's a person or a provision. If it's a person, we remember the name and create the hash element for that person. The **unless** test ensures that we won't delete someone's provision list if his or her list is split in two places in the data file.

For example, suppose that "The Skipper" and " sextant" (note the leading whitespace) are at the end of the data file in order to list an additional data item.

The key is the person's name, and the value is initially a reference to an empty anonymous array. If the line is a provision, push it to the end of the correct array, using the array reference.

This code works fine, but it actually says more than it needs to. Why? Because we can leave out the line that initializes the hash element's value to a reference to an empty array:

```
my %provisions;
my $person;

while (<>) {
  if (/^(\S.*)/) { # a person's name (no leading whitespace)
    $person = $1;
    ## $provisions{$person} = [  ] unless $provisions{$person};
  } elsif (/^\s+(\S.*)/) { # a provision
    die 'No person yet!' unless defined $person;
    push @{ $provisions{$person} }, $1;
  } else {
    die "I don't understand: $_";
  }
}
```

What happens when we try to store that blue shirt for the Skipper? While looking at the second line of input, we'll end up with this effect:

```
push @{ $provisions{'The Skipper'} }, "blue_shirt";
```

At this point, $provisions{"The Skipper"} doesn't exist, but we're trying to use it as an array reference. To resolve this, Perl automatically inserts a reference to a new empty anonymous array into the variable and continues the operation. Here, the reference to the newly created empty array is dereferenced, and we push the blue shirt to the provisions list.

This process is called *autovivification*. As long as we haven't already given the variable (or access to a single element in an array or hash) a value, Perl will automatically create the reference type we assume it already is. That is, if the value is undef but we treat it as an array reference, Perl replaces the undef with a new array reference.

This is actually the same behavior we've been using in Perl all along. Perl creates new variables as needed. Before that statement, $provisions{"The Skipper"} didn't exist, so Perl created %provisions so we could access a value in that hash. Then @{ $provisions{"The Skipper"} } didn't exist, so Perl created the key The Skipper so it could access it. We haven't given it a value, so it's undef. When we try to use that undefined value as an array reference, Perl makes the value an array reference so it can dereference it as an array.

For example, this works:

```
my $not_yet;                 # new undefined variable
@$not_yet = (1, 2, 3);
```

We dereference the value $not_yet as if it were an array reference. But because it's initially undef, Perl acts as if we had explicitly initialized $not_yet as an empty array reference:

```
my $not_yet;
$not_yet = [  ]; # inserted through autovivification
@$not_yet = (1, 2, 3);
```

In other words, an initially empty array becomes an array of three elements.

This autovivification also works for multiple levels of assignment:

```
my $top;
$top->[2]->[4] = 'lee-lou';
```

Initially, $top contains undef, but because we dereference it as if it were an array reference, Perl inserts a reference to an empty anonymous array into $top. Perl then accesses the third element (index value 2), which causes Perl to grow the array to be three elements long. That element is also undef, so Perl stuffs it with a reference to another empty anonymous array. We then spin out along that newly created array, setting the fifth element to lee-lou.

Autovivification and Hashes

Autovivification also works for hash references.[3] If we dereference a variable containing undef as if it were a hash reference, a reference to an empty anonymous hash is inserted, and the operation continues.

One place this comes in handy is in a typical data reduction task. For example, the Professor gets an island-area network up and running (perhaps using Coco-Net or maybe Vines), and now wants to track the traffic from host to host. He begins logging the number of bytes transferred to a log file, giving the source host, the destination host, and the number of transferred bytes:

```
professor.hut gilligan.crew.hut 1250
professor.hut lovey.howell.hut 910
thurston.howell.hut lovey.howell.hut 1250
professor.hut lovey.howell.hut 450
professor.hut laser3.copyroom.hut 2924
ginger.girl.hut professor.hut 1218
ginger.girl.hut maryann.girl.hut 199
...
```

Now the Professor wants to produce a summary of the source host, the destination host, and the total number of transferred bytes for the day. Tabulating the data is as simple as reading the input line by line, breaking it up, and adding the latest value to what we had previously:

```
my %total_bytes;
while (<>) {
  my ($source, $destination, $bytes) = split;
  $total_bytes{$source}{$destination} += $bytes;
}
```

We see how this works on the first line of data. We'll execute:

```
$total_bytes{'professor.hut'}{'gilligan.crew.hut'} += 1250;
```

Because %total_bytes is initially empty, Perl doesn't find the first key of professor.hut, but it establishes an undef value for the dereferencing as a hash reference. (Keep in mind that an implicit arrow is between the two sets of curly braces here.) Perl sticks in a reference to an empty anonymous hash in that element, which it then immediately extends to include the element with a key of gilligan.crew.hut. Its initial value is undef, which acts like a zero when we add 1,250 to it, and the result of 1,250 is inserted back into the hash (see Figure 5-2).

Any later data line that contains this same source host and destination host will reuse that same value, adding more bytes to the running total. But each new destination host extends a hash to include a new initially undef byte count, and each new source host uses autovivification to create a destination host hash. In other words, Perl does the right thing, as always.

3. Or, really, hash *dereferences*.

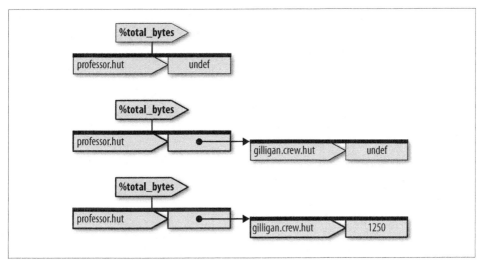

Figure 5-2. The autovivification of %total_bytes

Once we've processed the file, it's time to display the summary. First, we determine all the sources:

```
for my $source (keys %total_bytes) {
...
```

Now, we should get all destinations. The syntax for this is a bit tricky. We want all keys of the hash, resulting from dereferencing the value of the hash element, in the first structure:

```
for my $source (keys %total_bytes) {
  for my $destination (keys %{ $total_bytes{$source} }) {
....
```

For good measure, we should sort both lists to be consistent:

```
for my $source (sort keys %total_bytes) {
  for my $destination (sort keys %{ $total_bytes{$source} }) {
    print "$source => $destination:",
      " $total_bytes{$source}{$destination} bytes\n";
  }
  print "\n";
}
```

This is a typical strategy to reduce data for a report. Create a hash-of-hashrefs (perhaps nested even deeper, as we show later), using autovivification to fill in the gaps in the upper data structures as needed, and then walk through the resulting data structure to display the results.

The Perl Data Structures Cookbook, *perldsc*, has more examples of creating, accessing, and printing complex data structures.

Exercises

You can find the answers to these exercises in "Answers for Chapter 5" on page 318.

1. [5 minutes] Without running it, can you see what's wrong with this piece of a program? If you can't see the problem after a minute or two, see whether trying to run it will give you a hint of how to fix it (you might try turning on warnings):

```
my %passenger_1 = {
  name       => 'Ginger',
  age        => 22,
  occupation => 'Movie Star',
  real_age   => 35,
  hat        => undef,
};

my %passenger_2 = {
  name          => 'Mary-Ann',
  age           => 19,
  hat           => 'bonnet',
  favorite_food => 'corn',
};

my @passengers = (\%passenger_1, \%passenger_2);
```

2. [40 minutes] The Professor's data file (mentioned earlier in this chapter) is available as *coconet.dat* in the Download section of *http://www.intermediateperl.com/*. There may be comment lines (beginning with a #); be sure to skip them. (That is, your program should skip them. You might find a helpful hint if *you* read them!) Here are the first data lines in the file:

```
gilligan.crew.hut lovey.howell.hut 4721
thurston.howell.hut lovey.howell.hut 4046
professor.hut ginger.girl.hut 5768
gilligan.crew.hut laser3.copyroom.hut 9352
gilligan.crew.hut maryann.girl.hut 1180
fileserver.copyroom.hut thurston.howell.hut 2548
skipper.crew.hut gilligan.crew.hut 1259
fileserver.copyroom.hut maryann.girl.hut 248
fileserver.copyroom.hut maryann.girl.hut 798
skipper.crew.hut maryann.girl.hut 1921
```

Modify the code from this chapter so that each source machine's portion of the output shows the total bytes from that machine. List the source machines in order from most to least data transferred. Within each group, list the destination machines in order from most to least data transferred to that target from the source machine:

```
professor.hut => gilligan.hut: 1845
professor.hut => maryann.hut: 90
```

The result should be that the machine that sent the most data will be the first source machine in the list, and the first destination should be the machine to which it sent the most data. The Professor can use this printout to reconfigure the network for efficiency.

3. [40 minutes] Starting with your data structure from Exercise 2, rewrite the *coconet.dat* file so that it's in the same format, but sorted by source machine. Report each destination machine once per source machine along with total bytes transferred. The destination machines should be indented under the source machine name and be sorted by the machine name:

```
ginger.hut
  maryann.hut 13744
professor.hut
  gilligan.hut 1845
  maryann.hut 90
thurston.howell.hut
  lovey.howell.hut 97560
...
```

## CHAPTER 6

Manipulating Complex Data Structures

Now that we've shown the basics of references, we look at additional ways to manipulate complex data. We start by using the debugger to examine complex data structures and then use `Data::Dumper` to show the data under programmatic control. Next, we'll show how to store and retrieve complex data easily and quickly using `Storable`, and finally we'll wrap up with a review of `grep` and `map` and see how they apply to complex data.

Using the Debugger to View Complex Data

The Perl debugger can display complex data easily. For example, we can single-step through one version of the byte-counting program from Chapter 5:

```
my %total_bytes;
while (<>) {
  my ($source, $destination, $bytes) = split;
  $total_bytes{$source}{$destination} += $bytes;
}
for my $source (sort keys %total_bytes) {
  for my $destination (sort keys %{ $total_bytes{$source} }) {
    print "$source => $destination:",
      " $total_bytes{$source}{$destination} bytes\n";
  }
  print "\n";
}
```

Here's the data we'll use to test it:

```
professor.hut gilligan.crew.hut 1250
professor.hut lovey.howell.hut 910
thurston.howell.hut lovey.howell.hut 1250
professor.hut lovey.howell.hut 450
ginger.girl.hut professor.hut 1218
ginger.girl.hut maryann.girl.hut 199
```

We can do this in any number of ways. One of the easiest is to invoke Perl with a `-d` switch on the command line:

```
myhost% perl -d bytecounts bytecounts-in

Loading DB routines from perl5db.pl version 1.19
Editor support available.

Enter h or `h h' for help, or `man perldebug' for more help.

main::(bytecounts:2):        my %total_bytes;
  DB<1> s
main::(bytecounts:3):        while (<>) {
  DB<1> s
main::(bytecounts:4):          my ($source, $destination, $bytes) = split;
  DB<1> s
main::(bytecounts:5):            $total_bytes{$source}{$destination} += $bytes;
  DB<1> x $source, $destination, $bytes
0  'professor.hut'
1  'gilligan.crew.hut'
2  1250
```

Each new release of the debugger works slightly differently than previous releases, so our screen might not look exactly like what we show here. Also, if we get stuck at any time, we can type h for help, or look at *perldebug*.

The debugger shows each line of code before it executes it. That means that, at this point, we're about to invoke the autovivification, and we've got our keys established. The s command single-steps the program, while the x command dumps a list of values in a nice format. We can see that $source, $destination, and $bytes are correct, and now it's time to update the data:

```
DB<2> s
  main::(bytecounts:3):        while (<>) {
```

We've created the hash entries through autovivification. Here's what we have:

```
DB<2> x \%total_bytes
   0  HASH(0x132dc)
 'professor.hut' => HASH(0x37a34)
    'gilligan.crew.hut' => 1250
```

When we give x a hash reference, it dumps the entire contents of the hash, showing the key/value pairs. If any of the values are also hash references, it dumps those as well, recursively. What we'll see is that the %total_bytes hash has a single key of professor.hut, whose corresponding value is another hash reference. The referenced hash contains a single key of gilligan.crew.hut, with a value of 1250, as expected.

Here's what happens after the next assignment:

```
DB<3> s
  main::(bytecounts:4):          my ($source, $destination, $bytes) = split;
DB<3> s
  main::(bytecounts:5):            $total_bytes{$source}{$destination} += $bytes;
DB<3> x $source, $destination, $bytes
   0  'professor.hut'
   1  'lovey.howell.hut'
   2  910
```

```
DB<4> s
  main::(bytecounts:3):          while (<>) {
DB<4> x \%total_bytes
  0  HASH(0x132dc)
  'professor.hut' => HASH(0x37a34)
     'gilligan.crew.hut' => 1250
     'lovey.howell.hut' => 910
```

Now we've added bytes flowing from professor.hut to lovey.howell.hut. The top-level hash hasn't changed, but the second-level hash has added a new entry. We continue:

```
DB<5> s
  main::(bytecounts:4):          my ($source, $destination, $bytes) = split;
DB<6> s
  main::(bytecounts:5):          $total_bytes{$source}{$destination} += $bytes;
DB<6> x $source, $destination, $bytes
  0  'thurston.howell.hut'
  1  'lovey.howell.hut'
  2  1250
DB<7> s
  main::(bytecounts:3):          while (<>) {
DB<7> x \%total_bytes
  0  HASH(0x132dc)
  'professor.hut' => HASH(0x37a34)
     'gilligan.crew.hut' => 1250
     'lovey.howell.hut' => 910
  'thurston.howell.hut' => HASH(0x2f9538)
     'lovey.howell.hut' => 1250
```

Ah, now it's getting interesting. A new entry in the top-level hash has a key of thurston.howell.hut and a new hash reference, autovivified initially to an empty hash. Immediately after the new empty hash was put in place, a new key/value pair was added, indicating 1,250 bytes transferred from thurston.howell.hut to lovey.howell.hut. We step some more:

```
DB<8> s
  main::(bytecounts:4):          my ($source, $destination, $bytes) = split;
DB<8> s
  main::(bytecounts:5):          $total_bytes{$source}{$destination} += $bytes;
DB<8> x $source, $destination, $bytes
  0  'professor.hut'
  1  'lovey.howell.hut'
  2  450
DB<9> s
  main::(bytecounts:3):          while (<>) {
DB<9> x \%total_bytes
  0  HASH(0x132dc)
  'professor.hut' => HASH(0x37a34)
     'gilligan.crew.hut' => 1250
     'lovey.howell.hut' => 1360
  'thurston.howell.hut' => HASH(0x2f9538)
     'lovey.howell.hut' => 1250
```

Now we're adding in some more bytes from professor.hut to lovey.howell.hut, reusing the existing value place. Nothing too exciting there. We keep stepping:

```
DB<10> s
  main::(bytecounts:4):                my ($source, $destination, $bytes) = split;
DB<10> s
  main::(bytecounts:5):                $total_bytes{$source}{$destination} += $bytes;
DB<10> x $source, $destination, $bytes
  0  'ginger.girl.hut'
  1  'professor.hut'
  2  1218
DB<11> s
  main::(bytecounts:3):                while (<>) {
DB<11> x \%total_bytes
  0  HASH(0x132dc)
  'ginger.girl.hut' => HASH(0x297474)
     'professor.hut' => 1218
  'professor.hut' => HASH(0x37a34)
     'gilligan.crew.hut' => 1250
     'lovey.howell.hut' => 1360
  'thurston.howell.hut' => HASH(0x2f9538)
     'lovey.howell.hut' => 1250
```

This time, we added a new source, ginger.girl.hut. Notice that the top-level hash now has three elements, and each element has a different hash reference value. We step some more:

```
DB<12> s
  main::(bytecounts:4):                my ($source, $destination, $bytes) = split;
DB<12> s
  main::(bytecounts:5):                $total_bytes{$source}{$destination} += $bytes;
DB<12> x $source, $destination, $bytes
  0  'ginger.girl.hut'
  1  'maryann.girl.hut'
  2  199
DB<13> s
  main::(bytecounts:3):                while (<>) {
DB<13> x \%total_bytes
  0  HASH(0x132dc)
  'ginger.girl.hut' => HASH(0x297474)
     'maryann.girl.hut' => 199
     'professor.hut' => 1218
  'professor.hut' => HASH(0x37a34)
     'gilligan.crew.hut' => 1250
     'lovey.howell.hut' => 1360
  'thurston.howell.hut' => HASH(0x2f9538)
     'lovey.howell.hut' => 1250
```

Now we've added a second destination to the hash that records information for all bytes originating at ginger.girl.hut. Because that was the final line of data (in this run), a step brings us down to the lower foreach loop:

```
DB<14> s
  main::(bytecounts:8):                for my $source (sort keys %total_bytes) {
```

Even though we can't directly examine the list value from inside those parentheses, we can display it:

```
DB<14> x sort keys %total_bytes
    0  'ginger.girl.hut'
    1  'professor.hut'
    2  'thurston.howell.hut'
```

This is the list the foreach now scans. These are all the sources for transferred bytes seen in this particular logfile. Here's what happens when we step into the inner loop:

```
DB<15> s
    main::(bytecounts:9):                for my $destination (sort keys %{ $total_bytes{
    $source} }) {
```

At this point, we can determine from the inside out exactly what values will result from the list value from inside the parentheses. Here they are:

```
DB<15> x $source
    0  'ginger.girl.hut'
DB<16> x $total_bytes{$source}
    0  HASH(0x297474)
    'maryann.girl.hut' => 199
    'professor.hut' => 1218
DB<18> x keys %{ $total_bytes{$source } }
    0  'maryann.girl.hut'
    1  'professor.hut'
DB<19> x sort keys %{ $total_bytes{$source } }
    0  'maryann.girl.hut'
    1  'professor.hut'
```

Dumping $total_bytes{$source} shows that it was a hash reference. Also, the sort appears not to have done anything, but the output of keys is not necessarily in a sorted order. The next step finds the data:

```
DB<20> s
    main::(bytecounts:10):               print "$source => $destination:",
    main::(bytecounts:11):    .            " $total_bytes{$source}{$destination} bytes\n";
DB<20> x $source, $destination
    0  'ginger.girl.hut'
    1  'maryann.girl.hut'
DB<21> x $total_bytes{$source}{$destination}
    0  199
```

As we can see with the debugger, we can easily show the data, even structured data, to help us understand our program.

Viewing Complex Data with Data::Dumper

Another way to visualize a complex data structure rapidly is to *dump* it. Data::Dumper, which comes with Perl, provides a basic way to show a Perl data structure as Perl code. We replace the last half of the byte-counting program with a simple call to Data::Dumper:

```
use Data::Dumper;

my %total_bytes;
while (<>) {
  my ($source, $destination, $bytes) = split;
  $total_bytes{$source}{$destination} += $bytes;
}

print Dumper(\%total_bytes);
```

The `Data::Dumper` module defines the `Dumper` subroutine. This subroutine is similar to the `x` command in the debugger. We can give `Dumper` one or more values, and `Dumper` turns those values into a printable string. We pass reference arguments to keep the hash as a hash instead of a list of separate arguments. The difference between the debugger's `x` command and `Dumper`, however, is that the string generated by `Dumper` is Perl code:

```
% perl bytecounts < bytecounts-in
$VAR1 = {
          'thurston.howell.hut' => {
                                     'lovey.howell.hut' => 1250
                                   },
          'ginger.girl.hut' => {
                                 'maryann.girl.hut' => 199,
                                 'professor.hut' => 1218
                               },
          'professor.hut' => {
                               'gilligan.crew.hut' => 1250,
                               'lovey.howell.hut' => 1360
                             }
        };
```

The Perl code is fairly understandable; it shows that we have a reference to a hash of three elements, with each value of the hash being a reference to a nested hash. We can evaluate this code and get a hash that's equivalent to the original hash. However, if you're thinking about doing this in order to have a complex data structure persist from one program invocation to the next, please keep reading.

`Data::Dumper`, like the debugger's `x` command, handles shared data properly. For example, go back to that "leaking" data from Chapter 5:

```
use Data::Dumper;
$Data::Dumper::Purity = 1; # declare possibly self-referencing structures
my @data1 = qw(one won);
my @data2 = qw(two too to);
push @data2, \@data1;
push @data1, \@data2;
print Dumper(\@data1, \@data2);
```

Here's the output from this program:

```
$VAR1 = [
          'one',
          'won',
          [
```

```
                'two',
                'too',
                'to',
                [  ]
            ]
        ];
    $VAR1->[2][3] = $VAR1;
    $VAR2 = $VAR1->[2];
```

Notice how we've created two different variables now, since there are two parameters to Dumper. The element $VAR1 corresponds to a reference to @data1, while $VAR2 corresponds to a reference to @data2. The debugger shows the values similarly:

```
DB<1> x \@data1, \@data2
        0  ARRAY(0xf914)
    0  'one'
    1  'won'
    2  ARRAY(0x3122a8)
        0  'two'
        1  'too'
        2  'to'
        3  ARRAY(0xf914)
            -> REUSED_ADDRESS
    1  ARRAY(0x3122a8)
    -> REUSED_ADDRESS
```

The phrase REUSED_ADDRESS indicates that some parts of the data are actually references we've already seen.

Other Dumpers

Data::Dumper comes with Perl, so it's easy to use. However, it has a basic design decision that makes its output a bit ugly. It's specifically designed to represent a Perl data structure as a string that is valid Perl code. That means we could eval that string and get back the data structure, for the most part. If we don't care about reconstituting the data structure, we don't need Data::Dumper.

Other modules, which don't care about creating valid Perl code as output, can have nicer output formats. We have to install them from CPAN, but that's a small price to pay. We take the same data structure and look at their dumps with different modules. Here's $total_bytes again:

```
my %total_bytes = (
    'thurston.howell.hut' => {
        'lovey.howell.hut' => 1250
    },
    'ginger.girl.hut' => {
        'maryann.girl.hut' => 199,
        'professor.hut' => 1218
    },
    'professor.hut' => {
        'gilligan.crew.hut' => 1250,
        'lovey.howell.hut' => 1360
```

```
      }
    );
```

The Data::Dump module has a dump subroutine, which we give a reference argument as we did with Data::Dumper:

```
use Data::Dump qw(dump);

dump( \%total_bytes );
```

Its output is a little bit nicer than Data::Dumper, but still looks a lot like Perl code. We've wrapped the output lines here:

```
{
  "ginger.girl.hut"    =>
    { "maryann.girl.hut" => 199, "professor.hut" => 1218 },
  "professor.hut"      =>
    { "gilligan.crew.hut" => 1250, "lovey.howell.hut" => 1360 },
  "thurston.howell.hut" =>
    { "lovey.howell.hut" => 1250 },
}
```

The Data::Printer module does away with even more of the Perly bits. Its p subroutine doesn't need a reference argument because it does some magic to detect the argument type:

```
use Data::Printer;

p( %total_bytes );
```

The output is much easier to read:

```
{
    ginger.girl.hut      {
        maryann.girl.hut   199,
        professor.hut      1218
    },
    professor.hut        {
        gilligan.crew.hut  1250,
        lovey.howell.hut   1360
    },
    thurston.howell.hut  {
        lovey.howell.hut   1250
    }
}
```

Marshalling Data

We can take the output of Data::Dumper's Dumper routine, place it into a file, then load the file to a different program. Here's a program that has a circular data structure that we want to preserve:

```
use Data::Dumper;
```

```
my @data1 = qw(one won);
my @data2 = qw(two too to);
push @data2, \@data1;
push @data1, \@data2;
my $string =  Dumper( \@data1, \@data2 ); # to some filehandle
```

The text in `$string` is a Perl code which defines two variables, $VAR1 and $VAR2:

```
$VAR1 = [
          'one',
          'won',
          [
            'two',
            'too',
            'to',
            $VAR1
          ]
        ];
$VAR2 = $VAR1->[2];
```

To turn it back into a Perl data structure, we can use the string form of eval that we showed in Chapter 3. We can do this in the same program or a different program:

```
my $data_structure = eval $string
```

That's not very pretty. Those variables had names before and now they have prosaic identifiers. After the eval, we have variables named $VAR1 and $VAR2.

To fix that, we can call the Dump method with two array references. The first array reference is the list of variables we want to dump, and the second has the list of names we want to use:

```
print Data::Dumper->Dump(
  [ \@data1, \@data2 ],
  [ qw(*data1 *data2) ]
  );
```

We don't show typeglobs here, but we use the * prefix, which tells Data::Dumper to look at the references to figure out what variable type it should use in the string:

```
@data1 = (
           'one',
           'won',
           [
             'two',
             'too',
             'to',
             \@data1
           ]
         );
@data2 = @{$data1[2]};
```

When we eval this code, we get the same data and the variables that point to those data have the same names.

See *Mastering Perl* to learn about typeglobs.

Storing Complex Data with Storable

When we evaluate the code as Perl code, we end up with two package variables, $VAR1 and $VAR2, that are equivalent to the original data. This is called *marshalling* the data: converting complex data into a form that we can write to a file as a stream of bytes for later reconstruction.

However, another Perl core module is much better suited for marshaling: Storable. It's better suited because compared to Data::Dumper, Storable produces smaller and faster-to-process files. (The Storable module is standard in recent versions of Perl, but we can always install it from the CPAN if it's missing.)

The interface is similar to using Data::Dumper, except we must put everything into one reference. The freeze subroutine returns a binary string that represents the data structure:

```
use Storable;
my @data1 = qw(one won);
my @data2 = qw(two too to);
push @data2, \@data1;
push @data1, \@data2;
my $frozen = freeze [\@data1, \@data2];
```

The string in $frozen is 68 bytes, which is quite a bit shorter than the equivalent Data::Dumper output. It's also less readable for humans. We can save that string in a file, send it through a socket, or output it to a filehandle. Whoever gets this string can reconstitute the data structure:

```
use Storable;
my $data = thaw( $input );
```

We need to know something about the data structure to use it.

If we want to store the binary representation in a file, we can use nstore to freeze the data and save it in one step:

```
nstore [\@data1, \@data2], $filename;
```

On the other side, we use retrieve to reconstitute the data structure:

```
my $array_ref = retrieve $filename;
```

The binary format used by Storable is architecture byte-order dependent by default, but instead of using store, we used nstore, where the *n* stands for "network order." Different architectures agree, by convention, on "network order" for storing numbers so different architectures know how to interpret the data.

There's a useful task that `Storable` can now do for us. If we want to copy a data structure to have a completely separate existence, we can `freeze` then `thaw`. The original and reconstituted data structures don't affect each other.

Why is this interesting? We know that we can copy arrays then change one without changing the other:

```
use Data::Dumper;

my @provisions = qw( hat suncreen );
my @packed = @provisions;

push @packed, 'blue_shirt';

print Data::Dumper->Dump(
  [ \@provisions ],
  [ qw( *provisions ) ]
  );
print Data::Dumper->Dump(
  [ \@packed ],
  [ qw( *packed ) ]
  );
```

We copied `@provisions` into `@packed` then changed `@packed`, and `@provisions` stayed the same:

```
@provisions = (
                'hat',
                'suncreen'
              );
@packed = (
              'hat',
              'suncreen',
              'blue_shirt'
            );
```

This accidentally works because copying named arrays makes a *shallow copy*. It's a different story if one of the arrays holds a reference. Here's the same program with an additional twist. We push an array reference onto `@provisions`:

```
use Data::Dumper;

my @provisions = qw( hat suncreen );
my @science_kit = qw( microscope radio );
push @provisions, \@science_kit;

my @packed = @provisions;

push @packed, 'blue_shirt';

print Data::Dumper->Dump(
  [ \@provisions ],
  [ qw( *provisions ) ]
  );
```

```
print Data::Dumper->Dump(
  [ \@packed ],
  [ qw( *packed ) ]
  );
```

 A *shallow copy* of an array or hash only makes copies of the first level values. If one of the elements is a reference, however, the new array or hash gets the same reference. Everything below the reference (the *deep* part) is the same. Hence, a shallow copy.

The output shows the same thing happened. We copied the arrays and added an element to one of them. So far so good. We modify one of the arrays to add to the science kit:

```
use Data::Dumper;

my @provisions = qw( hat suncreen );
my @science_kit = qw( microscope radio );
push @provisions, \@science_kit;

my @packed = @provisions;

push @packed, 'blue_shirt';

push @{ $packed[2] }, 'batteries';

print Data::Dumper->Dump(
  [ \@provisions ],
  [ qw( *provisions ) ]
  );
print Data::Dumper->Dump(
  [ \@packed ],
  [ qw( *packed ) ]
  );
```

The output shows that both arrays changed. Each has `batteries` now!

```
@provisions = (
                'hat',
                'suncreen',
                [
                  'microscope',
                  'radio',
                  'batteries'
                ]
              );
@packed = (
            'hat',
            'suncreen',
            [
              'microscope',
              'radio',
```

```
        'batteries'
    ],
    'blue_shirt'
);
```

These arrays both have a reference to the same data, as shown in Figure 6-1, so changing the shared reference changes it for all of the other arrays.

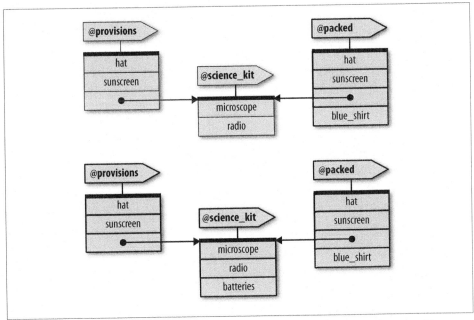

Figure 6-1. The arrays @provisions and @packed each contain a reference to @science_kit

We usually don't want a shallow copy. Instead, we want a *deep copy*, and Storable's freezing then thawing can do that for us:

```perl
use Data::Dumper;
use Storable qw(freeze thaw);

my @provisions = qw( hat suncreen );
my @science_kit = qw( microscope radio );
push @provisions, \@science_kit;

my $frozen = freeze \@provisions;
my @packed = @{ thaw $frozen };

push @packed, 'blue_shirt';

push @{ $packed[2] }, 'batteries';

print Data::Dumper->Dump(
    [ \@provisions ],
    [ qw( *provisions ) ]
```

```
    );
    print Data::Dumper->Dump(
    [ \@packed ],
    [ qw( *packed ) ]
    );
```

Now @provisions and @packed are completely separate. Only @packed gets batteries (see Figure 6-2):

```
    @provisions = (
                    'hat',
                    'suncreen',
                    [
                      'microscope',
                      'radio'
                    ]
                );
    @packed = (
                'hat',
                'suncreen',
                [
                  'microscope',
                  'radio',
                  'batteries'
                ],
                'blue_shirt'
            );
```

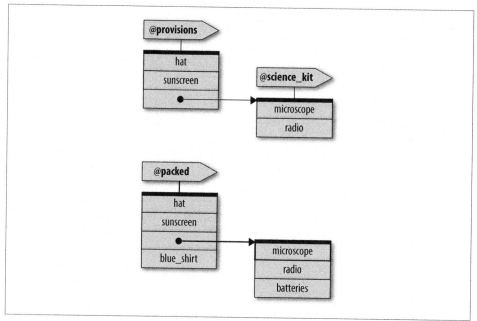

Figure 6-2. The @provisions and @packed after a deep copy

We don't need to do this in two steps. `Storable` anticipates this for us and does it in one step with `dclone`:

```
my @packed = @{ dclone \@provisions };
```

This makes `Storable` quite useful even if we don't want to exchange data with anyone.

YAML

Ingy döt Net[1] came up with Yet Another Markup Language (YAML) to provide a more readable (and more compact) format that different languages can all process.[2] It works in the same way as `Data::Dumper`. We'll see more about YAML when we talk about modules later, so we won't say much about it here.

From the earlier example, we plug in YAML where we had `Data::Dumper`, and use `Dump` where we had `Dumper`:

```
use YAML;

my %total_bytes;

while (<>) {
  my ($source, $destination, $bytes) = split;
  $total_bytes{$source}{$destination} += $bytes;
  }

print Dump(\%total_bytes);
```

When we use the same data from the earlier example, we get this output:

```
---
ginger.girl.hut:
  maryann.girl.hut: 199
  professor.hut: 1218
professor.hut:
  gilligan.crew.hut: 1250
  lovey.howell.hut: 1360
thurston.howell.hut:
  lovey.howell.hut: 1250
```

That's a lot easier to read because it takes up less space on the screen, which can be really handy when we have deeply nested data structures. And, if we want to share this with our Ruby or Python friends, they won't have any problem reading this data.

---

1. Yes, that's his name. Ingy's written many interesting modules, which we can see at *https://www.metacpan .org/author/INGY*.

2. "Acmeists believe that their ideas need to be shared across all language boundaries." See *http://acmeism .org/*.

JSON

JavaScript Object Notation, or JSON, is another popular format. We can easily exchange JSON data between programs, even if they are implemented in different languages. Our Perl program can send data to a web page, for example, and the web page's JavaScript can easily use the data right away. The JSON module has many ways to create the output, including the to_json:

```
use JSON;

print to_json( \%total_bytes, { pretty => 1 } );
```

We used the pretty attribute to make the output fit nicely on this page (which also makes it easier for us humans to read):

```
{
    "thurston.howell.hut" : {
        "lovey.howell.hut" : 1250
    },
    "ginger.girl.hut" : {
        "maryann.girl.hut" : 199,
        "professor.hut" : 1218
    },
    "professor.hut" : {
        "gilligan.crew.hut" : 1250,
        "lovey.howell.hut" : 1360
    }
}
```

We might get some JSON text from a file, a web request, or as the output from another program. We can easily recreate the Perl data structure, too:

```
use JSON;

my $hash_ref = from_json( $json_string );
```

Using the map and grep Operators

As the data structures become more complex, it helps to have higher level constructs deal with common tasks such as selection and transformation. In this regard, Perl's grep and map operators are worth mastering.

Applying a Bit of Indirection

Some problems that may appear complex are actually simple once we've seen a solution or two. For example, suppose we want to find the items in a list that have odd digit sums but don't want the items themselves. What we want to know is where they occurred in the original list.

All that's required is a bit of indirection.[3] First, we have a selection problem, so we use a grep. We don't want to grep the values themselves but the index for each item:

```
my @input_numbers = (1, 2, 4, 8, 16, 32, 64);
my @indices_of_odd_digit_sums = grep {
    ...
} 0..$#input_numbers;
```

Here, the expression `0..$#input_numbers` will be a list of indices for the array. Inside the block, `$_` is a small integer, from 0 to 6 (seven items total). Now, we don't want to decide whether `$_` has an odd digit sum. We want to know whether the array element at that index has an odd digit sum. Instead of using `$_` to get the number of interest, use `$input_numbers[$_]`:

```
my @indices_of_odd_digit_sums = grep {
    my $number = $input_numbers[$_];
    my $sum;
    $sum += $_ for split //, $number;
    $sum % 2;
} 0..$#input_numbers;
```

The result will be the indices at which 1, 16, and 32 appear in the list: 0, 4, and 5. We could use these indices in an array slice to get the original values again:

```
my @odd_digit_sums = @input_numbers[ @indices_of_odd_digit_sums ];
```

The strategy here for an indirect grep or map is to think of the `$_` values as identifying a particular item of interest, such as the key in a hash or the index of an array, and then use that identification within the block or expression to access the actual values.

Here's another example: we select the elements of @x that are larger than the corresponding value in @y. Again, we'll use the indices of @x as our `$_` items:

```
my @bigger_indices = grep {
    if ($_ > $#y or $x[$_] > $y[$_]) {
        1; # yes, select it
    } else {
        0; # no, don't select it
    }
} 0..$#x;
my @bigger = @x[@bigger_indices];
```

In the grep, `$_` varies from 0 to the highest index of @x. If that element is beyond the end of @y, we automatically select it. Otherwise, we look at the individual corresponding values of the two arrays, selecting only those that match our condition.

However, this is a bit more verbose than it needs to be. We could return the Boolean expression rather than a explicit 1 or 0:

---

3. A famous computing maxim states that "there is no problem so complex that it cannot be solved with appropriate additional layers of indirection." With indirection comes obfuscation, so there's got to be a magic middle ground somewhere.

```
my @bigger_indices = grep {
  $_ > $#y or $x[$_] > $y[$_];
} 0..$#x;
my @bigger = @x[@bigger_indices];
```

More easily, we can skip the step of building the intermediate array by returning the items of interest with a map:

```
my @bigger = map {
  if ($_ > $#y or $x[$_] > $y[$_]) {
    $x[$_];
  } else {
    ( );
  }
} 0..$#x;
```

If the index is good, return the resulting array value. If the index is bad, return an empty list, making that item disappear.

Selecting and Altering Complex Data

We can use these operators on more complex data. Taking the provisions list from Chapter 5 (see Figure 6-3):

```
my %provisions = (
  'The Skipper'    => [qw(blue_shirt hat jacket preserver sunscreen)      ],
  'The Professor'  => [qw(sunscreen water_bottle slide_rule batteries radio) ],
  'Gilligan'       => [qw(red_shirt hat lucky_socks water_bottle)         ],
);
```

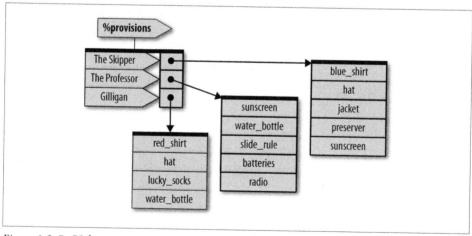

Figure 6-3. PeGS for provisions

Here, `$provisions{"The Professor"}` gives an array reference of the provisions brought by the Professor, and `$provisions{"Gilligan"}[-1]` gives the last item Gilligan thought to bring.

We run a few queries against this data. Who brought fewer than five items?

```perl
my @packed_light = grep @{ $provisions{$_} } < 5, keys %provisions;
```

Here, `$_` is the name of a person. We take that name, look up the array reference of the provisions for that person, dereference that in scalar context to get the count of provisions, and then compare it to 5. And wouldn't we know it; the only name is `Gilligan`.

Here's a trickier one. Who brought a water bottle?

```perl
my @all_wet = grep {
  my @items = @{ $provisions{$_} };
  grep $_ eq 'water_bottle', @items;
} keys %provisions;
```

Starting with the list of names again (`keys %provisions`), we pull up all the packed items first, and then use that list in an inner `grep` to count the number of those items that equal `water_bottle`. If the count is 0, there's no bottle, so the result is false for the outer `grep`. If the count is nonzero, we have a bottle, so the result is true for the outer `grep`. Now we see that the Skipper will be a bit thirsty later, without any relief.

We can also transform data. For example, we can turn a hash into a list of array references with each array containing two items. The first is the original person's name; the second is a reference to an array of the provisions for that person:

```perl
my @remapped_list = map {
  [ $_ => $provisions{$_} ];
} keys %provisions;
```

The keys of `%provisions` are names of the people. For each name, we construct a two-element list comprising the name and the corresponding provisions array reference. This list is inside an anonymous array constructor, so we get back a reference to a newly created array for each person. Three names in; three references out. Or, we can go a different way. We turn the input hash into a series of references to arrays. Each array will have a person's name and one of the items they brought:

```perl
my @person_item_pairs = map {
  my $person = $_;
  my @items = @{ $provisions{$person} };
  map [$person => $_], @items;
} keys %provisions;
```

Yes, a map within a map. The outer `map` selects one person at a time. We save this name in `$person`, and then we extract the item list from the hash. The inner `map` walks over this item list, executing the expression to construct an anonymous array reference for each item. The anonymous array contains the person's name and the provision item.

We had to use `$person` here to hold the outer `$_` temporarily. Otherwise, we can't refer to both temporary values for the outer `map` and the inner `map`.

Exercises

You can find the answers to these exercises in "Answers for Chapter 6" on page 320.

1. [20 minutes] The program from Exercise 3 in Chapter 5 needs to read the entire data file each time it runs. However, the Professor has a new router logfile each day and doesn't want to keep all that data in one giant file that takes longer and longer to process.

   Fix up that program to keep the running totals in a data file so the Professor can run it on each day's logs to get the new totals. Use the `Storable` module.

2. [20 minutes] Modify the program from Exercise 1 to use `JSON` instead of `Storable`.

## CHAPTER 7

Subroutine References

So far, we've shown references to three main Perl data types: scalars, arrays, and hashes. We can also take a reference to a *subroutine* (sometimes called a *coderef*).

Why would we want to do that? Well, in the same way that taking a reference to an array lets us have the same code work on different arrays at different times, taking a reference to a subroutine allows the same code to call different subroutines at different times. Also, references permit complex data structures. A reference to a subroutine allows a subroutine to effectively become part of that complex data structure.

Put another way, a variable or a complex data structure is a repository of values throughout the program. A reference to a subroutine can be thought of as a repository of *behavior* in a program. The examples in this section show how this works.

Referencing a Named Subroutine

The Skipper and Gilligan are having a conversation:

```
sub skipper_greets {
  my $person = shift;
  print "Skipper: Hey there, $person!\n";
}

sub gilligan_greets {
  my $person = shift;
  if ($person eq "Skipper") {
    print "Gilligan: Sir, yes, sir, $person!\n";
  } else {
    print "Gilligan: Hi, $person!\n";
  }
}

skipper_greets("Gilligan");
gilligan_greets("Skipper");
```

This results in:

```
Skipper: Hey there, Gilligan!
Gilligan: Sir, yes, sir, Skipper!
```

So far, nothing unusual has happened. Note, however, that Gilligan has two different behaviors, depending on whether he's addressing the Skipper or someone else.

Now, have the Professor walk into the hut. Both of the *Minnow* crew greet the newest participant:

```
skipper_greets('Professor');
gilligan_greets('Professor');
```

which results in:

```
Skipper: Hey there, Professor!
Gilligan: Hi, Professor!
```

Now the Professor feels obligated to respond:

```
sub professor_greets {
  my $person = shift;
  print "Professor: By my calculations, you must be $person!\n";
}

professor_greets('Gilligan');
professor_greets('Skipper');
```

resulting in:

```
Professor: By my calculations, you must be Gilligan!
Professor: By my calculations, you must be Skipper!
```

Whew. That's a lot of typing, and it's not general. If each person's behavior is in a separate named subroutine and a new person walks in the door, we have to figure out what other subroutines to call. We could certainly do it with enough hard-to-maintain code, but we can simplify the process by adding a bit of indirection, just as we did with arrays and hashes.

First, we use the "take a reference to" operator. It actually needs no introduction because it's that very same backslash as before:

```
my $ref_to_greeter = \&skipper_greets;
```

We're taking a reference to the subroutine `skipper_greets`. The preceding ampersand is mandatory here, and the lack of trailing parentheses is also intentional. Perl stores the reference to the subroutine (a coderef) within `$ref_to_greeter`, and like all other references, it fits nearly anywhere a scalar fits.

There's only one reason to get back to the original subroutine by dereferencing the coderef: to call it. Dereferencing a code reference is similar to dereferencing other references. First, start with the way we would have written it before we heard of references (including the optional ampersand prefix):

```
& skipper_greets ( 'Gilligan' )
```

Next, we replace the name of the subroutine with curly braces around the thing holding the reference:

```
& { $ref_to_greeter } ( 'Gilligan' )
```

There we have it. This construct calls the subroutine currently referenced by $ref_to_greeter, passing it the single Gilligan parameter.

But boy-oh-boy, is that ugly or what? Luckily, the same reference simplification rules apply. If the value inside the curly braces is a simple scalar variable, we can drop the braces:

```
& $ref_to_greeter ( 'Gilligan' )
```

We can also flip it around a bit with the arrow notation:

```
$ref_to_greeter -> ( 'Gilligan' )
```

That last form is particularly handy when the coderef is in a larger data structure, as we'll show in a moment.

To have both Gilligan and the Skipper greet the Professor, we merely need to iterate over all the subroutines:

```
for my $greet (\&skipper_greets, \&gilligan_greets) {
  $greet->('Professor');
}
```

First, inside the parentheses, we create a list of two items, each of which is a coderef. The coderefs are then individually dereferenced, calling the corresponding subroutine and passing it along the Professor string.

We've seen the coderefs in a scalar variable and as an element of a list. Can we put these coderefs into a larger data structure? Certainly. Create a table that maps people to the behavior they exhibit to greet others, and then rewrite that previous example using the table:

```
sub skipper_greets {
  my $person = shift;
  print "Skipper: Hey there, $person!\n";
}

sub gilligan_greets {
  my $person = shift;
  if ($person eq 'Skipper') {
    print "Gilligan: Sir, yes, sir, $person!\n";
  } else {
    print "Gilligan: Hi, $person!\n";
  }
}

sub professor_greets {
  my $person = shift;
  print "Professor: By my calculations, you must be $person!\n";
}
```

```
my %greets = (
  Gilligan  => \&gilligan_greets,
  Skipper   => \&skipper_greets,
  Professor => \&professor_greets,
);

for my $person (qw(Skipper Gilligan)) {
  $greets{$person}->('Professor');
}
```

Note that $person is a name, which we look up in the hash to get to a coderef. Then we dereference that coderef, passing it the name of the person being greeted, and we get the correct behavior, resulting in:

```
Skipper: Hey there, Professor!
Gilligan: Hi, Professor!
```

Now have everyone greet everyone, in a very friendly room:

```
sub skipper_greets {
  my $person = shift;
  print "Skipper: Hey there, $person!\n";
}

sub gilligan_greets {
  my $person = shift;
  if ($person eq 'Skipper') {
    print "Gilligan: Sir, yes, sir, $person!\n";
  } else {
    print "Gilligan: Hi, $person!\n";
  }
}

sub professor_greets {
  my $person = shift;
  print "Professor: By my calculations, you must be $person!\n";
}

my %greets = (
  Gilligan  => \&gilligan_greets,
  Skipper   => \&skipper_greets,
  Professor => \&professor_greets,
);

my @everyone = sort keys %greets;
for my $greeter (@everyone) {
  for my $greeted (@everyone) {
    $greets{$greeter}->($greeted)
      unless $greeter eq $greeted; # no talking to yourself
  }
}
```

This results in:

```
Gilligan: Hi, Professor!
Gilligan: Sir, yes, sir, Skipper!
```

```
Professor: By my calculations, you must be Gilligan!
Professor: By my calculations, you must be Skipper!
Skipper: Hey there, Gilligan!
Skipper: Hey there, Professor!
```

Hmmm. That's a bit complex. We let them walk into the room one at a time:

```perl
sub skipper_greets {
  my $person = shift;
  print "Skipper: Hey there, $person!\n";
}

sub gilligan_greets {
  my $person = shift;
  if ($person eq 'Skipper') {
    print "Gilligan: Sir, yes, sir, $person!\n";
  } else {
    print "Gilligan: Hi, $person!\n";
  }
}

sub professor_greets {
  my $person = shift;
  print "Professor: By my calculations, you must be $person!\n";
}

my %greets = (
  Gilligan  => \&gilligan_greets,
  Skipper   => \&skipper_greets,
  Professor => \&professor_greets,
);

my @room; # initially empty
for my $person (qw(Gilligan Skipper Professor)) {
  print "\n";
  print "$person walks into the room.\n";
  for my $room_person (@room) {
    $greets{$person}->($room_person); # speaks
    $greets{$room_person}->($person); # gets reply
  }
  push @room, $person; # come in, get comfy
}
```

The result is a typical day on that tropical island:

```
Gilligan walks into the room.

Skipper walks into the room.
Skipper: Hey there, Gilligan!
Gilligan: Sir, yes, sir, Skipper!

Professor walks into the room.
Professor: By my calculations, you must be Gilligan!
Gilligan: Hi, Professor!
Professor: By my calculations, you must be Skipper!
Skipper: Hey there, Professor!
```

Anonymous Subroutines

In that last example, we never explicitly called subroutines such as `professor_greets`; we only called them indirectly through the coderef. Thus, we wasted some brain cells to come up with a name for the subroutine used only in one other place, to initialize the data structure. But, just as we can create anonymous hashes and arrays, we can create anonymous subroutines!

We add another island inhabitant: Ginger. But rather than define her greeting behavior as a named subroutine, we create an anonymous subroutine:

```
my $ginger = sub {
  my $person = shift;
  print "Ginger: (in a sultry voice) Well hello, $person!\n";
};
$ginger->('Skipper');
```

An anonymous subroutine looks like an ordinary subroutine, but there's no name (or prototype) between sub and the block that follows. It's also part of a statement, so we usually need a trailing semicolon or other expression separator after it:

```
sub { ... body of subroutine ... };
```

The value in `$ginger` is a coderef, just as if we had defined the following block as a subroutine and then taken a reference to it. When we reach the last statement, we see:

```
Ginger: (in a sultry voice) Well hello, Skipper!
```

Although we kept the value in a scalar variable, we could have put that sub { ... } construct directly into the initialization of the greetings hash:

```
my %greets = (

  Skipper => sub {
    my $person = shift;
    print "Skipper: Hey there, $person!\n";
  },

  Gilligan => sub {
    my $person = shift;
    if ($person eq 'Skipper') {
      print "Gilligan: Sir, yes, sir, $person!\n";
    } else {
      print "Gilligan: Hi, $person!\n";
    }
  },

  Professor => sub {
    my $person = shift;
    print "Professor: By my calculations, you must be $person!\n";
  },

  Ginger => sub {
    my $person = shift;
```

```
      print "Ginger: (in a sultry voice) Well hello, $person!\n";
    },

);

my @room; # initially empty
for my $person (qw(Gilligan Skipper Professor Ginger)) {
  print "\n";
  print "$person walks into the room.\n";
  for my $room_person (@room) {
    $greets{$person}->($room_person); # speaks
    $greets{$room_person}->($person); # gets reply
  }
  push @room, $person; # come in, get comfy
}
```

Notice how much it simplifies the code. The subroutine definitions are right within the only data structure that references them directly. The result is straightforward:

```
Gilligan walks into the room.

Skipper walks into the room.
Skipper: Hey there, Gilligan!
Gilligan: Sir, yes, sir, Skipper!

Professor walks into the room.
Professor: By my calculations, you must be Gilligan!
Gilligan: Hi, Professor!
Professor: By my calculations, you must be Skipper!
Skipper: Hey there, Professor!

Ginger walks into the room.
Ginger: (in a sultry voice) Well hello, Gilligan!
Gilligan: Hi, Ginger!
Ginger: (in a sultry voice) Well hello, Skipper!
Skipper: Hey there, Ginger!
Ginger: (in a sultry voice) Well hello, Professor!
Professor: By my calculations, you must be Ginger!
```

Adding a few more castaways is as simple as putting the entry for the greeting behavior into the hash and adding them into the list of people entering the room. We get this scaling of effort because we've preserved the behavior as data over which we can iterate and look up, thanks to our friendly subroutine references.

Callbacks

A subroutine reference is often used for a *callback*. A callback defines what to do when a subroutine reaches a particular place in an algorithm. It gives us a chance to supply our own subroutine, the callback, for use at these points.

For example, the File::Find module exports a find subroutine that can efficiently walk through a given filesystem hierarchy in a fairly portable way. In its simplest form, we give the find subroutine two parameters: a starting directory and "what to do" for each file or directory name found recursively below that starting directory. The "what to do" is specified as a subroutine reference:

```
use File::Find;
sub what_to_do {
  print "$File::Find::name found\n";
}
my @starting_directories = qw(.);

find(\&what_to_do, @starting_directories);
```

The find starts at the current directory (.) and locates each file or directory. For each item, we call the subroutine what_to_do, passing it a few documented values through global variables. In particular, the value of $File::Find::name is the item's full pathname (beginning with the starting directory).

Here, we're passing both data (the list of starting directories) and *behavior* as parameters to the find routine.

It's a bit silly to invent a subroutine name to use the name only once, so we can write the previous code using an anonymous subroutine, such as:

```
use File::Find;
my @starting_directories = qw(.);

find(
  sub {
    print "$File::Find::name found\n";
  },
  @starting_directories,
);
```

Closures

We could also use File::Find to find out some other things about files, such as their size. For the callback's convenience, the current working directory is the item's containing directory, and the item's name within that directory is found in $_.

In the previous code, we used $File::Find::name for the item's name. So which name is real, $_ or $File::Find::name? $File::Find::name gives the name relative to the starting directory, but during the callback, the working directory is the one that holds the item just found. For example, suppose that we want find to look for files in the current working directory, so we give it (".") as the list of directories to search. If we call find when the current working directory is *usr*, find looks below that directory. When find locates *usr/bin/perl*, the current working directory (during the callback) is *usr/bin*. $_ holds *perl* and $File::Find::name holds ./bin/perl, which is the name relative to the directory where we started.

All of this means that the file tests, such as -s, automatically report on the just-found item. Although this is convenient, the current directory inside the callback is different from the search's starting directory.

What if we want to use File::Find to accumulate the total size of all files seen? The callback subroutine cannot take arguments, and the caller discards its result. But that doesn't matter. When dereferenced, a subroutine reference can see all visible lexical variables when the reference to the subroutine is taken. For example:

```
use File::Find;

my $total_size = 0;
find(sub { $total_size += -s if -f }, '.');
print $total_size, "\n";
```

As before, we call the find routine with two parameters: a reference to an anonymous subroutine and the starting directory. When it finds names within that directory (and its subdirectories), it calls the anonymous subroutine.

The subroutine accesses the $total_size variable. We declare this variable outside the scope of the subroutine but still visible to the subroutine. Thus, even though find calls the callback subroutine (and would not have direct access to $total_size), the callback subroutine accesses and updates the variable.

The kind of subroutine that can access all lexical variables that existed at the time we declared it is called a *closure* (a term borrowed from the world of mathematics). In Perl terms, a closure is a subroutine that references a lexical variable that has gone out of scope.

Furthermore, the access to the variable from within the closure ensures that the variable remains alive as long as the subroutine reference is alive. For example, we number the output files:

```
use File::Find;

my $callback;
{
  my $count = 0;
  $callback = sub { print ++$count, ": $File::Find::name\n" };
}
find($callback, '.');
```

We declare a variable to hold the callback. We cannot declare this variable within the bare block (the block following that is not part of a larger Perl syntax construct), or *perl* will recycle it at the end of that block. Next, the lexical $count variable is initialized to 0. We then declare an anonymous subroutine and place its reference into $callback. This subroutine is a closure because it refers to the lexical $count variable that goes out of scope at the end of the block. Remember the semicolon after the anonymous subroutine; this is a statement, not a normal subroutine definition.

At the end of the bare block, the $count variable goes out of scope. However, because it is still referenced by the subroutine in $callback, it stays alive as an anonymous scalar variable. When the callback is called from find, the value of the variable formerly known as $count is incremented from 1 to 2 to 3, and so on.

The closure declaration increases the reference count of the referent, as if another reference had been taken explicitly. Right at the end of the bare block, the reference count of $count is two, but after the block has exited, the value still has a reference count of one. Although no other code may access $count, it will still be kept in memory as long as the reference to the subroutine is available in $callback or elsewhere.

Returning a Subroutine from a Subroutine

Although a bare block worked nicely to define the callback, having a subroutine return that subroutine reference instead might be more useful:

```
use File::Find;

sub create_find_callback_that_counts {
  my $count = 0;
  return sub { print ++$count, ": $File::Find::name\n" };
}

my $callback = create_find_callback_that_counts(  );
find($callback, '.');
```

It's the same process here, just written a bit differently. When we call create_find_call back_that_counts, we initialize the lexical variable $count to 0. The return value from that subroutine is a reference to an anonymous subroutine that is also a closure because it accesses the $count variable. Even though $count goes out of scope at the end of the create_find_callback_that_counts subroutine, there's still a binding between it and the returned subroutine reference, so the variable stays alive until the subroutine reference is finally discarded.

If we reuse the callback, the same variable still has its most recently used value. The initialization occurred in the original subroutine (create_find_callback_that_counts), not the callback (unnamed) subroutine:

```
use File::Find;

sub create_find_callback_that_counts {
  my $count = 0;
  return sub { print ++$count, ": $File::Find::name\n" };
}

my $callback = create_find_callback_that_counts();
print "my bin:\n";
find($callback, 'bin');
```

```
print "my lib:\n";
find($callback, 'lib');
```

This example prints consecutive numbers starting at 1 for the entries below bin, but then continues the numbering when we start entries in lib. The same $count variable is used in both cases. However, if we call the create_find_callback_that_counts twice, we get two different $count variables:

```
use File::Find;

sub create_find_callback_that_counts {
  my $count = 0;
  return sub { print ++$count, ": $File::Find::name\n" };
}

my $callback1 = create_find_callback_that_counts( );
my $callback2 = create_find_callback_that_counts( );
print "my bin:\n";
find($callback1, 'bin');
print "my lib:\n";
find($callback2, 'lib');
```

Here, we have two separate $count variables, each accessed from within their own callback subroutine.

How would we get the total size of all found files from the callback? Earlier, we were able to do this by making $total_size visible. If we stick the definition of $total_size into the subroutine that returns the callback reference, we won't have access to the variable. But we can cheat a bit. For one thing, we can determine that we'll never call the callback subroutine with any parameters, so if the subroutine receives a parameter, we make it return the total size:

```
use File::Find;

sub create_find_callback_that_sums_the_size {
  my $total_size = 0;
  return sub {
    if (@_) { # it's our dummy invocation
      return $total_size;
    } else { # it's a callback from File::Find:
      $total_size += -s if -f;
    }
  };
}

my $callback = create_find_callback_that_sums_the_size( );
find($callback, 'bin');
my $total_size = $callback->('dummy'); # dummy parameter to get size
print "total size of bin is $total_size\n";
```

Distinguishing actions by the presence or absence of parameters is not a universal solution. Fortunately, we can create more than one subroutine reference in create_find_callbacks_that_sum_the_size:

```
use File::Find;

sub create_find_callbacks_that_sum_the_size {
  my $total_size = 0;
  return(sub { $total_size += -s if -f }, sub { return $total_size });
}

my ($count_em, $get_results) = create_find_callbacks_that_sum_the_size( );
find($count_em, 'bin');
my $total_size = &$get_results( );
print "total size of bin is $total_size\n";
```

Because we created both subroutine references from the same scope, they both have access to the same $total_size variable. Even though the variable has gone out of scope before we call either subroutine, they still share the same heritage and can use the variable to communicate the result of the calculation.

Returning the two subroutine references from the creating subroutine does not call them. The references are just data at that point. It's not until we invoke them as a callback or an explicit subroutine dereferencing that they actually do their job.

What if we call this new subroutine more than once?

```
use File::Find;

sub create_find_callbacks_that_sum_the_size {
  my $total_size = 0;
  return(sub { $total_size += -s if -f }, sub { return $total_size });
}

## set up the subroutines
my %subs;
foreach my $dir (qw(bin lib man)) {
  my ($callback, $getter) = create_find_callbacks_that_sum_the_size( );
  $subs{$dir}{CALLBACK}  = $callback;
  $subs{$dir}{GETTER}    = $getter;
}

## gather the data
for (keys %subs) {
  find($subs{$_}{CALLBACK}, $_);
}

## show the data
for (sort keys %subs) {
  my $sum = $subs{$_}{GETTER}->( );
  print "$_ has $sum bytes\n";
}
```

In the section to set up the subroutines, we create three instances of callback-and-getter pairs. Each callback has a corresponding subroutine to get the results. Next, in the section to gather the data, we call find three times with each corresponding callback subroutine reference. This updates the individual $total_size variables associated with each callback. Finally, in the section to show the data, we call the getter routines to fetch the results.

The six subroutines (and the three $total_size variables they share) are reference counted. When we modify %subs or it goes out of scope, the values have their reference counts reduced, recycling the contained data. (If that data also references further data, those reference counts are also reduced appropriately.)

Closure Variables as Inputs

While the previous examples showed closure variables being modified, closure variables are also useful to provide initial or lasting input to the subroutine. For example, we write a subroutine to create a File::Find callback that prints files exceeding a certain size:

```
use File::Find;

sub print_bigger_than {
  my $minimum_size = shift;
  return sub { print "$File::Find::name\n" if -f and -s >= $minimum_size };
}

my $bigger_than_1024 = print_bigger_than(1024);
find($bigger_than_1024, 'bin');
```

We pass the 1024 parameter into the print_bigger_than, which then gets shifted into the $minimum_size lexical variable. Because we access this variable within the subroutine referenced by the return value of the print_bigger_than variable, it becomes a closure variable, with a value that persists for the duration of that subroutine reference. Again, calling this subroutine multiple times creates distinct "locked-in" values for $minimum_size, each bound to its corresponding subroutine reference.

Closures are "closed" only on lexical variables, since lexical variables eventually go out of scope. Because a package variable (which is global) never goes out of scope, a closure never closes on a package variable. All subroutines refer to the same single instance of the global variable.

To illustrate this in our live *Intermediate Perl* class, we created File::Find::Closures, a collection of generator subroutines that each return two closures. One closure we give to find and the other we use to get the list of matching files:

```
use File::Find;
use File::Find::Closures qw(find_by_name);

my( $wanted, $list_reporter ) = find_by_name( qw(README) );

find( $wanted, @directories );

my @readmes = $list_reporter->();
```

We don't intend anyone to really use this module so much as steal from it. Here's find_by_min_size, which creates closures to find the files with a size equal to or larger than the byte size we pass in:

```
use File::Spec::Functions qw(canonpath no_upwards);

sub find_by_min_size {
  my $min   = shift;

  my @files = ();

  sub { push @files, canonpath( $File::Find::name )
    if -s $_ >= $min },
  sub { @files = no_upwards( @files );
    wantarray ? @files : [ @files ] }
}
```

We can easily adapt that for our own needs and put it right into our program.

Closure Variables as Static Local Variables

A subroutine doesn't have to be an anonymous subroutine to be a closure. If a named subroutine accesses lexical variables and those variables go out of scope, the named subroutine retains a reference to the lexicals, as we showed with anonymous subroutines. For example, consider two routines that count coconuts for Gilligan:

```
{
my $count;
sub count_one { ++$count }
sub count_so_far { return $count }
}
```

If we place this code at the beginning of the program, we declare the variable $count inside the bare block scope. The two subroutines that reference the variable become closures. However, because they have a name, they will persist beyond the end of the scope like any named subroutine. Since the subroutines persist beyond the scope and access variables declared within that scope, they become closures and thus can continue to access $count throughout the lifetime of the program.

So, with a few calls, we can see an incremented count:

```
count_one();
count_one();
count_one();
print 'we have seen ', count_so_far(), " coconuts!\n";
```

$count retains its value between calls to count_one or count_so_far, but no other section of code can access this $count at all.

What if we wanted to count down? Something like this will do:

```
{
my $countdown = 10;
sub count_down { $countdown-- }
sub count_remaining { $countdown }
}

count_down();
count_down();
count_down();
print "we're down to ", count_remaining(), " coconuts!\n";
```

That is, it'll do as long as we put it near the beginning of the program, before any invocations of count_down or count_remaining. Why?

This block doesn't work when we put it after those invocations because there are two functional parts to the first line:

```
my $countdown = 10;
```

One part is the declaration of $countdown as a lexical variable. That part is noticed and processed as the program is parsed during the *compile phase*. The second part is the assignment of 10 to the allocated storage. This is handled as *perl* executes the code during the *run phase*. Unless *perl* executes the run phase for this code, the variable has its initial undef value.

One practical solution to this problem is to change the block in which the static local appears into a BEGIN block:

```
BEGIN {
  my $countdown = 10;
  sub count_down { $countdown-- }
  sub count_remaining { $countdown }
}
```

The BEGIN keyword tells the Perl compiler that as soon as this block has been parsed successfully (during the compile phase), jump for a moment to run phase and run the block as well. Presuming the block doesn't cause a fatal error, compilation then continues with the text following the block. The block itself is also discarded, ensuring that the code within is executed precisely once in a program, even if it had appeared syntactically within a loop or subroutine.

state Variables

Perl v5.10 introduced another way to make a private, persistent variable for a subroutine. We introduced these in *Learning Perl*, but we'll give a brief review. Instead of creating a BEGIN block to create the scope for the lexical variable, we declare the variable inside the subroutine with state:

```
use v5.10;
sub countdown {
  state $countdown = 10;
  $countdown--;
}
```

We can use state in some places that some people don't normally consider a subroutine, like a sort block. If we wanted to watch the comparisons, we could also keep track
of the comparison number without creating a variable outside the sort block:

```
use v5.10;

my @array = qw( a b c d e f 1 2 3 );

print sort {
  state $n = 0;
  print $n++, ": a[$a] b[$b]\n";
  $a cmp $b;
  } @array;
```

We can also use state in a map block. If we want to sort lines but still remember their
original position, we can use a state variable to keep track of the line number:

```
use v5.10;

my @sorted_lines_tuples =
  sort { $b->[1] cmp $a->[1] }
  map  { state $l = 0; [ $l++, $_ ] }
  <>;
```

The state variable has a limitation, though. So far, we can initialize only scalar variables
with state. We can declare other types of variables, but we can't initialize them:

```
use v5.10;
sub add_to_tab {
  state @castaways = qw(Ginger Mary-Ann Gilligan); # compilation error
  state %tab = map { $_, 0 } @castaways;  # compilation error
  $countdown{'main'}--;
}
```

It gets messy to initialize them since we only want to do that once, not every time that
we run the subroutine. Instead of that mess, we'll stick to scalars. But, wait! References
are scalars, so we can initialize array or hash references:

```
use v5.10;
sub add_to_tab {
  my $castaway = shift;
  state $castaways = [ qw(Ginger Mary-Ann Gilligan) ]; # works!
  state $tab = { map { $_, 0 } @$castaways };  # works!
  $tab−>{$castaway}++;
}
```

Finding Out Who We Are

Anonymous subroutines have a problem with identity; they don't know who they are! We don't really care if they don't have a name, but when it comes to them telling us who they are, a name would be quite handy. Suppose we want to write a recursive subroutine using anonymous subroutines. What name do we use to call the same subroutine again when we haven't even finished creating it?

```perl
my $countdown = sub {
  state $n = 5;
  return unless $n > -1;
  say $n--;
  WHAT_NAME???->();
};
```

We could do it in two steps so the variable holding the reference already exists:

```perl
my $countdown;
$countdown = sub {
  state $n = 5;
  return unless $n > -1;
  say $n--;
  $countdown->();
};
$countdown->();
```

The output is our countdown:

```
5
4
3
2
1
0
```

That works because Perl doesn't care what is in $countdown until it actually wants to use it. To get around this, v5.16 introduces the _ _SUB_ _ token to return a reference to the current subroutine:

```perl
my $sub = sub {
  state $n = 5;
  return unless $n > -1;
  say $n--;
  _ _SUB_ _->();
};
$sub->();
```

This works with a named subroutine, too:

```perl
sub countdown {
  state $n = 5;
  return unless $n > -1;
  say $n--;
  _ _SUB_ _->();
};
countdown();
```

Enchanting Subroutines

How do we debug anonymous subroutines? When we start liberally passing them around, how do we know which one we have? For scalar, array, and hash values, we can dump their values:[1]

```
use v5.10;

my @array = ( \ 'xyz', [qw(a b c)], sub { say 'Buster' } );

foreach ( @array ) {
  when( ref eq ref \ ''   ) { say "Scalar $$_" }
  when( ref eq ref []     ) { say "Array @$_" }
  when( ref eq ref sub {} ) { say "Sub ???" }
}
```

The output lets us know what's on the inside, except for the subroutine, which we can't dereference without actually running it:

```
Scalar xyz
Array a b c
Sub ???
```

It's not that hard to make something useful here, but we have to pull out a lot of black magic we don't care to fully explain. This is some advanced kung fu, so don't worry if you don't feel comfortable with it right away. This isn't something you'd want to do in everyday programming anyway.

 For details, see the overload module.

First, we'll make the anonymous subroutine an object even though we haven't told you how to do that yet (after you read Chapter 15 you can come back to this). Inside this object, we overload stringification. We get to tell Perl how to stringify this reference, and we're going to add some useful information to it. That useful information is going to come from the B module, which can look into *perl*'s parse tree to do various things. We're going to use B to get the file and line number of the subroutine definition. This way we know where we have to go to fix things. Next, we use the B::Deparse module to turn *perl*'s internal code back into human-readable Perl with coderef2text. Finally, we put all of that together to form the string version of our subroutine reference:

---

1. Some of this example first appeared in "Enchant closures for better debugging output," *http://www .effectiveperlprogramming.com/blog/1345*.

```
use v5.14;

package MagicalCodeRef 1.00 {
  use overload '""' => sub {
    require B;

    my $ref = shift;
    my $gv = B::svref_2object($ref)->GV;

    require B::Deparse;
    my $deparse = B::Deparse->new;
    my $code = $deparse->coderef2text($ref);

    my $string = sprintf "---code ref---\n%s:%d\n%s\n---",
      $gv->FILE, $gv->LINE, $code;
  };

  sub enchant { bless $_[1], $_[0] }
}
```

When we create the anonymous subroutine, we pass it through our new mini-class and check for that when we want to stringify it:

```
my $sub = MagicalCodeRef->enchant( sub { say 'Gilligan!!!' } );

my @array = ( \ 'xyz', [qw(a b c)], $sub );

foreach ( @array ) {
  when( ref eq ref \ ''   )      { say "Scalar $$_" }
  when( ref eq ref []     )      { say "Array @$_" }
  when( ref eq 'MagicalCodeRef' ) { say "Sub $sub" }
}
```

Now, our output shows us where we defined the subroutine and what's in the subroutine (including any pragma settings in force at the time of the subroutine creation):

```
Scalar xyz
Array a b c
Sub ---code ref---
/Users/brian/Desktop/test.pl:14
{
    use strict 'refs';
    BEGIN {
        $^H{'feature_unicode'} = q(1);
        $^H{'feature_say'} = q(1);
        $^H{'feature_state'} = q(1);
        $^H{'feature_switch'} = q(1);
    }
    say 'Gilligan!!!';
}
---
```

We throw in another wrinkle by making this a closure so the value for the name isn't in the subroutine:

```
my $sub = do {
  my $name = 'Gilligan';
  MagicalCodeRef->enchant( sub { say "$name!!!" } );
};
```

Now the output is less useful because we don't know what the value for $name is:

```
Scalar xyz
Array a b c
Sub ---code ref---
/Users/brian/Desktop/test.pl:16
{
    use strict 'refs';
    BEGIN {
        $^H{'feature_unicode'} = q(1);
        $^H{'feature_say'} = q(1);
        $^H{'feature_state'} = q(1);
        $^H{'feature_switch'} = q(1);
    }
    say "$name!!!";
}
---
```

There's a module, PadWalker, that can look further back into *perl*'s parsing to find those closure variables. We used its closed_over function to get a hash of those variables then dump it with Data::Dumper:

```
use v5.14;

package MagicalCodeRef 1.01 {
  use overload '""' => sub {
    require B;

    my $ref = shift;
    my $gv = B::svref_2object($ref)->GV;

    require B::Deparse;
    my $deparse = B::Deparse->new;
    my $code = $deparse->coderef2text($ref);

    require PadWalker;
    my $hash = PadWalker::closed_over( $ref );

    require Data::Dumper;
    local $Data::Dumper::Terse = 1;
    my $string = sprintf "---code ref---\n%s:%d\n%s\n---\n%s---",
      $gv->FILE, $gv->LINE,
      $code,
      Data::Dumper::Dumper( $hash );
  };

  sub enchant { bless $_[1], $_[0] }
}
```

Now we see the values for $name:

```
Scalar xyz
Array a b c
Sub ---code ref---
debug.pl:38
{
  use warnings;
  use strict 'refs';
  BEGIN {
    $^H{'feature_unicode'} = q(1);
    $^H{'feature_say'} = q(1);
    $^H{'feature_state'} = q(1);
    $^H{'feature_switch'} = q(1);
  }
  say "$name!!!";
}
---
{
  '$name' => \'Gilligan'
}
---
```

Still with us? Pat yourself on the back. That was tricky stuff. Now that you understand it, we hope you never have to use it. We wouldn't want your coworkers to strand you on a desert island. However, you will know what's happening under the hood in the next section.

Dumping Closures

Now that we've shown the hard way to dump closures, we'll show you an easier way. We're like a good murder mystery; the first suspect is never the killer.

The Data::Dump::Streamer module is Data::Dumper on steroids, and it can handle code references and closures:

```
use Data::Dump::Streamer;

my @luxuries = qw(Diamonds Furs Caviar);

my $hash = {
  Gilligan    => sub { say 'Howdy Skipper!'      },
  Skipper     => sub { say 'Gilligan!!!!'        },
  'Mr. Howell' => sub { say 'Money money money!' },
  Ginger      => sub { say $luxuries[rand @luxuries] },
  };

Dump $hash;
```

We dump the value for hash, which gives this output (minus some boring stuff we left out). Notice it also dumps @luxuries since it knows that the Ginger subroutine needs it:

```
my (@luxuries);
@luxuries = (
        'Diamonds',
```

```
             'Furs',
             'Caviar'
         );
$HASH1 = {
        Gilligan     => sub {...},
        Ginger       => sub {
                use warnings;
                use strict 'refs';
                BEGIN {
                  $^H{'feature_unicode'} = q(1);
                  $^H{'feature_say'} = q(1);
                  $^H{'feature_state'} = q(1);
                  $^H{'feature_switch'} = q(1);
                }
                say $luxuries[rand @luxuries];
                },
        "Mr. Howell" => sub {...},
        Skipper      => sub {...}
};
```

Exercise

You can find the answer to this exercise in "Answer for Chapter 7" on page 323.

 You don't have to type all of this code. This program should be available as the file named *ex7-1.pl* in the downloadable files, available at *http:// www.intermediateperl.com/*.

1. [50 minutes] The Professor modified some files on Monday afternoon and now he's forgotten which ones they were. This happens all the time. He wants you to make a subroutine called gather_mtime_between, which, given a starting and ending timestamp, returns a pair of coderefs. The first one will be used with File::Find to gather the names of only the items that were modified between those two times; the second one you can use to get the list of items found.

Here's some code to try; it should list only items that were last modified on the most recent Monday, although you could easily change it to work with a different day.

Hint: We can find a file's timestamp (*mtime*) with code such as:

```
my $timestamp = (stat $file_name)[9];
```

Because it's a slice, remember that those parentheses are mandatory. Don't forget that the working directory inside the callback isn't necessarily the starting directory from which we called find:

```
use File::Find;
use Time::Local;
```

```perl
my $target_dow = 1;          # Sunday is 0, Monday is 1, ...
my @starting_directories = (".");

my $seconds_per_day = 24 * 60 * 60;
my($sec, $min, $hour, $day, $mon, $yr, $dow) = localtime;
my $start = timelocal(0, 0, 0, $day, $mon, $yr);          # midnight today
while ($dow != $target_dow) {
  # Back up one day
  $start -= $seconds_per_day;          # hope no DST! :-)
  if (--$dow < 0) {
    $dow += 7;
  }
}
my $stop = $start + $seconds_per_day;

my($gather, $yield) = gather_mtime_between($start, $stop);
find($gather, @starting_directories);
my @files = $yield->( );

for my $file (@files) {
  my $mtime = (stat $file)[9];          # mtime via slice
  my $when = localtime $mtime;
  print "$when: $file\n";
}
```

Note the comment about DST. In many parts of the world, on the days when daylight saving time or summer time kicks in and out, the civil day is no longer 86,400 seconds long. The program glosses over this issue, but a more careful coder might take it into consideration appropriately.

## CHAPTER 8

Filehandle References

We've seen arrays, hashes, and subroutines passed around in references, permitting a level of indirection to solve certain types of problems. We can also store `filehandles` in references, and we can open filehandles on more than files. We look at the old problems then the new solutions.

The Old Way

In the olden days, Perl used barewords for programmer-defined filehandle names, and still does for the special filehandles such as STDIN, ARGV, and others. The filehandle is another Perl data type, although people don't talk about it as a data type much since it doesn't get its own special sigil. You've probably already seen a lot of code that uses these bareword filehandles:[1]

```
open LOG_FH, '>>', 'castaways.log'
  or die "Could not open castaways.log: $!";
```

What happens if we want to pass around these filehandles so we could share them with other parts of our code, such as libraries? You've probably seen some tricky looking code that uses a typeglob or a reference to a typeglob:[2]

```
log_message( *LOG_FH, 'The Globetrotters are stranded with us!' );

log_message( \*LOG_FH, 'An astronaut passes overhead' );
```

In the `log_message` routine, we take the first element off the argument list and store it in another typeglob. Without going into too many details, a typeglob stores pointers to all the package variables of that name. When we assign one typeglob to another, we create aliases to the same data. We can now access the data, including the details of the filehandle, from another name. Then, when we use that name as a filehandle, Perl

---

1. We covered filehandle basics in *Learning Perl*.

2. Learn more about typeglobs in *Mastering Perl*.

knows to look for the filehandle portion of the typeglob. We'd have a much easier time if filehandles had sigils!

```
sub log_message {
  local *FH = shift;

  print FH @_, "\n";
}
```

Notice our use of `local` there. A typeglob works with the symbol table, which means it's dealing with package variables. Package variables can't be lexical variables, so we can't use `my`. Since we don't want to stomp on anything else that might be named FH somewhere else in the script, we must use `local` to denote that the name FH has a temporary value for the duration of the `log_message` subroutine and that when the subroutine finishes, *perl* should restore any previous values to FH as if we were never there.

If all of that makes you nervous and wish that none of this stuff existed, that's good. Don't do this anymore! We put it in a section called "The Old Way" because there is a much better way to do it now. Pretend this section never existed and move on to the next one.

The Improved Way

Starting with v5.6, open can create a filehandle reference in a normal scalar variable as long as the variable's value is undefined. Instead of using a bareword for the filehandle name, we use a scalar variable whose value is undefined:

```
my $log_fh;
open $log_fh, '>>', 'castaways.log'
  or die "Could not open castaways.log: $!";
```

If the scalar already has a value, this doesn't work because Perl won't stomp on our data. In the next example, Perl tries to use the value 5 as a symbolic reference, so it looks for a filehandle named 5. That is, it tries to look for that filehandle, but `strict` will stop it:

```
my $log_fh = 5;
open $log_fh, '>>', 'castaways.log'
  or die "Could not open castaways.log: $!";
print $log_fh "We need more coconuts!\n";   # doesn't work
```

However, the Perl idiom is to do everything in one step. We can declare the variable right in the open statement. It looks funny at first, but after doing it a couple (okay, maybe several) times, you'll get used to it and like it better:

```
open my $log_fh, '>>', 'castaways.log'
  or die "Could not open castaways.log: $!";
```

When we want to print to the filehandle, we use the scalar variable instead of a bareword. Notice that there is still no comma after the filehandle:

```
print $log_fh "We have no bananas today!\n";
```

That syntax might look funny to you though, and even if it doesn't look funny to you, it might look odd to the person who has to read your code later. There's another problem, though. You may remember that $_ is the default argument to print, even if you specify bareword filehandle:

```
$_ = 'Salt water batteries';
print;
print STDOUT;
print STDERR;
```

However, Perl doesn't know at compile-time what $log_fh is if that's your only argument to print. Should that be a filehandle or the value to send to standard output? Perl guesses that you want the value of $log_fh to go to standard output:

```
print $log_fh; # sends "GLOB(0x9bcd5c)" to standard output
```

We have the same problem if we accidently put a comma after our scalar filehandle. Perl thinks you want to send the value of $log_fh to standard output again:

```
# sends "GLOB(0x9bcd5c)Salt water batteries" to standard output
print $log_fh, 'Salt water batteries';
```

In *Perl Best Practices*, Damian Conway recommends putting braces around the filehandle portion to explicitly state what we intend. This syntax makes it look more like grep and map with inline blocks:

```
print {$log_fh} "We have no bananas today!\n";
```

Now we treat the filehandle reference just like any other scalar. We don't have to do any tricky magic to make it work:

```
log_message( $log_fh, 'My name is Mr. Ed' );

sub log_message {
  my $fh = shift;

  print $fh @_, "\n";
}
```

We can also create filehandle references from which we can read. We put the right thing in the second argument:

```
open my $fh, '<', 'castaways.log'
    or die "Could not open castaways.log: $!";
```

Now we use the scalar variable in place of the bareword in the line input operator. Before, we would have seen the bareword between the angle brackets:

```
while( <LOG_FH> ) { ... }
```

And now we see the scalar variable in its place:

```
while( <$log_fh> ) { ... }
```

In general, where we've seen the bareword filehandle we can substitute the scalar variable filehandle reference:

```
while( <$log_fh> ) { ... }
if( -t $log_fh ) { ... }
my $line = readline $log_fh;
close $log_fh;
```

In any of these forms, when the scalar variable goes out of scope (or we assign another value to it), Perl closes the file. We don't have to explicitly close the file ourselves.

Filehandles to Strings

Since v5.6, we can open a filehandle to a reference to a scalar instead of to a file. That filehandle either reads from or writes to that string instead of a file (or pipe or socket).

Perhaps we need to capture the output that would normally go to a filehandle. If we open a write filehandle to a string and use that, the output never really has to leave our program and we don't have to pull any stunts to capture it:

```
open my $string_fh, '>', \ my $string;
```

For instance, we could save the state of a CGI.pm program, but we have to give save a filehandle. If we use our $string_fh, the data never have to leave our program:

```
use CGI;

open my $string_fh, '>', \ my $string;
CGI->save( $string_fh );
```

Similarly, Storable lets us pack data into a string (see Chapter 6), but nstore wants to save it to a named file, and nstore_fd will send it to a filehandle. If we want to capture it in a string, we use a string filehandle again:

```
use Storable;

open my $string_fh, '>', \ my $string;
nstore_fd \@data, $string_fh;
```

We can also use filehandles to strings to capture output to STDOUT or STDERR for those pesky programs that want to clutter our screens. Sometimes, we just want to keep our programs quiet, and sometimes, we want to redirect the output. Here, we have to close STDOUT first then reopen the filehandle. Since we usually don't want to lose the real STDOUT, we can localize it within a scope so our replacement has a limited effect:

 This sort of trick won't pass the new version of STDOUT to external programs through system.

```
print "1. This goes to the real standard output\n";

my $string;
{
  local *STDOUT;
  open STDOUT, '>', \ $string;

  print "2. This goes to the string\n";

  $some_obj->noisy_method(); # this STDOUT goes to $string too
}

print "3. This goes to the real standard output\n";
```

We can design our own programs to be flexible so that others can decide where to send their data. If we let them specify the filehandle, they can decide if the output goes into a file, down a socket, or into a string. The best part of this flexibility is that the implementation is simple and the same for each of them:

```
sub output_to_fh {
  my( $fh, @data ) = @_;
  print $fh @data;
}
```

If we want to specialize output_to_fh, we have to wrap it to provide the right sort of filehandle:

```
sub as_string {
  my( @data ) = @_;
  open my $string_fh, '>', \ my $string;
  output_to_fh( $string_fh, @data );
  $string;
}
```

Processing Strings Line by Line

When we can treat a string as a file, many common tasks become much easier since we can use the filehandle interface. Consider, for instance, breaking a multiline string into lines. We could use split to break it up:

```
my @lines = split /$/, $multiline_string;
foreach my $line ( @lines ) {
  ... do something ...
}
```

Now, however, we have the data in two places, and the slightly annoying fragility of this solution shows that our pattern to split might not be the right one. Instead, we can open a filehandle for reading on a reference to that scalar, and then get its lines from the line input operator:

```
open my $string_fh, '<', \ $multiline_string;
while( <$string_fh> ) {
  ... do something ...
}
```

If our data come in from another source later, we need a filehandle that we can read.

Collections of Filehandles

Since, like any other reference, filehandle references are scalars, we can treat them as scalars. Specifically, we can store them as array elements or hash values. We can have several filehandles open at the same time and decide later which one to use.

For instance, we want to go through our data from Chapter 6 and separate it into files based on the source machine (the first column):

```
professor.hut gilligan.crew.hut 1250
professor.hut lovey.howell.hut 910
thurston.howell.hut lovey.howell.hut 1250
professor.hut lovey.howell.hut 450
ginger.girl.hut professor.hut 1218
ginger.girl.hut maryann.girl.hut 199
```

We could read a line, open a filehandle based on the source machine name, store the filehandle in a hash, and print the rest of the line to that filehandle:

```
use v5.10;  # for state

while( <> ) {
  state $fhs;

  my( $source, $destination, $bytes ) = split;

  unless( $fhs->{$source} ) {
    open my $fh, '>>', $source or die '...';
    $fhs->{$source} = $fh;
  }

  say { $fhs->{$source} } "$destination $bytes";
}
```

We declare the $fhs variable with state so it's private to the while loop but retains its value between iterations. Each time we need to create a new filehandle, we add it as a value to that hash reference. When the while is done, the $fhs goes out of scope, closing our filehandles for us.

If you are using an older Perl, you can get the same thing by moving $fhs out of the while, but scoping it with a bare block:

```
use v5.10;  # for state

{ # bare block to scope $fhs
  my $fhs;

  while( <> ) {
    ...
  }
}
```

IO::Handle and Friends

Behind the scenes, Perl is really using the IO::Handle module to work its filehandle magic, so our filehandle scalar is really an object for an IO::Handle object. We could instead write our operations as methods:

```
use IO::Handle;

open my $fh, '>', $filename or die '...';
$fh->print( 'Coconut headphones' );
$fh->close;
```

 Have you ever wondered why there is no comma after the filehandle portion of the print? It's really the indirect object notation (which we haven't mentioned yet unless you've read the whole book before you read the footnotes, like we told you to do in the introduction!).

As of v5.14, we don't have to explicitly load IO::Handle, but with earlier versions we need to do that ourselves.

The IO::Handle package is a base class for input–output things, so it handles a lot more than just files. Most of the time, we want to use some of the handy modules built on top of it instead of using it directly. We haven't told you about object-oriented programming yet (it's in Chapter 13, so we almost have), but in this case you just have to follow the example in its documentation.

Some of these modules do some of the same things that we can already do with Perl's built-in open (depending on which version of Perl we have), but they can be handy when we want to decide as late as possible which module should handle input or output. Instead of using the built-in open, we use the module interface. To switch the behavior, we change the module name. Since we've set up our code to use a module interface, it's not that much work to switch modules.

IO::File

The IO::File module subclasses IO::Handle to work with files. It comes with the standard Perl distribution, so you should already have it. There are a variety of ways to create an IO::File object.

We can create the filehandle reference with the one argument form of the constructor. We check the result of the operation by looking for a defined value in the filehandle reference variable:

```
use IO::File;

my $fh = IO::File->new( '> castaways.log' )
    or die "Could not create filehandle: $!";
```

Since we don't like combining the open mode with the filename (for the same reasons as regular open), we'll use one of the other calling conventions. The optional second argument is the filehandle mode:

```
my $read_fh  = IO::File->new( 'castaways.log', 'r' );

my $write_fh = IO::File->new( 'castaways.log', 'w' );
```

 These are the ANSI C fopen mode strings. We can also use these with the built-in open. Indeed, IO::File uses the built-in open behind-the-scenes.

Using a bitmask as the mode allows for more granular control. The IO::File module supplies the constants:

```
my $append_fh = IO::File->new( 'castaways.log', O_WRONLY|O_APPEND );
```

Besides opening named files, we might want to open an anonymous temporary file. On systems that support this sort of thing, we create the new object to get a read/write filehandle:

```
my $temp_fh = IO::File->new_tmpfile;
```

As before, Perl closes these files when the scalar variable goes out of scope, but if that's not enough, we can do it ourselves explicitly by either calling close or undefining the filehandle:

```
$temp_fh->close or die "Could not close file: $!";

undef $append_fh;
```

Perl v5.6 and later can open an anonymous, temporary file if we give it undef as a filename. We probably want to both read and write from that file at the same time. Otherwise, it's a bit pointless to have a file we can't find later:

```
open my $fh, '+>', undef
    or die "Could not open temp file: $!";
```

IO::Scalar

If we're using an ancient version of Perl that can't create filehandles to a scalar reference, we can use the IO::Scalar module. It uses the magic of tie behind-the-scenes to give us a filehandle reference that appends to a scalar. This module doesn't come with the standard Perl distribution so we'll have to install it ourselves:

```
use IO::Scalar;

my $string_log = '';
my $scalar_fh = IO::Scalar->new( \$string_log );

print $scalar_fh "The Howells' private beach club is closed\n";
```

Now our log message ends up in the scalar variable `$string_log` instead of a file. What if we want to read from our logfile though? We do the same thing. In this example, we create `$scalar_fh` just as we did before, then read from it with the line input operator. In our `while` loop we'll extract the log messages that contain Gilligan (which is most of them, since he's always part of the mess):

```perl
use IO::Scalar;

my $string_log = '...'; # assume many lines
my $scalar_fh = IO::Scalar->new( \$string_log );

while( <$scalar_fh> ) {
  next unless /Gilligan/;
  print;
}
```

IO::Tee

What if we want to send output to more than one place at a time? What if we want to send it to a file *and* save it in a string at the same time? Using what we know already, we'd have to do something like this:

```perl
open my $log_fh, '>>', 'castaways.log'
  or die "Could not open castaways.log";
open my $scalar_fh, '>>', \ my $string;

my $log_message = "The Minnow is taking on water!\n"
print $log_fh    $log_message;
print $scalar_fh $log_message;
```

We could shorten that a bit so we only have one `print` statement. We use `foreach` to iterate through the filehandle references, alias each in `$fh` in turn, and print to each one:

```perl
foreach my $fh ( $log_fh, $scalar_fh ) {
  print $fh $log_message;
}
```

That's still a bit too much work. In the `foreach` we had to decide which filehandles to include. What if we could define a group of filehandles that answered to the same name? Well, that's what `IO::Tee` does for us. Imagine it like a tee connector on a bilge output pipe; when the water gets to the tee, it can flow it two different directions at the same time. When our output gets to `IO::Tee`, it can go to two (or more) different channels at the same time. That is, `IO::Tee` *multiplexes* output. In this example, the castaways' log message goes to both the logfile and the scalar variable:

```perl
use IO::Tee;

my $tee_fh = IO::Tee->new( $log_fh, $scalar_fh );

print $tee_fh "The radio works in the middle of the ocean!\n";
```

That's not all though. If the first argument to IO::Tee is an input filehandle (the succeeding arguments must be output filehandles), we can use the same teed filehandle to read from input and write to the output. The source and destination channels are different but we get to treat them as a single filehandle. IO::Tee does something special in this case: when it reads a line from the input filehandle, it immediately prints them to the output filehandles:

```
use IO::Tee;

my $tee_fh = IO::Tee->new( $read_fh, $log_fh, $scalar_fh );

# reads from $read_fh, prints to $log_gh and $scalar_fh
my $message = <$tee_fh>;
```

The $read_fh doesn't have to be connected to a file, either. It might also be connected to a socket, a scalar variable, or an external command's output. We can create readable filehandles to external commands with IO::Pipe or anything else we can dream up.

IO::Pipe

Sometimes our data don't come from a file or a socket, but from an external command. We can use a piped open to read the output of a command. The | after $command notes that output is coming out of the command and flowing through the pipe into our program:

```
open my $pipe, '-|', $command
  or die "Could not open filehandle: $!";

while( <$pipe> ) {
  print "Read: $_";
}
```

This might be a bit easier with a module to handle the details for us. IO::Pipe is a front end to IO::Handle. Given a command, it handles the fork and the exec for us and leaves us with a filehandle from which we can read the output of the command:

```
use IO::Pipe;

my $pipe = IO::Pipe->new;

$pipe->reader( "$^X -V" ); # $^X is the current perl executable

while( <$pipe> ) {
  print "Read: $_";
}
```

Similarly, we can write to a command, too. We put the pipe in front of $command to show that data are coming into our program:

```
open my $pipe, "| $command"
  or die "Could not open filehandle: $!";
```

```perl
foreach ( 1 .. 10 ) {
  print $pipe "I can count to $_\n";
}
```

We can let `IO::Pipe` handle that, too:

```perl
use IO::Pipe;

my $pipe = IO::Pipe->new;

$pipe->writer( $command );

foreach ( 1 .. 10 ) {
  print $pipe "I can count to $_\n";
}
```

IO::Null and IO::Interactive

Sometimes we don't want to send our output anywhere, but we are forced to send it somewhere. In that case, we can use `IO::Null` to create a filehandle that discards anything that we give it. It looks and acts like a filehandle, but does nothing:

```perl
use IO::Null;

my $null_fh = IO::Null->new;

some_printing_thing( $null_fh, @args );
```

Other times, we want output in some cases but not in others. If we are logged in and running our program in our terminal, we want to see lots of output. However, if we schedule the job through *cron*, we don't care so much about the output so long as it does the job. The `IO::Interactive` module is smart enough to tell the difference:

```perl
use IO::Interactive;

print { interactive } 'Bamboo car frame';
```

The `interactive` subroutine returns a filehandle. Since the call to the subroutine is not a simple scalar variable, we surround it with braces to tell Perl that it's the filehandle.

Now that we know "do nothing" filehandles, we can replace some ugly code that everyone tends to write. Sometimes we want output and sometimes we don't, so we can use a statement modifier to turn off a statement in some cases:

```perl
print STDOUT "Hey, the radio's not working!" if $Debug;
```

Instead, we can assign different values to `$debug_fh` based on whatever condition we want, then leave off the ugly `if $Debug` at the end of every `print`:

```perl
use IO::Null;

my $debug_fh = $Debug ? *STDOUT : IO::Null->new;

$debug_fh->print( "Hey, the radio's not working!" );
```

The magic behind IO::Null might give a warning about "print() on unopened filehandle GLOB" with the indirect object notation (e.g., print $debug_fh), even though it works just fine. We don't get that warning with the arrow form.

Directory Handles

In the same way that we can create references to filehandles, we can create directory handle references:

```
opendir my $dh, '.' or die "Could not open directory: $!";

foreach my $file ( readdir( $dh ) ) {
  print "Skipper, I found $file!\n";
}
```

The directory handle reference obeys the same rules we laid out before. This only works if the scalar variable does not already have a value and the handle automatically closes when the variable goes out of scope or we assign it a new value.

Directory Handle References

We can use object-oriented interfaces for directory handles, too. The IO::Dir module has been part of the standard Perl distribution since v5.6. It doesn't add interesting new features but wraps the *perl* built-in functions:[3]

```
use IO::Dir;

my $dir_fh = IO::Dir->new( '.' )
  or die "Could not open dirhandle! $!\n";

while( defined( my $file = $dir_fh->read ) ) {
  print "Skipper, I found $file!\n";
}
```

We don't have to create a new directory handle if we decide we want to go through the list again (perhaps later in the program). We can rewind the directory handle to start over:

```
while( defined( my $file = $dir_fh->read ) ) {
  print "I found $file!\n";
}

# time passes
$dir_fh->rewind;

while( defined( my $file = $dir_fh->read ) ) {
  print "I can still find $file!\n";
}
```

---

3. For each IO::Dir method name, append "dir" and look at the documentation in *perlfunc*.

Exercises

You can find the answers to these exercises in "Answers for Chapter 8" on page 324.

1. [20 minutes] Write a program that prints the today's date and the day of the week, but allows the user to choose to send the output to a file, a scalar, or both at the same time. No matter which one the user selects, send the output with a single print statement. If the user chooses to send the output to a scalar, at the end of the program print the scalar's value to standard output.

2. [30 minutes] The Professor has to read a logfile that looks like the example we show here. You can get sample data files from the Downloads section of *http://www.intermediateperl.com/*:

```
Gilligan: 1 coconut
Skipper: 3 coconuts
Gilligan: 1 banana
Ginger: 2 papayas
Professor: 3 coconuts
MaryAnn: 2 papayas
...
```

He wants to write a series of files, called gilligan.info, maryann.info, and so on. Each file should contain all the lines that begin with that name. (Names are always delimited by the trailing colon.) At the end, gilligan.info should start with:

```
Gilligan: 1 coconut
Gilligan: 1 banana
```

Now, the logfile is large and the coconut-powered computer is not fast, so he wants to process the input file in one pass and write all output files in parallel. How does he do it?

Hint: Use a hash keyed by castaway name and whose values are filehandle references for each output file. Create those files if they don't exist yet, and overwrite them if they do.

3. [15 minutes] Write a program that takes multiple directory names from the command line and then prints out their contents. Use a function that takes a directory handle reference that you made with opendir.

## CHAPTER 9

Regular Expression References

Beginning with v5.5, we can compile regular expressions and keep references to them without using a match or substitution operator. We can do all of our regular expression handling and preparation before we actually want to use them. Since a regular expression reference is just a scalar like any other reference, we can store it in an array or hash, pass it as an argument, interpolate it into a string, or use it in the many other ways we can use a scalar.

Before Regular Expression References

Most people usually see regular expressions as part of a match or substitution operator:

```
m/\bcoco.*/
s/\bcoconut\b/coconet/
split /coconut/, $string
```

The pattern, however, is separate from the operator, and the operator merely applies the pattern to a string.

We might already have an inkling of this since we can interpolate a regular expression into one of the operators:

```
my $pattern = 'coco.*';

if( m/$pattern/ ) {
  ...
}
```

In that case, $pattern is just a string like any other string, and it has no idea how we are going to use it. After the match operator interpolates the variable, it has to compile the resulting regular expression. The match has no idea ahead of time whether the pattern is valid, like it would in a literal pattern. Given an invalid pattern, the match might cause a fatal runtime error. To handle that, we can catch that at match time with an eval:

```
print 'Enter a pattern: ';
chomp( my $pattern = <STDIN> );

print "Enter some lines:\n";
while( <STDIN> ) {
  if( eval { m/$pattern/ } ) {
    print "Match: $_";
  }

  if( $@ ) {
    die "There was a regex problem: $@\n";
  }
}
```

The error message shows where the pattern goes wrong when we use an invalid pattern that has an unmatched parenthesis:

```
% perl match.pl
Enter a pattern: Gilligan)
Enter some lines:
Gilligan & Skipper
There was a regex problem: Unmatched ) in regex;
marked by <-- HERE in m/Gilligan) <-- HERE /
at test line 8, <STDIN> line 2.
```

We have to do a similar thing to use a regular expression as a subroutine argument. We pass a string as the argument, then compile the pattern inside the subroutine:

```
find_match( 'Gilligan)' );

sub find_match {
  my( $pattern ) = @_;

  if( eval { m/$pattern/ } ) {
    ...
  }
}
```

As with the previous case, we get the error too late to do anything about it. We could write a subroutine to test a pattern before we try to use it. We try a match against an empty string:

```
sub is_valid_pattern {
  my( $pattern ) = @_;
  local( $@ );

  eval { '' =~ /$pattern/ };
  return length $@ ? 0 : 1;
}
```

We can then use this subroutine to try a pattern before we actually use it. This isn't ideal for a many reasons, including the side effects of the match variables and the possibility that a regex can run arbitrary code. We don't want to trigger either of those just to validate a pattern. Besides, this is pretty messy and annoying. We'd have a much easier time if we could precompile the regular expression without actually matching.

Precompiled Patterns

Perl v5.5 introduced a new quoting mechanism, the qr// operator. It's like other generalized quoting mechanisms, but it gives us a reference to a compiled regular expression:

```
my $regex = qr/Gilligan|Skipper/;
```

 See "Quote and Quote-like Operators" in *perlop*.

This doesn't apply the pattern to anything yet; we'll do that later. We can even check our pattern by printing it:

```
print $regex
```

Perl stringifies the pattern:

```
(?^:Gilligan|Skipper)
```

 Different versions of Perl may stringify the reference differently, so we shouldn't rely on a particular string form. This form comes from v5.14.

We'll show more about those extra parts in the stringified version in a moment.

The qr// doesn't solve our invalid pattern problem though, so we should still use the eval if we are going to interpolate a string:

```
my $regex = eval { qr/$pattern/ };
```

Like the other generalized quoters, we can choose different delimiters, which we typically do to avoid a problem with a literal character that we want to use in the pattern:

```
my $regex = qr(/usr/local/bin/\w+);
```

There's one delimiter that's special, just as with the match operator. If we use the single quotes as our delimiter, Perl treats our pattern as a single-quoted string. That is, Perl will not do any double-quoted interpolation:

```
my $regex = qr'$var'; # four characters
```

Even though the single quote delimiter disables interpolation, regular expression meta characters are still special. For instance, the $ is still the end-of-string anchor. If we want a literal $, we need to escape it so Perl doesn't think it's the end-of-string anchor:

```
my $regex = qr'\$\d+\.\d+';
```

The rest of the regular expression is as normal; the \d is still the digit character class, the + is still a quantifier, and so on.

Regular Expression Options

When we use the match or substitution operators, we can put all of the flags at the end, after the final delimiter:

```
m/Gilligan$/migc
s/(\d+)/ $1 + 1 /eg
```

Since we put all of the options at the end of the operator, we didn't have to distinguish between flags that affect the pattern and flags that affect the operator.[1]

When we use the qr// quoting, we can add only flags that affect the pattern (/x, / i, /s, /m, /p, /o, /a, /l, /d, or /u). We have two ways to do this. First, we can add the flags to the end of the qr// just like we did with the operators:

```
qr/Gilligan$/mi;
```

We can also add the flags directly in the pattern itself. This isn't a feature of the qr//—you can use it in any pattern. The special sequence (?flags:pattern) allows us to specify the modifiers within the pattern itself:

```
qr/(?mi:Gilligan$)/;
```

The modifiers apply to only the part of the pattern enclosed in its parentheses. Suppose that we wanted only part of the pattern to be case-insensitive. We can group those parts with (?) and apply the pattern flags we want:

```
qr/abc(?i:Gilligan)def/;
```

We can remove modifiers from part of a pattern by prefixing the flags with a -:

```
qr/abc(?-i:Gilligan)def/i;
```

We can even add and remove modifiers at the same time. First, we specify those that we want to add then take away the ones we don't want:

```
qr/abc(?x-i:G i l l i g a n)def/i;
```

Applying Regex References

When we want to apply our regular expression reference, we have many options. We can interpolate it into a match or substitution operator:

```
my $regex = qr/Gilligan/;
$string =~ m/$regex/;
$string =~ s/$regex/Skipper/;
```

---

1. "Know the difference between regex and match operator flags," *http://www.effectiveperlprogramming .com/blog/174.*

We can also bind to it directly without the explicit match operator. The binding operator recognizes the regular expression reference and runs the match:

```
$string =~ $regex;
```

A smart match is the same thing:

```
$string ~~ $regex;
```

Regexes as Scalars

Now that we can store precompiled regular expressions in scalars, we can use them in the same ways that we use other scalars. We can store them in arrays and hashes, and we can pass them as arguments to subroutines.

Suppose you want to match multiple patterns at the same time. You could store each pattern in an array, and then go through each of them until you find a match:

```
use v5.10.1;

my @patterns = (
  qr/(?:Willie )?Gilligan/,
  qr/Mary-Ann/,
  qr/Ginger/,
  qr/(?:The )?Professor/,
  qr/Skipper/,
  qr/Mrs?\. Howell/,
);

my $name = 'Ginger';

foreach my $pattern ( @patterns ) {
  if( $name ~~ $pattern ) {
    say "Match!";
    last;
  }
}
```

That's not nice. We have an `if` surrounded by a `foreach`. With a smart match, we can match against an array of patterns. The smart match will distribute over the elements:

```
use v5.10.1;

my @patterns = (
  qr/(?:Willie )?Gilligan/,
  qr/Mary-Ann/,
  qr/Ginger/,
  qr/(?:The )?Professor/,
  qr/Skipper/,
  qr/Mrs?\. Howell/,
);
```

```
my $name = 'Ginger';

say "Match!" if $name ~~ @patterns;
```

That's still not good. Which patterns matched? We can put them in a hash so we can give them labels:

```
use v5.10.1;

my %patterns = (
  Gilligan    => qr/(?:Willie )?Gilligan/,
  'Mary-Ann' => qr/Mary-Ann/,
  Ginger      => qr/Ginger/,
  Professor   => qr/(?:The )?Professor/,
  Skipper     => qr/Skipper/,
  'A Howell' => qr/Mrs?\. Howell/,
);

my $name = 'Ginger';

my( $match ) = grep { $name =~ $patterns{$_} } keys %patterns;

say "Matched $match" if $match;
```

We will make one more refinement. The grep will keep looking even after it finds a match, so we'll use first from List::Util:

```
use v5.10.1;
use List::Util qw(first);

my %patterns = (
  Gilligan    => qr/(?:Willie )?Gilligan/,
  'Mary-Ann' => qr/Mary-Ann/,
  Ginger      => qr/Ginger/,
  Professor   => qr/(?:The )?Professor/,
  Skipper     => qr/Skipper/,
  'A Howell' => qr/Mrs?\. Howell/,
);

my $name = 'Ginger';

my( $match ) = first { $name =~ $patterns{$_} } keys %patterns;

say "Matched $match" if $match;
```

We can get a bit more fancy. What if there are multiple names that match, but we want the rightmost match? As you should already know from *Learning Perl*, Perl's regular expression engine finds the leftmost longest match. We'll create a subroutine called rightmost which, given a string and a list of patterns, returns the starting position of the rightmost match:

```
my $position = rightmost(
  'Mary-Ann and Ginger',
  qr/Mary/, qr/Gin/,
);
```

Here's how we'll do it. We'll start with $rightmost at –1. If we get that position as the return value, we know nothing matched. Remember, the first position is 0, so if we get that, we know the pattern matched at the beginning of the string.

We can go through @patterns with each. In its v5.12 form, it returns the index and the value for the next element.[2] Inside the while, we use the conditional operator to select a value based on the result of the match. If it's a successful match, we choose $-[0], and -1 otherwise. The @- special variable remembers the starting match positions of the entire pattern and the capture groups. The number in $-[0] is the starting position of the entire match.[3] If the match position is higher (so, more to the right) than a previously remembered position, we store that in $rightmost:

```
use v5.12;

sub rightmost {
  my( $string, @patterns ) = @_;

  my $rightmost = -1;
    while( my( $i, $pattern ) = each @patterns ) {
    $position = $string =~ m/$pattern/ ? $-[0] : -1;
    $rightmost = $position if $position > $rightmost;
  }

return $rightmost;
}
```

We put that all together now. We'll get the patterns as a hash slice with the sorted list of keys from our %patterns hash:

```
use v5.12;

my %patterns = (
  Gilligan   => qr/(?:Willie )?Gilligan/,
  'Mary-Ann' => qr/Mary-Ann/,
  Ginger     => qr/Ginger/,
  Professor  => qr/(?:The )?Professor/,
  Skipper    => qr/Skipper/,
  'A Howell' => qr/Mrs?\. Howell/,
);

my $position = rightmost(
  'There is Mrs. Howell, Ginger, and Gilligan',
  @patterns{ sort keys %patterns }
);

say "Rightmost match at position $position";
```

---

2. It's only mildly more annoying to do this without each. You go through the indices and extract the value yourself. You're missing out on the fun of the new features though.

3. There's also @+, which has the ending positions.

There are some other ways that we can improve on this, but we're going to leave some of that fun for you in the exercises. You don't have to remember everything going on here; just know that you can pass a regular expression reference as a subroutine argument. After all, like all references, it's just a scalar.

Build Up Regular Expressions

We can precompile patterns and interpolate them into the match operators. We can also interpolate the patterns into other patterns. This way, we build up complicated patterns from smaller, more manageable pieces:

```
my $howells    = qr/Thurston|Mrs/;
my $tagalongs  = qr/Ginger|Mary-Ann/;
my $passengers = qr/$howells|$tagalongs/;
my $crew       = qr/Gilligan|Skipper/;

my $everyone   = qr/$crew|$passengers/;
```

Any regular expression metacharacters are still special when we use the regular expression references in bigger patterns. Those alternations in $howells and $tagalongs are still alternations in $passengers.

This lets us decompose long, complicated patterns into smaller, easily digestible chunks that we can put together any way that we like. Not only that, we can put them together in different ways. If we want to match a different group of people, we put different parts together:

```
my $poor_people = qr/$tagalongs|$passengers|$crew/;
```

Here's a longer example, although you shouldn't ever have to write this regular expression on your own. RFC 1738 specifies the format for URLs, and we can turn that specification into regular expressions. This series of regular expression references is almost a direct translation of RFC 1738:

```
my $alpha      = qr/[a-z]/;
my $digit      = qr/\d/;
my $alphadigit = qr/(?i:$alpha|$digit)/;
my $safe       = qr/[\$_.+-]/;
my $extra      = qr/[!*'\(\),]/;
my $national   = qr/[{}|\\^~\[\]`]/;
my $reserved   = qr|[;/?:@&=]|;
my $hex        = qr/(?i:$digit|[A-F])/;
my $escape     = qr/%$hex$hex/;
my $unreserved = qr/$alpha|$digit|$safe|$extra/;
my $uchar      = qr/$unreserved|$escape/;
my $xchar      = qr/$unreserved|$reserved|$escape/;
my $ucharplus  = qr/(?:$uchar|[;?&=])*/;
my $digits     = qr/(?:$digit){1,}/;

my $hsegment   = $ucharplus;
my $hpath      = qr|$hsegment(?:/$hsegment)*|;
my $search     = $ucharplus;
```

```
my $scheme      = qr|(?i:https?://)|;
my $port        = qr/$digits/;
my $password    = $ucharplus;
my $user        = $ucharplus;

my $toplevel    = qr/$alpha|$alpha(?:$alphadigit|-)*$alphadigit/;
my $domainlabel = qr/$alphadigit|$alphadigit
  (?:$alphadigit|-)*$alphadigit/x;
my $hostname    = qr/(?:$domainlabel\.)*$toplevel/;
my $hostnumber  = qr/$digits\.$digits\.$digits\.$digits/;
my $host        = qr/$hostname|$hostnumber/;
my $hostport    = qr/$host(?::$port)?/;
my $login       = qr/(?:$user(?::$password)\@)?/;

my $urlpath     = qr/(?:(?:$xchar)*)/;
```

These patterns don't interfere with each other because the qr// puts virtual noncapturing parentheses around the patterns for us. Finally, we can put it all together to represent the URL to make a program to look for URLs in text:

```
# ... all of those other lines
use v5.10.1;

my $httpurl = qr|$scheme$hostport(?:/$hpath(?:\?$search)?)?|;

while( <> ) {
  say if /$httpurl/;
}
```

That is, we could put it all together like that, but there's a better way to do it. Keep reading.

Regex-Creating Modules

Since we can create precompiled regular expressions, many people have created modules that create patterns for us. Instead of creating complicated patterns ourselves, and perhaps missing an edge case or specifying part of it incorrectly, we can rely on these well-known modules to supply the patterns for us.

Using Common Patterns

Abigail, one of Perl's regex masters, put together a module to supply most of the complicated patterns that people try to make themselves (and usually mess up). Instead of creating our own pattern, we can use the one that Regexp::Common provides. It exports a hash reference named $RE that has as its values the regular expression references that we need. That long program from the previous section reduces to this much simpler one:

```
use v5.10.1;
use Regexp::Common qw(URI);
```

```
while( <> ) {
  print if /$RE{URI}{HTTP}/;
}
```

The hash gives us a regular expression reference, which we can stringify like any other reference:

```
use v5.10.1;
use Regexp::Common qw(zip);

say $RE{zip}{US};
```

The string we get is a bit complicated:

```
(?:(?:(?:USA?)-){0,1}(?:(?:(?:[0-9]{3})(?:[0-9]{2}))
(?:(?:-)(?:(?:[0-9]{2})(?:[0-9]{2}))){0,1}))
```

There are many other sorts of regular expressions that we can get from this module. If we wanted to find IPv4 addresses, such as *10.1.0.37*, we can use one of the patterns from the net facilities of the module:

```
use v5.10.1;
use Regexp::Common qw(net);

while( <> ) {
  print if /$RE{net}{IPv4}/;
}
```

Behind the scenes, the Regexp::Common uses ties, so it can activate a lot of special magic from the keys that we decide to use. Suppose that we wanted to match numbers. We can start with one of the Regexp::Common patterns for numbers:

```
use v5.10.1;
use Regexp::Common qw(number);

while( <> ) {
  print if /$RE{num}{int}/;
}
```

 To learn about ties, see *Mastering Perl* or *perltie*.

That finds decimal integers just fine, but we can modify the pattern to find hexadecimal integers:

```
use v5.10.1;
use Regexp::Common qw(number);

while( <> ) {
  print if /$RE{num}{int}{ -base => 16 }/;
}
```

That program prints lines that contain numbers, but if we want the number and not the entire line, we can add a {-keep} key so the pattern captures the match:

```
use v5.10.1;
use Regexp::Common qw(number);

while( <> ) {
  print $1 if /$RE{num}{int}{ -base => 16 }{-keep}/;
}
```

Since $RE is a magic hash, we don't even have to put the keys in any particular order. We can put the special keys starting with - anywhere that we like:

```
use v5.10.1;
use Regexp::Common qw(number);

while( <> ) {
  print $1 if /$RE{ -base => 16 }{num}{ -keep }{int}/;
}
```

Assembling Regular Expressions

The Regexp::Common module gives us predefined patterns, but there are also modules to help us build regular expressions. For instance, the Regexp::Assemble module helps us build efficient alternations. Consider the situation where we have an alternation in which most of the branches have a common prefix. Suppose we want to match either Mr. Howell, Mrs. Howell, or Mary Ann. We could make a simple alternation:

```
my $passenger = qr/(?:Mr. Howell|Mrs\. Howell|Mary-Ann)/;
```

All alternatives start with an *M*, but our simple approach checks for that *M* each time. Two or them have an *r* as the second letter.

That's not efficient because the match might have to look at the same character several times to make sure it's the same thing it matched last time. Using the Regexp::Assemble module, we can put together the different parts:

```
use v5.10.1;
use Regexp::Assemble;

my $ra = Regexp::Assemble->new;
for ( 'Mr. Howell', 'Mrs. Howell', 'Mary-Ann' ) {
  $ra->add( "\Q$_" );
}

say $ra->re;
```

The module figures out a good way to put those together as an alternation so we don't check any character more than we should:

```
(?^:M(?:rs?\. Howell|ary Ann))
```

If you are using v5.10 or later, Perl already does this for you.

Exercises

You can find the answers to these exercises in "Answers for Chapter 9" on page 326.

1. [30 minutes] Get the `rightmost` program running (you can get the program from the Downloads section of *http://www.intermediateperl.com/* if you don't want to type the whole thing yourself). Once you have the example working, modify the `rightmost` program, take a hash reference of patterns, and return the key of the rightmost match. Instead of calling it like:

   ```
   my $position = rightmost(
     'There is Mrs. Howell, Ginger, and Gilligan',
     @patterns{ sort keys %patterns }
   );
   ```

   call it like:

   ```
   my $key = rightmost(
     'There is Mrs. Howell, Ginger, and Gilligan',
     \%patterns
   );
   ```

2. [45 minutes] Write a program to read in a list of patterns from a file. Precompile the patterns and store them in an array. For example, your patterns file might look like:

   ```
   cocoa?n[ue]t
   Mary[-\s]+Anne?
   (The\s+)?(Skipper|Professor)
   ```

   Prompt the user for lines of input, printing the line number and text for each line that matches. The `$.` variable is useful here.

3. Modify the program from Exercise 2 to use `Regexp::Assemble` so you have one pattern instead of an array of patterns.

## CHAPTER 10

Practical Reference Tricks

This chapter looks at optimizing, sorting, and dealing with recursively defined data.

Fancier Sorting

Perl's built-in **sort** operator sorts text strings in their code point text order[1] by default. This is fine if we want to sort text strings:

```
my @sorted = sort qw(Gilligan Skipper Professor Ginger Mary-Ann);
```

but gets pretty messy when we want to sort numbers:

```
my @wrongly_sorted = sort 1, 2, 4, 8, 16, 32;
```

The resulting list is 1, 16, 2, 32, 4, 8. Why didn't **sort** order these properly? It treats each item as a string and sorts them in string order. Any string that begins with 3 sorts before any string that begins with 4.

If we don't want the default sorting order, we don't need to write an entire sorting *algorithm*, which is good news since Perl already has a good one of those. But no matter what sorting algorithm we use, at some point we have to look at item A and item B, and decide which one comes first. That's the part we'll write: code to handle two items. Perl will do the rest.

By default, as Perl orders the items, it uses a string comparison. We can specify a new comparison using a *sort block* that we place between the **sort** keyword and the list of things to sort.[2] Within the sort block, $a and $b stand in for two of the items **sort** will compare. If we're sorting numbers, then $a and $b will be two numbers from our list.

---

1. We'll say "string order" to be the ascending numeric order of their code numbers, ignoring normalization, casing, and everything else that humans think might matter. Some call this the "ASCIIbetical" ordering. However, modern Perl doesn't use ASCII; instead, it uses a default sort order, depending on the current locale and character set. See *perllocale*.

2. We can also use a named subroutine that **sort** invokes for each comparison.

The sort block must return a coded value to indicate the sort order. If $a comes before $b in our desired sorting order, it should return -1; it should return +1 if $b comes before $a; if the order doesn't matter, it should return 0. The order might not matter, for example, if it's a case-insensitive sort comparing "FRED" to "Fred", or if it's a numeric sort comparing 42 to 42.[3]

For example, to sort those numbers in their proper order, we can use a sort block comparing $a and $b, like so:

```perl
my @numerically_sorted = sort {
  if ($a < $b)    { -1 }
  elsif ($a > $b) { +1 }
  else            {  0 }
} 1, 2, 4, 8, 16, 32;
```

Now we have a proper numeric comparison, so we have a proper numeric sort. This is far too much typing, so we can use the spaceship operator, <=>, instead:

```perl
my @numerically_sorted = sort { $a <=> $b } 1, 2, 4, 8, 16, 32;
```

The spaceship operator returns -1, 0, and +1, according to the rules we laid out. A descending sort is simple in Perl:[4]

```perl
my @numerically_descending =
    reverse sort { $a <=> $b } 1, 2, 4, 8, 16, 32;
```

But there is more than one way to do it. The spaceship operator is nearsighted; it can't see which one of its parameters comes from $a and which from $b; it sees only which value is to its left and which is to its right. If we reverse the positions of $a and $b, the spaceship will sort in the opposite order:

```perl
my @numerically_descending =
    sort { $b <=> $a } 1, 2, 4, 8, 16, 32;
```

In every place the previous sort expression returned -1, this expression returns +1, and vice versa. Thus, the sort is in the opposite order, and so it doesn't need a reverse. It's also easy to remember because if $a is to the left of $b, we get out the least items first. If $b is leftmost in our expression, we get the higher items first.

Which way is better? When should we use a reverse sort, and when should we switch $a and $b? Well, it usually shouldn't matter much for efficiency, so it's probably best to optimize for clarity and use reverse. For a more complex comparison, however, a single reverse may not be up to the task.

---

3. Actually, we can use any negative or positive number in place of -1 and +1, respectively. Recent Perl versions include a default sorting engine that is *stable*, so zero returns from the sort block cause the relative ordering of $a and $b to reflect their order in the original list. Older versions of Perl didn't guarantee such stability, and a future version might not use a stable sort, so don't rely on it. The use sort "stable"; declaration guarantees stability or dies.

4. As of v5.8.6, Perl recognizes the reverse sort and does it without generating the temporary, intermediate list.

Like the spaceship operator, we can indicate a string sort with `cmp`, although this is rarely used alone because it is the default comparison. The `cmp` operator is most often used in more complex comparisons, as we'll show shortly.

Sorting with Indices

In the same way we used indices to solve a few problems with `grep` and `map` back in Chapter 3, we can also use indices with `sort` to get some interesting results. For example, we sort the list of names from earlier:

```
my @sorted = sort qw(Gilligan Skipper Professor Ginger Mary-Ann);
print "@sorted\n";
```

which necessarily results in:

```
Gilligan Ginger Mary-Ann Professor Skipper
```

But what if we wanted to look at the original list and determine which element of the original list now appears as the first, second, third, and so on element of the sorted list? For example, Ginger is the second element of the sorted list and was the fourth element of the original list. How do we determine that the second element of the final list was the fourth element of the original list?

Well, we can apply a bit of indirection. We don't sort the actual names but rather the indices of each name:

```
     #        0        1        2        3       4
   my @input = qw(Gilligan Skipper Professor Ginger Mary-Ann);
   my @sorted_positions =
     sort { $input[$a] cmp $input[$b] } 0 .. $#input;
   print "@sorted_positions\n";
```

This time, `$a` and `$b` aren't the elements of the list, but the indices. So instead of comparing `$a` to `$b`, we use `cmp` to compare `$input[$a]` to `$input[$b]` as strings. The result of the `sort` are the indices, in an order defined by the corresponding elements of `@input`. This prints `0 3 4 2 1`, which means that the first element of the sorted list is element 0 of the original list, Gilligan. The second element of the sorted list is element 3 of the original list, which is Ginger, and so on. Now we can rank information rather than just move the names around.

Actually, we have the inverse of the rank. We still don't know for a given name in the original list about which position it occupies in the output list. But with a bit more magic, we can get there as well:

```
     #        0        1        2        3       4
   my @input = qw(Gilligan Skipper Professor Ginger Mary-Ann);
   my @sorted_positions =
     sort { $input[$a] cmp $input[$b] } 0 .. $#input;
   my @ranks;
   @ranks[@sorted_positions] = (0..$#sorted_positions);
   print "@ranks\n";
```

The code prints 0 4 3 1 2. This means that Gilligan is position 0 in the output list, Skipper is position 4, Professor is position 3, and so on. The positions here are 0-based, so add 1 to get "human" ordinal values. One way to cheat is to use 1..@sorted_positions instead of 0..$#sorted_positions. So, a way to dump it all out looks like:

```
    #             0        1        2        3        4
my @input = qw(Gilligan Skipper Professor Ginger Mary-Ann);
my @sorted_positions = sort { $input[$a] cmp $input[$b] } 0..$#input;
my @ranks;
@ranks[@sorted_positions] = (1 .. @sorted_positions);
foreach (0..$#ranks) {
  print "$input[$_] sorts into position $ranks[$_]\n";
}
```

This results in:

```
Gilligan sorts into position 1
Skipper sorts into position 5
Professor sorts into position 4
Ginger sorts into position 2
Mary-Ann sorts into position 3
```

This general technique can be convenient if we need to look at our data in more than one way. Perhaps we keep many records in order by a numeric code for efficiency reasons, but we occasionally want to view them in alphabetical order as well. Or maybe the data items themselves are impractical to sort, such as a month's worth of server logs.

Sorting Efficiently

As the Professor tries to maintain the community computing facility (built entirely out of bamboo, coconuts, and pineapples, and powered by a certified Perl-hacking monkey), he continues to discover that people are leaving entirely too much data on the single monkey-powered filesystem, so he decides to print a list of offenders.

The Professor has written a subroutine called ask_monkey_about, which, given a castaway's name, returns the number of pineapples of storage they use. We have to ask the monkey because he's in charge of the pineapples. An initial naïve approach to find the offenders from greatest to least might be something like:

```
my @castaways =
  qw(Gilligan Skipper Professor Ginger Mary-Ann Thurston Lovey);
my @wasters = sort {
  ask_monkey_about($b) <=> ask_monkey_about($a)
} @castaways;
```

In theory, this would be fine. For the first pair of names (Gilligan and Skipper), we ask the monkey "How many pineapples does Gilligan have?" and "How many pineapples does Skipper have?" We get back two values from the monkey and use them to order Gilligan and Skipper in the final list.

However, at some point, we have to compare the number of pineapples that Gilligan has with another castaway as well. For example, suppose the pair is Ginger and Gilligan. We ask the monkey about Ginger, get a number back, and then ask the monkey about Gilligan. . . again. This will probably annoy the monkey a bit, since we already asked. But we need to ask for each value two, three, or maybe even four times just to put the seven values into order.

This can be a problem because it irritates the monkey.

How do we keep the number of monkey requests to a minimum? Well, we can build a table first. We use a map with seven inputs and seven outputs, turning each castaway item into a separate array reference, with each referenced array consisting of the castaway name and the pineapple count reported by the monkey:

```
my @names_and_pineapples = map {
  [ $_, ask_monkey_about($_) ]
} @castaways;
```

At this point, we asked the monkey seven questions in a row, but that's the last time we have to talk to the monkey! We now have everything we need to finish the task.

For the next step, we sort the arrayrefs, ordering them by the monkey-returned value:

```
my @sorted_names_and_pineapples = sort {
  $b->[1] <=> $a->[1];
} @names_and_pineapples;
```

In this subroutine, $a and $b are still two elements from the list of things to be sorted. When we're sorting numbers, $a and $b are numbers; when we're sorting references, $a and $b are references. We dereference them to get to the corresponding array itself, and pick out item 1 from the array (the monkey's pineapple value). Because $b appears to the left of $a, it'll be a descending sort. We want a descending sort because the Professor wants the first name on the list to be the person who uses the most pineapples.

We're almost done, but what if we just wanted the top names alone, rather than the names and pineapple counts? We merely need to use another map to transform the references back to the original data:

```
my @names = map $_->[0], @sorted_names_and_pineapples;
```

Each element of the list ends up in $_, so we'll dereference that to pick out element 0 of that array, which is the name.

Now we have a list of names, ordered by their pineapple counts, and the monkey's off our backs, all in three easy steps.

The Schwartzian Transform

The intermediate variables between each of these steps were not necessary, except as input to the next step. We can save ourselves some brainpower by stacking all the steps together:

```
my @names =
  map $_->[0],
  sort { $b->[1] <=> $a->[1] }
  map [ $_, ask_monkey_about($_) ],
  @castaways;
```

Because the map and sort operators are right to left, we have to read this construct from the bottom up. Take a list of @castaways, create some arrayrefs by asking the monkey a simple question, sort the list of arrayrefs, and then extract the names from each arrayref. This gives us the list of names in the desired order.

This construct is commonly called the *Schwartzian Transform*,[5] which was named after Randal (but not by Randal), thanks to a Usenet posting he made many years ago. The Schwartzian Transform has since proven to be a good thing to have in our bag of sorting tricks.

If this transform looks like it might be too complex to memorize or come up with from first principles, it might help to look at the flexible and constant parts:

```
my @output_data =
  map  { EXTRACTION },
  sort { COMPARISON }
  map  [ CONSTRUCTION ],
  @input_data;
```

The basic structure maps the original list into a list of arrayrefs, computing the expensive function only once for each; sorts those array refs, looking at the cached value of each expensive function invocation;[6] and then extracts the original values back out in the new order. All we have to do is plug in the proper two operations, and we're done. For example, to use the Schwartzian Transform to implement a case-insensitive sort, we could use code like this:[7]

```
use v5.16;

my @output_data =
  map $_->[0],
  sort { $a->[1] cmp $b->[1] }
  map [ $_, "\F$_" ],   # \F is the full case folder from v5.16
  @input_data;
```

---

5. The Schwartzian Transform is actually a pun from Tom Christiansen, who named it the "Black Transform," but, *schwartz* being the German word for black as well as the the inventor's surname, he ended up with the name most people now use.

6. An *expensive* operation is one that takes a relatively long time or a relatively large amount of memory.

7. This is an efficient way to do this only if the uppercasing operation is sufficiently expensive, which it might be if our strings tend to be very long or if we have a large enough number of them. For a small number of not-long strings, a simple my @output_data = sort { "\F$a" cmp "\F$b"} @input_data is probably more efficient. If in doubt, benchmark.

There's nothing special about the array reference here. If we can't remember what we put into which array element, we can use a hash reference instead. We use the FOLDED key to describe what the sort value represents:

```
my @output_data =
  map $_->{ORGINAL},
  sort { $a->{FOLDED} cmp $b->{FOLDED} }
  map { ORIGINAL => $_, FOLDED => "\F$_" ],
  @input_data;
```

Multilevel Sort with the Schwartzian Transform

If we need to sort on more than one criterion, the Schwartzian Transform is still up to the task. We just have to add sort keys to the anonymous array then use them in the comparison:

```
my @output_data =
  map $_->[0],
  sort {
    $a->[1] cmp $b->[1] or
    $a->[2] <=> $b->[2] or
    $a->[3] cmp $b->[3] }
  map [ $_, lc, get_id($_), get_name($_) ],
  @input_data;
```

This code skeleton has a three-level **sort** comparison, using three computed values saved in the anonymous array (alongside the original data item to be sorted, which always comes first).

That's a bit hard to remember though. There's nothing special about the array reference. We could use a hash reference and give each comparison level a descriptive name:

```
map $_->{VALUE},
sort {
  $a->{LOWER} cmp $b->{LOWER}  or
  $a->{ID}    <=> $b->{ID}     or
  $a->{NAME}  AND $b->{NAME} }
map {
  VALUE  => $_,
  LOWER  => lc,
  ID     => get_id($_),
  NAME   => get_name($_),
  },
@input_data;
```

Recursively Defined Data

While the data we've processed with references up to this point has been rather fixed structure, sometimes we have to deal with hierarchical data, which is often defined recursively.

For example, consider an HTML table that has rows containing cells—some of those cells may also contain entire tables. Example Two could be a visual representation of a filesystem consisting of directories containing files and other directories. Example Three is a company organization chart, which has managers with direct reports, some of which may be managers themselves. And Example Four is a more complex organization chart, which can contain instances of the HTML tables of Example One, the filesystem representations of Example Two, or even entire organization charts.

We can use references to acquire, store, and process such hierarchical information. Frequently, the routines to manage the data structures end up as recursive subroutines.

Recursive algorithms deal with the unlimited complexity of their data by beginning with a base case and building on that. Recursive functions should all have a base or trivial case, where it doesn't need to recurse and that all other recursions can eventually reach. That is, unless we have a lot of time on our hands to let the function recurse forever. The base case considers what to do in the simplest case: when the leaf node has no branches, when the array is empty, when the counter is at zero. It's common to have more than one base case in various branches of a recursive algorithm. A recursive algorithm with no base case is an infinite loop.

A recursive subroutine has a branch from which it calls itself to handle a portion of the task, and a branch that doesn't call itself to handle the base cases. In Example One, the base case could be a table cell that is empty. There could also be base cases for empty tables and table rows. In Example Two, base cases would be needed for files and perhaps for empty directories.

For example, a recursive subroutine handling the factorial function, which is one of the simplest recursive functions, might look like:

```
sub factorial {
  my $n = shift;
  if ($n <= 1) {
    return 1;
  } else {
    return $n * factorial($n - 1);
  }
}
```

 Other languages have something called *tail recursion* where the compiler can recognize this and convert it to an iterative solution so it doesn't actually recurse. A dynamic language such as Perl can't do this because the subroutine definition might change before we can call it again. This means we have to be careful with Perl's recursion.

Here we have a base case where $n is less than or equal to 1, which does not invoke the recursive instance, along with a recursive case for $n greater than 1, which calls the routine to handle a portion of the problem (i.e., compute the factorial of the next lower number).

This task would be solved better using iteration rather than recursion, even though the classic definition of factorial is often given as a recursive operation.

Building Recursively Defined Data

Suppose we wanted to capture information about a filesystem, including the filenames and directory names, and their included contents. We'll represent a directory as a hash, in which the keys are the names of the entries within the directory and values are undef for plain files. A sample /bin directory looks like:

```
my $bin_directory = {
  cat  => undef,
  cp   => undef,
  date => undef,
  ... and so on ...
};
```

Similarly, the Skipper's home directory might also contain a personal *bin* directory (at something like *~skipper/bin*) that contains personal tools:

```
my $skipper_bin = {
  navigate           => undef,
  discipline_gilligan => undef,
  eat                => undef,
};
```

Nothing in either structure tells where the directory is located in the hierarchy. It represents the contents of some directory.

Go up one level to the Skipper's home directory, which is likely to contain a few files along with the personal *bin* directory:

```
my $skipper_home = {
  '.cshrc'                      => undef,
  'Please_rescue_us.pdf'        => undef,
  'Things_I_should_have_packed' => undef,
  bin                           => $skipper_bin,
};
```

Ahh, notice that we have three files, but the fourth entry bin doesn't have undef for a value but rather the hash reference created earlier for the Skipper's personal *bin* directory. This is how we indicate subdirectories. If the value is undef, it's a plain file; if it's a hash reference, we have a subdirectory, with its own files and subdirectories. We have combined these two initializations (see Figure 10-1):

```
my $skipper_home = {
  '.cshrc'                      => undef,
  'Please_rescue_us.pdf'        => undef,
  'Things_I_should_have_packed' => undef,
```

```
  bin => {
    navigate            => undef,
    discipline_gilligan => undef,
    eat                 => undef,
  },
};
```

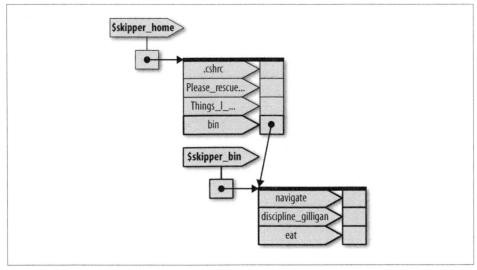

Figure 10-1. Skipper home PeGS

Now the hierarchical nature of the data starts to come into play.

Obviously, we don't want to create and maintain a data structure by changing literals in the program. We should fetch the data by using a subroutine. Write a subroutine that returns undef for a given pathname if the path is a file, or a hash reference of the directory contents if the path is a directory. The base case of looking at a file is the easiest, so we write that:

```
sub data_for_path {
  my $path = shift;
  if (-f $path) {
    return undef;
  }
  if (-d $path) {
    ...
  }
  warn "$path is neither a file nor a directory\n";
  return undef;
}
```

If the Skipper calls this on *.cshrc*, he'll get back an undef value, indicating that a file was seen.

Now for the directory part. We need a hash reference, which we declare as a named hash inside the subroutine. For each element of the hash, we call ourselves to populate the value of that hash element. It goes something like this:

```
sub data_for_path {
  my $path = shift;
  if (-f $path or -l $path) {          # files or symbolic links
    return undef;
  }
  if (-d $path) {
    my %directory;
    opendir PATH, $path or die "Cannot opendir $path: $!";
    my @names = readdir PATH;
    closedir PATH;
    for my $name (@names) {
      next if $name eq '.' or $name eq '..';
      $directory{$name} = data_for_path("$path/$name");
    }
    return \%directory;
  }
  warn "$path is neither a file nor a directory\n";
  return undef;
}
```

The base cases in this recursive algorithm are the files and symbolic links. This algorithm wouldn't correctly traverse the filesystem if it followed symbolic links to directories as if they were true (hard) links since it could end up in a circular loop if the symlink pointed to a directory that contained the symlink.[8] It would also fail to correctly traverse a malformed filesystem—that is, one in which the directories form a ring rather than a tree structure, say. Although malformed filesystems may not often be an issue, recursive algorithms in general are vulnerable to errors in the structure of the recursive data.

For each file within the directory being examined, the response from the recursive call to data_for_path is undef. This populates most elements of the hash. When the reference to the named hash is returned, the reference becomes a reference to an anonymous hash because the name immediately goes out of scope. (The data itself doesn't change, but the number of ways in which we can access the data changes.)

If there is a subdirectory, the nested subroutine call uses readdir to extract the contents of that directory and returns a hash reference, which is inserted into the hash structure created by the caller.

At first, it may look a bit mystifying, but if we walk through the code slowly, we'll see it's always doing the right thing. Test the results of this subroutine by calling it on . (the current directory) and inspecting the result:

---

8. Not that any of us have ever done that and wondered why the program took forever. The second time really wasn't our fault anyway, and the third time was just bad luck. That's our story, and we're sticking to it.

```
use Data::Dumper;
print Dumper(data_for_path('.'));
```

Obviously, this will be more interesting if our current directory contains subdirectories.

Displaying Recursively Defined Data

The Dumper routine of Data::Dumper displays the output nicely, but what if we don't like the format being used? We can write a routine to display the data. Again, for recursively defined data, a recursive subroutine is usually the key.

To dump the data, we need to know the name of the directory at the top of the tree because that's not stored within the structure:

```
sub dump_data_for_path {
  my $path = shift;
  my $data = shift;

  if (not defined $data) { # plain file
    print "$path\n";
    return;
  }
  ...
}
```

For a plain file, dump the pathname; for a directory, $data is a hash reference. We walk through the keys and dump the values:

```
sub dump_data_for_path {
  my $path = shift;
  my $data = shift;

  if (not defined $data) { # plain file
    print "$path\n";
    return;
  }

  foreach (sort keys %$data) {
    dump_data_for_path("$path/$_", $data->{$_});
  }
}
```

For each element of the directory, we pass a path consisting of the incoming path followed by the current directory entry, and the data pointer is either undef for a file or a subdirectory hash reference for another directory. We can see the results by running:

```
dump_data_for_path('.', data_for_path('.'));
```

Again, this is more interesting in a directory that has subdirectories, but the output should be similar to calling find from the shell prompt:

```
% find . -print
```

Avoiding Recursion

We used recursion in the previous examples so that we could show how to do it, but it's not the only way to get the job done. Now we'll code our solutions using iterative solutions. Why? Most people learn recursion because some other language has a feature that can take what looks like recursive code and turn it into an iterative solution. It's easier to conceive as a recursive algorithm, but that doesn't mean that the program actually recurses. In Perl, however, we don't get that benefit of that behind-the-scenes rearrangement.

There are other benefits to iterative solutions. In the recursive version of data_ for_path, we constructed the directory tree depth first, and we can only do it depth first. With a recursive solution, we have to work all the way down to the bottom before we can move on to the next thing at the top level.

To make an iterative solution, we follow a basic template. We have to manage our own queue of things that we need to process. As long as we have things in the queue, we keep going. When we exhaust the queue, we return the data structure we created. The template looks like:

```perl
sub iterative_solution {
  my( $start ) = @_;

  my $data = {};
  my @queue = ( [ $start, $data ] );

  while( my $next = shift @queue ) {
    ... process current element ...
    ... add new things to @queue ...
  }

  return $data;
}
```

In the template, each item in @queue carries along everything we need to process that element as an anonymous array. Here, $start is the thing we need to process and $data is the reference where we need to store the result. Although we only have two things in that anonymous array, we'll add some more later to add an additional, attractive, feature.

First, we merely translate the recursive solution into an iterative one, using the same depth-first behavior:

```perl
use File::Basename;
use File::Spec::Functions;

my $data = data_for_path( '/Users/Gilligan/Desktop' );

sub data_for_path {
  my( $path ) = @_;
```

```
    my $data = {};

    my @queue = ( [ $path, $data ] );

    while( my $next = shift @queue ) {
      my( $path, $ref ) = @$next;

      my $basename = basename( $path );

      $ref->{$basename} = do {
        if( -f $path or -l $path ) { undef }
        else {
          my $hash = {};
          opendir my ($dh), $path;
          my @new_paths = map {
            catfile( $path, $_ )
            } grep { ! /^\.\.?\z/ } readdir $dh;

          unshift @queue, map { [ $_, $hash ] } @new_paths;
          $hash;
        }
      };
    }

    $data;
  }
```

Inside the while loop, we get the next element to process. It has the path it needs to process and the reference for its result. Since $path is the full path and we only want the filename, we get the basename to use as the key. Once we have the key to add to $ref, we have to decide what the value should be. Inside the do block, we have two branches: in the file or link case, the value is undef, and in the directory case, we have to create new items to process and add them to the queue.

To create the new element, we create a new reference in $hash. This is a reference we're going to store as the result for the new item we need to process. This is the reference that is going into the anonymous array for the item to process. This is the cool reference trick: even though we create the reference separately, when we assign it as the value to $ref->{$basename}, even as the empty anonymous hash, it becomes part of the data structure. We don't know where it is in the data structure, but we don't have to know.

Since we want to make this a depth-first algorithm, when we have a new element to process, we put it at the front of @queue by using unshift. There's nothing in this version that makes it better than the recursive solution. It's a bit longer, it's more complicated to understand the first time we see it, and it doesn't necessarily run any faster.

The Breadth-First Solution

Now that we've created the iterative solution, we can do quite a bit more than the recursive version ever could. We can easily change it to a breadth-first algorithm, and it's just a matter of changing a single keyword. With unshift, we put the newly discovered items at the front of the queue. If we use push instead, we put newly discovered items at the end of the queue:

```
# unshift @queue, map { [ $_, $hash ] } @new_paths;
push @queue, map { [ $_, $hash ] } @new_paths;
```

The depth-first version is last in–first out (LIFO) and the breadth-first version is first in–first out (FIFO). The code for either is almost identical. If we're a computer science purist, we may point out that the depth-first version is actually a stack instead of a queue, but we'll just say it's a queue with a VIP section where more important VIPs keep cutting in line.

The breadth-first has an extremely attractive ability: we can easily stop at any level that we like. If we only want to go three levels deep, we don't add any items to process that would be deeper than that. We could engineer the recursive solution to do this too, but it looks pretty ugly.

In our iterative solution, we keep track of our level in the anonymous arrays that we store in @queue. In the else branch in the do block, we add elements to @queue only if the current level is below the threshold since the elements we add are one level deeper:

```
use Data::Dumper;
use File::Basename;
use File::Spec::Functions;

my $data = data_for_path( "/Users/brian/Desktop", 2 );
print Dumper( $data );

sub data_for_path {
  my( $path, $threshold ) = @_;

  my $data = {};

  my @queue = ( [ $path, 0, $data ] );

  while( my $next = shift @queue ) {
    my( $path, $level, $ref ) = @$next;

    my $basename = basename( $path );

    $ref->{$basename} = do {
      if( -f $path or -l $path ) { undef }
      else {
        my $hash = {};
        if( $level < $threshold ) {
          opendir my ($dh), $path;
          my @new_paths = map {
            catfile( $path, $_ )
            } grep { ! /^\.\.?\z/ } readdir $dh;

          push @queue, map { [ $_, $level + 1, $hash ] } @new_paths;
        }
        $hash;
      }
```

```
    };
  }

  $data;
}
```

Nifty, eh? It gets even better, though. It's not too tough to let the user decide if he or she wants depth-first or breadth-first traversals. That might be interesting if the user wants to process a certain number of items at a time, leaving some of them unprocessed. We aren't going to spoil the fun you'll have as you work on that in Exercise 5, though.

Exercises

You can find the answers to these exercises in "Answers for Chapter 10" on page 329.

1. [15 minutes] Using the glob operator, a naïve sort of every name in your home directory by their relative sizes might be written as:

   ```
   chdir;  # the default is our home directory
   my @sorted = sort { -s $a <=> -s $b } glob '*';
   ```

   Rewrite this using the Schwartzian Transform technique.

2. [15 minutes] Read up on the Benchmark module, included with Perl. Write a program that will answer the question, "How much does using the Schwartzian Transform speed up the task of Exercise 1?"

3. [10 minutes] Using a Schwartzian Transform, read a list of words and sort them in "dictionary order." Dictionary order ignores all capitalization and internal punctuation. Hint: The following transformation might be useful:

   ```
   my $string = 'Mary-Ann';
   $string =~ tr/A-Z/a-z/;      # force all lowercase
   $string =~ tr/a-z//cd;       # strip all but a-z from the string
   print $string;               # prints "maryann"
   ```

   Be sure you don't mangle the data! If the input includes the Professor and The Skipper, the output should have them listed in that order, with that capitalization.

4. [20 minutes] Modify the recursive directory dumping routine so it shows the nested directories through indentation. An empty directory should show up as:

   ```
   sandbar, an empty directory
   ```

   while a nonempty directory should appear with nested contents, indented two spaces:

   ```
   uss_minnow, with contents:
     anchor
     broken_radio
     galley, with contents:
       captain_crunch_cereal
       gallon_of_milk
   ```

```
    tuna_fish_sandwich
    life_preservers
```

5. [20 minutes] Modify the iterative version of `data_for_path` to handle both depth-first or breadth-first traversal. Use an optional third argument to allow the user to decide which to use:

```
my $depth   =
    data_for_path( $start_dir, $threshold, 'depth-first' );

my $breadth =
    data_for_path( $start_dir, $threshold, 'breadth-first' );
```

## CHAPTER 11

Building Larger Programs

As our programs get larger, we start to realize that some of our code applies to other jobs we have. We can move some of that code to a *library* that we can share among several programs, and even with other people. We can also use libraries to compartmentalize code by its function or use, keeping it separate from code that does unrelated tasks.

The Cure for the Common Code

The Skipper writes many Perl programs to provide navigation for all the common ports of call for the *Minnow*. He finds himself cutting and pasting a very common routine into each program:

```
sub turn_toward_heading {
  my $new_heading = shift;
  my $current_heading = current_heading( );
  print "Current heading is ", $current_heading, ".\n";
  print "Come about to $new_heading ";
  my $direction = 'right';
  my $turn = ($new_heading - $current_heading) % 360;
  if ($turn > 180) { # long way around
    $turn = 360 - $turn;
    $direction = 'left';
  }
  print "by turning $direction $turn degrees.\n";
}
```

This routine gives the shortest turn to make from the current heading returned by the subroutine current_heading to a new heading given as the first parameter to the subroutine.

The first line of this subroutine might have read instead:

```
my ($new_heading) = @_;
```

This is mostly a style call: in both cases, the first parameter ends up in $new_heading. However, removing the items from @_ as they are identified does have some advantages.

So, we stick (mostly) with the "shifting" style of argument parsing. Now back to the matter at hand.

After writing a dozen programs using this routine, the Skipper realizes that the output is excessively chatty when he's already taken the time to steer the proper course (or perhaps started drifting in the proper direction). After all, if the current heading is 234 degrees and he needs to turn to 234 degrees, we see:

```
Current heading is 234.
Come about to 234 by turning right 0 degrees.
```

How annoying! The Skipper decides to fix this problem by checking for a zero turn value:

```
sub turn_toward_heading {
  my $new_heading = shift;
  my $current_heading = current_heading( );
  print "Current heading is ", $current_heading, ".\n";
  my $direction = 'right';
  my $turn = ($new_heading - $current_heading) % 360;
  unless ($turn) {
    print "On course (good job!).\n";
    return;
  }
  print "Come about to $new_heading ";
  if ($turn > 180) { # long way around
    $turn = 360 - $turn;
    $direction = 'left';
  }
  print "by turning $direction $turn degrees.\n";
}
```

Great. The new subroutine works nicely in the current navigation program. However, because he had previously cut-and-pasted it into a half dozen other navigation programs, those other programs still annoy the Skipper with extraneous turning messages.

The Skipper needs a way to write the code in one place and then share it among many programs. And like most things in Perl, there's more than one way to do it.

Inserting Code with eval

The Skipper can save disk space (and brain space) by putting the definition for turn_toward_heading into a separate file. For example, suppose the Skipper figures out a half-dozen common subroutines related to navigating the *Minnow* that he seems to use in most or all of the programs he's writing for the task. He can put them in a separate file called *Navigation.pm*, which comprises the needed subroutines.

The .pm extension stands for "Perl Module" and is important, as we show later. We don't need any particular filename or extension here because we tell require exactly which filename we want. In the earlier days of Perl, people used .pl (for "Perl library"), but now people use that extension for Perl programs, too.

But now, how can we tell Perl to pull in that program snippet from another file? We could do it the hard way, using the string form of eval that we showed in Chapter 3:

```
sub load_common_subroutines {
  open my $more_fh, '<', 'Navigation.pm' or die "Navigation.pm: $!";
  undef $/; # enable slurp mode
  my $more_code = <$more_fh>;
  close $more_fh;
  eval $more_code;
  die $@ if $@;
}
```

Perl reads the code from *Navigation.pm* into the $more_code variable. We then use eval to process that text as Perl code. Any lexical variables in $more_code remain local to the evaluated code. If there's a syntax error, Perl sets the $@ variable and we die with the appropriate error message.

 An eval can access any lexical variables in the scope where we call it. It doesn't create a new scope like a subroutine call would.

Now, instead of a few dozen lines of common subroutines to place in each file, we have one subroutine to insert in each file:

```
load_common_subroutines();
```

But that's not very nice, especially if we need to keep doing this kind of task repeatedly. Luckily, Perl has several ways to help us out.

Using do

The Skipper placed a few common navigation subroutines into *Navigation.pm*. If the Skipper merely inserts:

```
do 'Navigation.pm';
die $@ if $@;
```

into his typical navigation program it's almost the same as if the eval code were executed right at that point in the program.[1]

---

1. Except in regard to @INC, %INC, and missing file handling, which we'll show later.

That is, the do operator acts as if the code from *Navigation.pm* were incorporated into the current program although in its own scope block so that lexicals (my variables) and most directives (such as use strict) from the included file don't leak into the main program.

Now the Skipper can safely update and maintain one copy of the common subroutines without having to copy and recopy all the fixes and extensions into the many separate navigation programs he creates and uses.

This requires a bit of discipline because breaking the expected interface of a given subroutine now breaks many programs instead of one.[2] Once we let other people use our code, we're virtually stuck with our interface because our new customers will complain about anything that makes them change their code.

By placing some of the code into a separate file, other programmers can reuse the Skipper's routines and vice versa by sharing the file without sharing their entire application. If Gilligan writes a routine to drop_anchor and places it in the file *DropAnchor.pm* then the Skipper can use Gilligan's code by including his library:

```
do 'DropAnchor.pm';
die $@ if $@;
...
drop_anchor() if at_dock() or in_port();
```

Thus, the code that we bring in from separate files permits easy maintenance and interprogrammer cooperation. That doesn't mean it's *sufficient* for either of those, so we still have to be good team members.

 The do does not search the module directories like use and require that we showed in Chapter 2. We have to give do the absolute or relative path to the file.

While the code we brought in from a *.pm* file can have direct executable statements that run when we load the file, it's much more common to define subroutines that we can load using do.

Going back to that *DropAnchor.pm* library for a second, what if the Skipper wrote a program that needed to "drop anchor" as well as navigate? He would need to load two files:

```
do 'DropAnchor.pm';
die $@ if $@;
do 'Navigation.pm';
die $@ if $@;
...
```

2. In Chapter 14, we show how to set up tests to be used while maintaining reused code.

```
turn_toward_heading(90);
...
drop_anchor() if at_dock();
```

That works fine and dandy. The subroutines defined in both libraries are available to this program.

Using require

Suppose *Navigation.pm* itself also pulls in *DropAnchor.pm* for some common navigation task. Perl reads the file once directly and then again while processing the navigation package. This needlessly redefines drop_anchor. Worse than that, if we have warnings enabled we get a warning from Perl that we redefined the subroutine, even if it's the same definition.

We need a mechanism that tracks which files we've brought in and then brings them in only once. Perl has such an operation, called require. Change the previous code to:

```
require 'DropAnchor.pm';
require 'Navigation.pm';
```

The require operator keeps track of the files Perl has read. Once Perl has processed a file successfully, it ignores any further require operations on that same file. This means that even if *Navigation.pm* contains require "DropAnchor.pm", Perl imports the *Drop Anchor.pm* file exactly once, and we'll get no annoying error messages about duplicate subroutine definitions (see Figure 11-1). Most importantly, we'll also save time by not processing the file more than once.

 Perl uses the %INC hash to track loaded modules, as described in the entry for require in *perlfunc*.

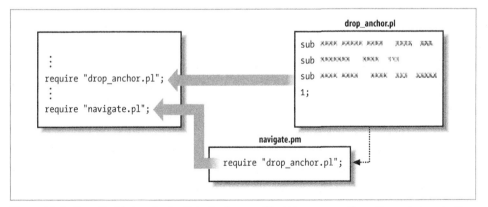

Figure 11-1. Once Perl brings in the DropAnchor.pm file, it ignores another attempt to require it

The `require` operator also has two additional features:

- Any syntax error in the required file causes the program to die, thus many `die $@` `if $@` statements are unnecessary.

- The last expression evaluated in the file must return a true value so `require` knows it worked.

Because of the second point, most files evaluated for `require` have a cryptic `1;` as their last line of code. This ensures that the last evaluated expression is true. Try to carry on this tradition as well.

The Problem of Namespace Collisions

Sometimes the Skipper runs a ship into an island, but sometimes the collision involved is just a couple of names in a Perl program. Suppose that the Skipper has added all his cool and useful routines to *Navigation.pm* and that Gilligan has incorporated the library into his own navigation package `head_toward_island`:

```
require 'Navigation.pm';

sub turn_toward_port {
  turn_toward_heading(compute_heading_to_island( ));
}

sub compute_heading_to_island {
  .. code here ..
}

.. more program here ..
```

Gilligan then has his program debugged (perhaps with the aid of the Professor), and everything works well.

However, now the Skipper decides to modify his *Navigation.pm* library, adding a routine called `turn_toward_port` that makes a 45-degree turn toward the left (known as "port" in nautical jargon).

Gilligan's program will fail in a catastrophic way as soon as he tries to head to port: he'll start steering the ship in circles! The problem is that the Perl compiler first compiles `turn_toward_port` from Gilligan's main program, then when Perl evaluates the `require` at runtime, it redefines `turn_toward_port` as the Skipper's definition. Sure, if Gilligan has warnings enabled, he'll notice something is wrong, but why should he have to count on that?

The problem is that Gilligan defined `turn_toward_port` as meaning "turn toward the port on the island," while the Skipper defined it as "turn toward the left." How do we resolve this?

One way is to require that the Skipper put an explicit prefix in front of every name defined in the library, say `navigation_`. Thus, Gilligan's program ends up looking like:

```
require 'Navigation.pm';

sub turn_toward_port {
  navigation_turn_toward_heading(compute_heading_to_island(  ));
}

sub compute_heading_to_island {
  .. code here ..
}

.. more program here ..
```

Clearly, the `navigation_turn_toward_heading` comes from the *Navigation.pm* file. This is great for Gilligan, but awkward for the Skipper, as his file now has longer subroutine names:

```
sub navigation_turn_toward_heading {
  .. code here ..
}

sub navigation_turn_toward_port {
  .. code here ..
}

1;
```

Yes, every scalar, array, hash, filehandle, or subroutine now has to have a `navigation_` prefix in front of it to guarantee that the names won't collide with any potential users of the library. Obviously, for that old sailor, this ain't gonna float his boat. What do we do instead?

Packages as Namespace Separators

If the name prefix of the last example didn't have to be spelled out on every use, things would work much better. We can improve the situation by using a package:

```
package Navigation;

sub turn_toward_heading {
  .. code here ..
}

sub turn_toward_port {
  .. code here ..
}

1;
```

The `package` declaration at the beginning of this file tells Perl to virtually insert `Navigation::` in front of most names within the file. Thus, the previous code implicitly uses the fully qualified package name for the subroutines:

```
sub Navigation::turn_toward_heading {
  .. code here ..
}

sub Navigation::turn_toward_port {
  .. code here ..
}

1;
```

Now when Gilligan uses this file he adds `Navigation::` to the subroutines defined in the library, and leaves the `Navigation::` prefix off for subroutines he defines on his own:

```
require 'Navigation.pm';

sub turn_toward_port {
  Navigation::turn_toward_heading(compute_heading_to_island( ));
}

sub compute_heading_to_island {
  .. code here ..
}

.. more program here ..
```

Package names are like variable names: they consist of alphanumerics and underscores but can't begin with a digit. Also, for reasons explained in the *perlmodlib* documentation, a package name should begin with a capital letter and not overlap an existing CPAN or core module name.

 The Perl Authors Upload Server, or PAUSE, has advice for naming conventions and how your module fits in with everything else already on CPAN. Read more about this in Chapter 21.

Package names can also have multiple names separated by double colons, such as `Minnow::Navigation` and `Minnow::Food::Storage`.

Nearly every scalar, array, hash, subroutine, and filehandle name[3] is actually implicitly prefixed by the current package, unless the name already contains one or more double-colon markers.

So, in *Navigation.pm*, we can use variables such as:

```
package Navigation;
@homeport = (21.283, -157.842);

sub turn_toward_port {
  .. code ..
}
```

3. Except lexicals, as we'll show in a moment.

Trivia note: 21.283 degrees north, 157.842 degrees west is the location of the real-life marina where the opening shot of a famous television series was filmed. Check it out on Google Maps if you don't believe us.

We can refer to the `@homeport` variable in the main code with its full package specification:

```
@destination = @Navigation::homeport;
```

If every name has a package name inserted in front of it, what about names in the main program? Yes, they are also in a package, called `main`. It's as if `package main;` were at the beginning of each file. Thus, to keep Gilligan from having to say `Navigation::turn_toward_heading`, the *Navigation.pm* file can say:

```
sub main::turn_toward_heading {
  .. code here ..
}
```

Now the subroutine is defined in the `main` package, not the `Navigation` package. This isn't an optimal solution (we'll show better solutions in Chapter 17 when we talk about `Exporter`), but at least there's nothing sacred or terribly unique about `main` compared to any other package.

If we know the package, we can access the package's variables and subroutines from anywhere in the program.

This is what the modules in Chapter 2 were doing when they imported symbols into our scripts, but we didn't tell you the whole story then. Those modules imported the subroutines and variables into the current package (again, that's `main` in our scripts, usually). That is, those symbols are only available in that package unless we use the full package specification. We'll get more into how this works later.

Scope of a Package Directive

Perl doesn't make us create an explicit `main` loop like C. Perl knows that every script needs one, so it gives it to us for free.

All Perl files start as if we had said `package main;` at the beginning. Any package directive remains in effect until the next `package` directive unless that `package` directive is inside a curly braced scope. In that case, Perl remembers the prior package and restores it when that scope ends. Here's an example:

```
package Navigation;

{  # start scope block
  package main;  # now in package main

  sub turn_toward_heading {  # main::turn_toward_heading
    .. code here ..
  }

}  # end scope block

# back to package Navigation

sub turn_toward_port { # Navigation::turn_toward_port
  .. code here ..
}
```

The current package is lexically scoped, similar to the scope of my variables, narrowed to the innermost-enclosing brace pair or file in which we introduced the package.

Most libraries have only one package declaration at the top of the file. Most programs leave the package as the default main package. However, it's nice to know that we can temporarily have a different current package

 Some names are always in package main regardless of the current package: ARGV, ARGVOUT, ENV, INC, SIG, STDERR, STDIN, and STDOUT. We can always refer to @INC and be assured of getting @main::INC. The punctuation mark variables such as $_, $2, and $! are either all lexicals or forced into package main, so when we write $. we never get $Navigation::. by mistake.

Packages and Lexicals

A lexical variable (a variable introduced with my) isn't prefixed by the current package because package variables are always global: we can always reference a package variable if we know its full name. A lexical variable is usually temporary and accessible for only a portion of the program. If we declare a lexical variable, then using that name without a package prefix gets the lexical variable. A package prefix ensures that we are accessing a package variable and never a lexical variable.

For example, suppose a subroutine within *Navigation.pm* declares a lexical @homeport variable. Any mention of @homeport will then be the newly introduced lexical variable, but a fully qualified mention of @Navigation::homeport accesses the package variable instead:

```
package Navigation;
our @homeport = (21.283, -157.842); # package version
```

```
sub get_me_home {
  my @homeport;

  .. @homeport .. # refers to the lexical variable
  .. @Navigation::homeport .. # refers to the package variable

}

.. @homeport .. # refers to the package variable
```

Obviously, this can lead to confusing code, so we shouldn't introduce such duplication needlessly. The results are completely predictable if we know the rules, though.

Package Blocks

Starting with v5.12, we can use a new syntax that allows us to use a block with our package statements:

```
package Navigation {
  my @homeport = (21.283, -157.842); # package version

  sub get_me_home {
    my @homeport;

    .. @homeport .. # refers to the lexical variable
    .. @Navigation::homeport .. # refers to the package variable

  }

  .. @homeport .. # refers to the package variable
}
```

This isn't much different than a package in a bare block, even if it looks a little nicer:

```
{
  package Navigation;
  my @homeport = (21.283, -157.842); # package version

  sub get_me_home {
    my @homeport;

    .. @homeport .. # refers to the lexical variable
    .. @Navigation::homeport .. # refers to the package variable

  }

  .. @homeport .. # refers to the package variable
}
```

Either way, we can use a lexical variable that's scoped to that block, which only that package happens to use. We don't have to define a package all at once, so this only works if we don't define other parts of the package elsewhere and expect access to that variable.

This is also useful for defining multiple small packages in the same file:

```
use v5.12;

package Navigation {
  ...
}

package DropAnchor {
  ...
}
```

Typically, we use one package per file, which gives us much the same effect but usually accidentally since the lexical variables we use are also scoped to the file (and not the package). Denoting the scope of the package also explicitly scopes the lexical variables we use.

We don't talk about versions until Chapter 12, but the new `package` syntax allows us to specify a version, with or without a block:

```
use v5.12;

package Navigation 0.01;

package DropAnchor 1.23 { ... }
```

This is really a shortcut for setting the `$VERSION` variable, which other code looks for when it wants a package version. It's a regular Perl scalar, though, and we can set it ourselves directly if we like.

Exercises

You can find the answers to these exercises in "Answers for Chapter 11" on page 333.

1. [30 minutes] The Oogaboogoo natives on the island have unusual names for the days and months. Here is some simple but not very well-written code from Gilligan. Fix it up, add a conversion function for the month names, and make the whole thing into a library. For extra credit, add suitable error checking and consider what should be in the documentation:

```
@day = qw(ark dip wap sen pop sep kir);
sub number_to_day_name { my $num = shift @_; $day[$num]; }
@month = qw(diz pod bod rod sip wax lin sen kun fiz nap dep);
```

2. [10 minutes] Make a program that uses your library and the following code to print out a message, such as Today is dip sen 15 2011, meaning that today is a Monday in August. You might use localtime:

```
my($sec, $min, $hour, $mday, $mon, $year, $wday) = localtime;
```

Hint: The year and month numbers returned by localtime may not be what you'd expect, so you need to check the documentation.

## CHAPTER 12

Creating Your Own Perl Distribution

So far, we've shown Perl as a language. The rest of this book starts your education for the Perl development process. We're almost to the point of making modules, but before we do that, we want to show how to create a Perl distribution. We don't need a distribution to create modules, but a distribution makes development easier; most of Perl's tools are built around the concept of the distribution. Along with that, we want to test the code as we develop it, not when we think we're done.

Perl's Two Build Systems

A *build system* takes the files that we distribute and turns them into the files we actually install. It might compile files, insert configuration into code, or anything else the developer might want to do. Once it's transformed the files, the builder installs them.

There are two common build systems in Perl. The ExtUtils::Makemaker is built on top of make, a dependency management tool that originated with Unix developers. These distributions use a *Makefile.PL* to control the build. If we want to customize our build script, we have to know the language of make and we have to ensure that our additions are portable. Although ExtUtils::Makemaker is well supported, it's at the end of its life and no new features will be added. Still, many of the CPAN distributions still use ExtUtils::Makemaker so many developers continue to use it because it's stable and works well for common cases.

The newer system uses Module::Build, a pure-Perl tool. If we want to install Perl modules, we likely already have Perl. Using a build system that only needs Perl means we don't need to install anything extra. However, Module::Build has only been in the Standard Library since v5.10. These distributions have a *Build.PL*.

Some distributions come with both a *Makefile.PL* and a *Build.PL*. Some of those use either system, and some of those merely provide a thin wrapper around the other.

No matter which one we choose, the distribution structure is mostly the same, so almost everything in this chapter applies to either build system. We'll note where there is a difference between the two.

Inside Makefile.PL

ExtUtils::Makemaker typically uses *Makefile.PL*, but there's really nothing special about that name other than the toolchain using it by convention. As its file extension denotes, it's just a program. The WriteMakefile subroutine takes some settings, in the form of keys and values, and turns them into a *Makefile*, the powerful dependency management system that is common to Unix.

The starter *Makefile.PL* looks something like this, as created by *module-starter*:

```
use 5.006;
use strict;
use warnings;
use ExtUtils::MakeMaker;

WriteMakefile(
    NAME                => 'Animal',
    AUTHOR              => q{Willie Gilligan <gilligan@island.example.com>},
    VERSION_FROM        => 'lib/Animal.pm',
    ABSTRACT_FROM       => 'lib/Animal.pm',
    PL_FILES            => {},
    PREREQ_PM => {
        'Test::More' => 0,
    },
    dist                => { COMPRESS => 'gzip -9f', SUFFIX => 'gz', },
    clean               => { FILES => 'Animal2-*' },
);
```

The ExtUtils::Makemaker documentation explains each of these. The interesting one here is PREREQ_PM, which lists the modules and their versions that we need to run our code. When we list these dependencies here, the CPAN clients can automatically fetch, build, and install them.

The PREREQ_PM setting is a catchall, but we can use other keys to give the CPAN clients more information. The CONFIGURE_REQUIRES and BUILD_REQUIRES use the same format, but list the dependencies for those steps. We may need some modules to setup or run the build, but not need them after we install the modules. The test modules, which we show in Chapters 14 and 20, only need to be there for the build portion. If we need a particular module or version to run the build file, we can specify those. ExtUtils::Makemaker didn't support BUILD_REQUIRES until version 6.56, so if we want to use that, we need to specify that version as a requirement. We do that in the *Makefile.PL* and as an argument in CONFIGURE_REQUIRES:

```
use ExtUtils::Makemaker 6.56;

WriteMakefile(
    ...
```

```
    CONFIGURE_REQUIRES => {
        'ExtUtils::Makemaker' => 6.56,
    },
    BUILD_REQUIRES => {
        'Test::More' => 0,
    },
    PREREQ_PM => {
        ...,
    },
    ...
);
```

It may seem strange to specify an ExtUtils::Makemaker dependency when we've already required it to run, but when we package everything for distribution, the build program will create a *META.yml* or *META.json* file with all these settings. The CPAN clients can then unpack a distribution and look at the *META* file to see what it needs to do before it runs *Makefile.PL*.

Another useful setting is EXE_FILES, where we can list the installable programs our distribution contains. We give it an array reference of programs:

```
use ExtUtils::Makemaker 6.56;

WriteMakefile(
    ...
    EXE_FILES => [ qw( scripts/barnyard.pl ) ],
    ...
);
```

As we create programs in our examples, we'll put them in the *scripts* directory. The name of the directory isn't special; it just has to be the relative path we give to EXE_FILES.

Although we typically think of Perl distributions as archives of modules, with EXE_FILES we can distribute programs with no modules.

Inside Build.PL

If we use Module::Build, we have a *Build.PL* instead of a *Makefile.PL*. It looks similar, but does it slightly differently. Instead of calling a subroutine, we create an object and then call create_build_script. In the common case, we don't care much about this. For complicated build processes, we can subclass Module::Build to accomplish whatever we need to do. Indeed, one of the motivations for Module::Build was that sort of flexibility:

```
use 5.006;
use strict;
use warnings;
use Module::Build;

my $builder = Module::Build->new(
    module_name         => 'Animal',
    license             => 'perl',
    dist_author         => q{Willie Gilligan <gilligan@island.example.com>},
```

```
        dist_version_from   => 'lib/Animal.pm',
        build_requires => {
            'Test::More' => 0,
        },
        requires => {
            'perl' => 5.006,
        },
        add_to_cleanup      => [ 'Animal-*' ],
    );

    $builder->create_build_script();
```

The Module::Build::API documentation explains all of the valid keys for new. Instead of EXE_FILES, Module::Build uses script_files:

```
    my $builder = Module::Build->new(
        ...
        script_files     => [ qw(scripts/barnyard.pl) ],
        ...
    );
```

Our First Distribution

There are several ways that we can create a Perl distribution, but we are only going to show a couple of them. The tool we use depends on the level of control that we want and if we like the choices they make for us. Most give us the same basic directory structure, so once we make the distribution, the tool doesn't matter any more.

We're going to make some modules to represent the animals in a barnyard.

h2xs

The *h2xs* tool comes with Perl. As its name says, it's designed to turn *.h* C header files to *.xs* files, the glue language that connects Perl and C code. It does a lot more than that now, and its main advantage is that it's the module creation tool that comes with the standard Perl library. If we have Perl, we should already have this tool.

To start off our Animal module, we run *h2xs* with the -A and -X to turn off AUTOLOAD and XS[1] features (curiously, the two features that implement most of the reason that *h2xs* exists), and use the -n switch to set the name:

```
% h2xs -AX -n Animal

Writing Animal/lib/Animal.pm
Writing Animal/Makefile.PL
Writing Animal/README
Writing Animal/t/Animal.t
```

---

1. You can find out more about XS in *Extending and Embedding Perl* by Simon Cozens and Tim Jenness (Manning).

```
Writing Animal/Changes
Writing Animal/MANIFEST
```

The output shows that *h2xs* created an *Animal* directory and several files under it. We'll explain each of those files in a moment. The files that *h2xs* produces are completely serviceable, but there are other tools that do a bit more for us.

Module::Starter

A more common practice uses `Module::Starter`, although it does not come with the Standard Library. It gives us greater control over the output by filling in some details for us. With its *module-starter* program, we specify our name and email so it can insert into the appropriate places in the files. We also like the `--verbose` option so we can see what *module-starter* is doing for us:

```
% module-starter --module=Animal --author="Gilligan" /
  --email=gilligan@island.example.com --verbose
Created Animal
Created Animal/lib
Created Animal/lib/Animal.pm
Created Animal/t
Created Animal/t/pod-coverage.t
Created Animal/t/pod.t
Created Animal/t/boilerplate.t
Created Animal/t/00-load.t
Created Animal/.cvsignore
Created Animal/Makefile.PL
Created Animal/Changes
Created Animal/README
Created Animal/MANIFEST
Created starter directories and files
```

By default, *module-starter* creates a distribution with *Makefile.PL*. To use `Module::Build` instead, we use the `--builder` switch to specify the build system that we want to use:

```
% module-starter --module=Animal --builder="Module::Build" --author="Gilligan" /
  --email=gilligan@island.example.com --verbose
```

We don't have to type out the whole `--builder` line because *module-starter* provides a shortcut as the `--mb` switch:

```
% module-starter --module=Animal --mb --author="Gilligan" /
  --email=gilligan@island.example.com --verbose
```

We don't want to type that long command line every time, so *module-starter* can get that information from a configuration file *$HOME/.module-starter/config*. If we're on Windows, that *.module-starter* name is a bit of a problem, so we can set the `MODULE_STARTER_DIR` environment variable to the name of the directory that contains *config*.

Inside *config*, we can list the parameter names and values separated by a colon:

```
author: Willie Gilligan
email: gilligan@island.example.com
builder: Module::Build
verbose: 1
```

Once we have our configuration file setup, life is much easier since we only need to specify the name of the distribution that we want to create:

```
% module-starter --module=Animal
```

Custom Templates

Before we have worked on enough distributions to develop our own preferences, the distributions that `Module::Starter` creates are probably good enough. Eventually, however, we're going to want to customize our distributions beyond what *module-starter* creates for us. There are several ways that we can handle this.

If we really like `Module::Starter` but need slight changes, we can customize and change how it works by using plug-ins or creating our own plug-in. There are several already on CPAN, and the `Module::Starter::Plugin` documentation shows us how to create our own plug-ins.

A bit easier, however, is to get a set of templates that we like and merely process them every time we need to create a new distribution. We can add any files that we like and put anything we like in those files. This is the approach that `Distribution::Cooker` takes. We set up exactly what we want as `Template Toolkit` templates. We might even start the initial templates with the output from *module-starter*. When we are ready for a new distribution, we run the *dist_cooker* program.

For really sophisticated module creation, we could use `Dist::Zilla`. Not only does `Dist::Zilla` create the new distribution for us, but it also knows how to update things after we've changed the files. If we want to change the copyright message, author credits, or something similar, `Dist::Zilla` can handle that without making us start over.

Or, we can create our own distribution creator, since that's what everyone else seems to do.[2]

Inside Your Perl Distribution

We've created our `Animal` distribution, and it contains the skeleton of a distribution. It doesn't do anything interesting yet, but it is a complete distribution and everything works. To get started, we create the build script by running *Build.PL*:

```
% perl Build.PL
Checking whether your kit is complete...
Looks good
```

---

2. And, one of the authors did create his own distribution creator and snuck it into this section.

```
Checking prerequisites...
Looks good

Creating new 'Build' script for 'Animal' version '0.01'
```

That first line of output shows *Build.PL* checking the distribution to ensure it has all the files it needs. Each distribution keeps track of those in the *MANIFEST* file. Since we haven't done anything yet, we haven't created any problems. When we give our distribution to someone else, the *MANIFEST* file helps that person figure out if we gave them everything they need.

The next part of the output shows *Build.PL* checking the prerequisites for our distribution. We'll look at *Build.PL* more closely later to show how to specify any other modules that we need to make our own code work.

Once *Build.PL* has done its check, it creates a *Build* program that knows about our *perl* setup, module paths, and other things. We're ready to play with our distribution. First we build it:

```
% ./Build
Copying lib/Animal.pm -> blib/lib/Animal.pm
Manifying blib/lib/Animal.pm -> blib/libdoc/Animal.3
```

Two things happened when we ran *Build*. First, it copied our module files from *lib* into the build library, *blib*. This is the staging area where the build system gets everything ready for installation. Next, `Module::Build` translated the embedded documentation in Animal into its Unix manpage equivalent and put the result in *blib/libdoc*.

After we build the distribution, we can test it. This is the most frequent command that we run. We'll make some changes to the module in *lib/Animal.pm* then run the tests to see how badly we messed up. *module-starter* created some test stubs in the *t* directory. Since we haven't done anything yet, all of the tests should pass:

```
% ./Build test
t/00-load.t ....... ok
t/boilerplate.t ... ok
t/pod-coverage.t .. skipped: Test::Pod::Coverage 1.08 required for testing POD coverage
t/pod.t ........... ok
All tests successful.
Files=4, Tests=5,  0 wallclock secs ( ... )
Result: PASS
```

We'll look at these tests more as we work on our distribution and go though Perl's testing framework in Chapter 14.

When we're ready to give our distribution to someone else, we can first try `disttest`. This is a bit different. During `disttest`, *Build* creates a subdirectory for the archive it's about to create, copies all of the files in *MANIFEST* into it, changes into that directory, and runs the tests again. This ensures that what we're about to archive and distribute has everything our tests need:

```
% ./Build disttest
Creating Makefile.PL
```

```
Added to MANIFEST: Makefile.PL
Creating META.yml
Added to MANIFEST: META.yml
Creating Animal-0.01
/usr/local/perls/perl-5.10.0/bin/perl Build.PL
Checking whether your kit is complete...
Looks good

Checking prerequisites...
Looks good

Creating new 'Build' script for 'Animal' version '0.01'
/usr/local/perls/perl-5.10.0/bin/perl Build
Copying lib/Animal.pm -> blib/lib/Animal.pm
Manifying blib/lib/Animal.pm -> blib/libdoc/Animal.3
/usr/local/perls/perl-5.10.0/bin/perl Build test
t/00-load.t ....... ok
t/pod-coverage.t .. skipped: Test::Pod::Coverage 1.08 required for testing POD coverage
t/pod.t ........... ok
All tests successful.
Files=3, Tests=2,  1 wallclock secs ( ... )
Result: PASS
```

When we're ready to distribute it, we run the `dist` action, which takes all of the files we listed in *MANIFEST*:

```
% ./Build dist
Creating Makefile.PL
Deleting META.yml
Creating META.yml
Deleting Animal-0.01
Creating Animal-0.01
Creating Animal-0.01.tar.gz
Deleting Animal-0.01
```

Now we have a *Animal-0.01.tar.gz* archive that we can send to our friends and family, or upload to CPAN as we show in Chapter 21.

The META File

The *build dist* output showed a line `Creating META.yml`, and, depending on our builder version, `Creating META.json`. These are special files that contain the digested information from the build file in a language-agnostic text format, either YAML and JSON, which we showed in Chapter 6. This way, the CPAN clients can read this text file to determine what it needs to do. Clients are especially interested in the fields that contain `_requires` so they can use that information before they run the build file. In this *META.yml* example, the client would check that it has `Module::Build` 0.38 before it tries to run *Build.PL*:

```
---
abstract: 'The great new Animal!'
author:
  - 'Willie Gilligan <gilligan@island.example.com>'
```

```
build_requires:
  Test::More: 0
configure_requires:
  Module::Build: 0.38
dynamic_config: 1
generated_by: 'Module::Build version 0.38, CPAN::Meta::Converter version 2.112150'
license: perl
meta-spec:
  url: http://module-build.sourceforge.net/META-spec-v1.4.html
  version: 1.4
name: Animal
provides:
  Animal:
    file: lib/Animal.pm
    version: 0.01
  Horse:
    file: lib/Horse.pm
    version: 0.01
requires:
  perl: 5.006
resources:
  license: http://dev.perl.org/licenses/
version: 0.01
```

We could also add to this file with the META_MERGE key in *Makefile.PL* or the meta_merge key in *Build.PL*. To see what we might do, we can check the META spec, which is conveniently listed in the meta-spec key.

Adding Additional Modules

Eventually, we'll want to add another module to our distribution, and we're going to do that as we create our object-oriented modules in the upcoming chapters.

If we know that we want multiple modules in the distribution before we start, we can specify them in our initial run of *module-starter* as a comma-separated list to --module:

```
% module-starter --module=Animal,Cow,Horse,Mouse
```

More likely, though, we are going to want to add a new module after we create the initial distribution. Module::Starter::AddModule can do the job, but we have to install it ourselves and then add it to our *module-starter* configuration file as a plug-in:

```
author: Willie Gilligan
email: gilligan@island.example.com
builder: Module::Build
verbose: 1
plugins: Module::Starter::AddModule
```

Starting in our Animal directory, we run *module-starter* again. We use the --dist argument with the full stop, ., to tell it to work with the distribution in the current working directory. The output is a bit noisy, but there are two lines with Created that show our new Sheep module:

```
% module-starter --module=Sheep --dist=.
Found .. Use --force if you want to stomp on it.
Skipped lib/Animal.pm
Skipped lib/Cow.pm
Skipped lib/Horse.pm
Skipped lib/Mouse.pm
Created lib/Sheep.pm
Skipped t/pod-coverage.t
Skipped t/pod.t
Skipped t/manifest.t
Skipped t/boilerplate.t
Skipped t/00-load.t
Created ./ignore.txt
Skipped ./Build.PL
Skipped ./Changes
Skipped ./README
Regenerating MANIFEST
Created MYMETA.yml and MYMETA.json
Creating new 'Build' script for 'Animal' version '0.01'
File 'MANIFEST.SKIP' does not exist: Creating a temporary 'MANIFEST.SKIP'
Added to MANIFEST: lib/Sheep.pm
Created starter directories and files
```

If our distribution wasn't the current working directory, we could specify the directory by name. For instance, we realize immediately that we left out the Sheep directory, so we add it to the distribution we just created:

```
% module-starter --module=Animal,Cow,Horse,Mouse
% module-starter --module=Sheep --dist=Animal
```

If we are inside our distribution directory already, we can use . as the distribution location:

```
% module-starter --module=Sheep --dist=.
```

Inside a Module

Now that we have a module waiting for us, we look on the inside of the module to see what the tool created for us. Here's most of the text in *lib/Animal.pm*, although we've removed some of the boring boilerplate to save a couple pages of this book:

```
package Animal;

use 5.006;
use strict;
use warnings;

=head1 NAME

Animal - The great new Animal!

=head1 VERSION

Version 0.01
```

```
=cut

our $VERSION = '0.01';


=head1 SYNOPSIS

Quick summary of what the module does.

Perhaps a little code snippet.

    use Animal;

    my $foo = Animal->new();
    ...

=head1 EXPORT

A list of functions that can be exported.  You can delete this section
if you don't export anything, such as for a purely object-oriented module.

=head1 SUBROUTINES/METHODS

=head2 function1

=cut

sub function1 {
}

=head2 function2

=cut

sub function2 {
}

=head1 AUTHOR

Willie Gilligan, C<< <gilligan at island.example.com> >>

=head1 BUGS

...

=head1 SUPPORT

You can find documentation for this module with the perldoc command.

    perldoc Animal

...

=head1 LICENSE AND COPYRIGHT
```

```
Copyright 2012 Willie Gilligan.

=cut

1; # End of Animal
```

Instead of going through that code line by line, we get rid of the noncode portions. Perl has an embedded documentation format called *Pod*, short for plain ol' documentation. We can put Pod between code parts, so this file has some code, then some Pod, then some code, and so on.

Plain Ol' Documentation

This section is a brief introduction to Pod, and there is a lot more to it than we show. However, the parts we don't show aren't that common. The Pod format is specified in *perlpod* and *perlpodspec*, and we should check them in that order.

When *perl* expects to see the start of a new statement but finds a = at the start of a line, such as =head1, it changes to its Pod processing mode. To compile the code, *perl* skips the documentation (just like most programmers). The *perldoc* program does the inverse. It skips the code bits, parses the Pod portions, and displays the result. So far, we've used *perldoc* to read the documentation of installed modules, but we can read the documentation of files, too:

```
% perldoc lib/Animal.pm
```

By default, *perldoc* uses *nroff* (or a variant), which looks dull in black and white on this page, but can be colorful in our terminal:

```
Animal(3) User Contributed Perl Documentation Animal(3)

NAME
        Animal - The great new Animal!

VERSION
        Version 0.01

SYNOPSIS
        Quick summary of what the module does.

        Perhaps a little code snippet.

            use Animal;

            my $foo = Animal->new();
```

We can get other formats. The *pod2html* program produces—wait for it—HTML:

```
% pod2html lib/Animal.pm
<?xml version="1.0" ?>
<!DOCTYPE html PUBLIC "-//W3C//DTD XHTML 1.0 Strict//EN"
  "http://www.w3.org/TR/xhtml1/DTD/xhtml1-strict.dtd">
```

```
<html xmlns="http://www.w3.org/1999/xhtml">
<head>
<title>Animal - The great new Animal!</title>
<meta http-equiv="content-type" content="text/html; charset=utf-8" />
<link rev="made" href="mailto:gilligan@example.com" />
</head>

<body style="background-color: white">
```

Pod Command Paragraphs

Pod *command paragraphs* do what they say. The =headn directives specify a heading. The =head1 is a first level heading, =head2 a second level heading, and so on:

```
=head1 NAME

=head1 DESCRIPTION

=head2 Functions
```

When we are ready to go back to code, we use =cut:

```
=head1 NAME

=head1 DESCRIPTION

=head2 Functions

=cut
```

To create a list, we start with =over n then start each item with =item. When we are done, we end the list with =back:

```
=over 4

=item 1. Gilligan

=item 2. Skipper

=item 3. Ginger

=back
```

After the =item, we use something to denote the type of list. A number, like 1, creates a numbered list. If we use a *, we get a bulleted list:

```
=over 4

=item * Gilligan

=item * Skipper

=item * Ginger

=back
```

Pod Paragraphs

To add text to our documentation, we just add it. We don't need to mark it in any way. Under the SYNOPSIS heading, we have two paragraphs:

```
=head1 SYNOPSIS

Quick summary of what the module does.

Perhaps a little code snippet.
```

Pod formatters can rewrap these paragraphs. If we don't want the text to wrap, we can use a *verbatim paragraph*. Any paragraph that starts with whitespace won't wrap, so that's what we use for code:

```
=head1 SYNOPSIS

Quick summary of what the module does.

Perhaps a little code snippet.

    use Animal;

    my $foo = Animal->new();
```

Pod Formatting Codes

Inside an ordinary paragraph, and in some command paragraphs, we can style text with formatting codes, also known as *interior sequences*. Each formatting code starts with a capital letter and surrounds its text with < and >. For instance, to make italic text, we use I<italic this>. Here are the formatting codes:

- B<bold text>
- C<code text>
- E<named entity>
- I<italic text>
- L<linked text>

If the text in our formatting code has angle brackets, we can double up the delimiters. The Pod parsers are smart enough to find the right ending sequence. For example, we could write C<< $a <=> $b >>. Curiously, in the Pod source for this book, we had to triple up the delimiter to show the doubled up ones: C<<< C<< $a <=> $b >> >>>. Oh, wait, to do that we had to. . .

If we need special characters, we can use E<name> to specify it. It understands HTML entity names and code numbers, like E<eacute>, E<lt>, or E<0x0414>. However, the Pod parsers can handle UTF-8, so we can usually type the characters directly as long as we declare the encoding:

```
=encoding utf8

Gilligan tried to download Björk Guðmundsdóttir's latest album,
but the Professor's Internet connection was down. The Professor
pointed out that Gilligan should just say Björk.
```

Checking the Pod Format

Once we have added Pod to our program or module, we can check that we've done it correctly by using the *podchecker* program:

```
% podchecker lib/Animal.pm
*** WARNING: =head4 without preceding higher level at line 45 in file lib/Animal.pm
*** ERROR: unterminated L<...> at line 82 in file lib/Animal.pm
*** ERROR: =over on line 74 without closing =back (at head1) at line 93 in
    file lib/Animal.pm
*** WARNING: empty section in previous paragraph at line 96 in file lib/Animal.pm
lib/Animal.pm has 2 pod syntax errors.
```

We normally don't do this ourselves because we use a test file to do it for us, as we show in Chapter 14.

The Module Code

When we remove the Pod from *Animal.pm*, we are left with a little code:

```
package Animal;

use 5.006;
use strict;
use warnings;

our $VERSION = '0.01';

sub function1 {
}

sub function2 {
}

1; # End of Animal
```

We showed the package statements in Chapter 11, and strict and warnings are old friends by now.

By convention, Perl modules declare their versions with the $VERSION package variable, declared with our in this code:

```
our $VERSION = '0.01';
```

The version is a string, which seems odd since we tend to think versions are numbers because they use digits. In Chapter 21, we show how $VERSION is important for PAUSE indexing and CPAN clients, so we need to treat its value carefully. If we start with version 1.9 and make our next version 1.10, for instance, we've actually *lowered* the version "number" because the Perl toolchain compares them as numbers (so, 1.10 is less than 1.9). This is the same problem we showed in *Learning Perl* when we introduced sort.

We can declare the version as "version strings" with a leading v. We separate the major, minor, and point releases with a ... When we compare these, the first numbers are compared, as numbers, then the second numbers, and so on:

```
use v5.10;  # v-strings are unreliable before v5.10;
our $VERSION = v0.1;
our $VERSION = v1.2.3;
```

 To read more about the version math, see the version module's documentation.

The *module-starter* program added two stub functions, function1 and function2. It doesn't intend us to keep either of these subroutines or the names.

The last statement of the module is 1;. It doesn't have to be that particular value, but it needs to be a true value. When we require or use a module, *perl* knows that it successfully loaded and compiled the file if the file returns a true value (a compilation error would return false).[3]

That's the basic module setup. In the upcoming chapters, we add to this basic setup as we use other module features.

Module Building Summary

We went through a lot of stuff in this chapter. Since there are several steps, we provide a summary of the process for both Module::Build-based and ExtUtils::Makemaker-based distributions.

Creating a Module::Build Distribution

Create our initial distribution:

```
% module-starter --mb --module="Animal"
```

We run *Build.PL* to create the *Build* script:

```
% perl Build.PL
```

We build the distribution by running Build:

---

3. Some people have fun with their true values, using strings such as 'false'.

```
% ./Build
```

We ensure the tests pass before we do anything with the `test` action:

```
% ./Build test
```

We ensure that the tests still pass with the `disttest` action:

```
% ./Build disttest
```

We create the distribution with the `dist` action:

```
% ./Build dist
```

Creating a ExtUtils::Makemaker Distribution

Although we used `Module::Build` throughout the chapter, if we're using *Makefile.PL*, we follow the same process and the same things happen.

We create the distribution with `Module::Starter`:

```
% module-starter --builder="ExtUtils::Makemaker" --module="Animal"
```

We run the *Makefile.PL* to create the *Makefile*:

```
% perl Makefile.PL
```

We build the distribution by running `make`:

```
% make
```

We ensure the tests pass before we do anything with the `test` target:

```
% make test
```

We ensure that the tests still pass with the `disttest` target:

```
% make disttest
```

We create the distribution with the `dist` target:

```
% make dist
```

Exercises

You can find the answers to these exercises in "Answers for Chapter 12" on page 334.

1. [20 minutes] Create your own `Animal` distribution with `Module::Starter` by running *module-starter* from the command line. Build the distribution and run the tests. Since you haven't changed anything, all the tests should pass.

   To see what happens when you have an error in your module, create some sort of syntax error in *Animal.pm*. Rerun the tests. The tests should fail this time. Don't worry about messing anything up because you can just rerun `module-starter`!

2. [20 minutes] Setup your `Module::Starter` configuration file with your name and email address then redo Exercise 1, replacing the `Animal` distribution.

3. [20 minutes] Download and install the `Module::Starter::AddModule`. Add the plug-in to your `Module::Starter` configuration file. Add the `Cow` module to your distribution.

## CHAPTER 13

Introduction to Objects

Object-oriented programming (often called OOP) helps us run code sooner and maintain it easier by organizing the code into things that we can name and compartmentalize. We need a little more infrastructure to get going with objects, but in the long run, it's worth it.

The benefits of OOP become worthwhile when our program (including all external libraries and modules) exceeds about *N* lines of code. Unfortunately, nobody can agree on what the value of *N* is, but for Perl programs, it's arguably around 1,000 lines of code. If our whole program is only a couple hundred lines of code, using objects is probably overkill.

Like references, Perl's object architecture was grafted on after a substantial amount of existing pre-v5 code was already in use, so we had to ensure that it wouldn't break existing syntax. Amazingly, the only additional syntax to achieve object nirvana is the *method call*, which we'll introduce shortly. The meaning of that syntax requires a bit of study, and we're going to cover just those syntax basics.

 If you want to learn about OOP in Perl in all the gory details, try Damian Conway's *Object Oriented Perl* (Manning), which also covers the theory and architecture behind these ideas.

The Perl object architecture relies heavily on packages, subroutines, and references, so if you're skipping around in this book, go back to the beginning. Ready? Here we go.

If We Could Talk to the Animals. . .

Obviously, the castaways can't survive on coconuts and pineapples alone. Luckily for them, a barge carrying random farm animals crashed on the island not long after they arrived, and the castaways began farming and raising animals.

Starting with the `Animal` distribution we created in the previous chapter, we add some specific animals with *module-starter*:

```
% module-starter --module=Cow,Horse,Sheep --dist=
```

Now we have three extra files in *lib*: *Cow.pm*, *Horse.pm*, and *Sheep.pm*. In each of those files, we'll add a `speak` subroutine that's special to that animal. Although we build up these files piece by piece, we can look at the end of this chapter to see the complete code for each file as they would be after all of our changes.

We listen to those animals for a moment by giving them a way to speak. In the stub modules that *module-starter* created, we find some starter subroutines that we replace with our `speak` subroutines:

In *Cow.pm*:

```
sub speak {
  print "a Cow goes moooo!\n";
}
```

In *Horse.pm*:

```
sub speak {
  print "a Horse goes neigh!\n";
}
```

In *Sheep.pm*:

```
sub speak {
  print "a Sheep goes baaaah!\n";
}
```

We now create a script in *scripts/pasture* (and add that to our build file). We load each of our new modules then call the `speak` subroutines in each class:

```
use Cow;
use Horse;
use Sheep;

Cow::speak;
Horse::speak;
Sheep::speak;
```

Since we haven't installed our modules, running our script initially fails because Perl doesn't know where to find the modules:

```
% perl scripts/pasture
Can't locate Cow.pm in @INC (...)
```

Until we decide to install the modules, we can tell *perl* to use the versions that we have in *lib* through any of the ways we showed in Chapter 2:

```
% perl -Ilib scripts/pasture
```

Now we get the right output:

```
a Cow goes moooo!
a Horse goes neigh!
a Sheep goes baaaah!
```

Nothing spectacular here: simple subroutines, albeit from separate packages, and called using the full package name. We create an entire pasture using the subroutines we defined:

```
use Cow;
use Horse;
use Sheep;

my @pasture = qw(Cow Cow Horse Sheep Sheep);
foreach my $beast (@pasture) {
  no strict 'refs';
  &{$beast."::speak"};                 # Symbolic coderef
}
```

Now we have many more animals making noise:

```
a Cow goes moooo!
a Cow goes moooo!
a Horse goes neigh!
a Sheep goes baaaah!
a Sheep goes baaaah!
```

Wow. That symbolic coderef dereferencing there in the body of the loop is pretty nasty. We're counting on no strict 'refs' mode, certainly not recommended for larger programs. And why was that necessary? Because the name of the package seems inseparable from the name of the subroutine we want to invoke within that package.

Or is it?

Although all examples in this book should be valid Perl code, some examples in this chapter will break the rules enforced by strict to make them easier to understand. By the end of the chapter, though, we'll show how to make strict-compliant code again.

Introducing the Method Invocation Arrow

A *class* is a group of things with similar behaviors and traits. For now, we say that Class->method invokes subroutine method in package Class. A method is the object-oriented version of the subroutine, so we'll say "method" from now on.[1] That's not completely accurate, but we'll go on one step at a time. We use it like so:

---

1. In Perl, there really isn't a difference between a subroutine and a method. They both get an argument list in @_, and we have to make sure we do the right thing.

```
use Cow;
use Horse;
use Sheep;

Cow->speak;
Horse->speak;
Sheep->speak;
```

This outputs the same thing that we saw before:

```
a Cow goes moooo!
a Horse goes neigh!
a Sheep goes baaaah!
```

That's not fun yet. We've got the same number of characters, all constant, no variables. However, the parts are separable now. We can put the class name in a variable and use that:

```
my $beast = 'Cow';
$beast->speak;              # invokes Cow->speak
```

Ahh! Now that the package name is separated from the subroutine name, we can use a variable package name. This time, we've got something that works even when we enable use strict 'refs'.

Take the arrow invocation and put it back in the barnyard example:

```
use Cow;
use Horse;
use Sheep;

my @pasture = qw(Cow Cow Horse Sheep Sheep);
foreach my $beast (@pasture) {
  $beast->speak;
}
```

There! Now all the animals are talking, and safely at that, without the use of symbolic coderefs.

But look at all that common code. Each speak method has a similar structure: a print operator and a string that contains common text, except for two words. One of OOP's core principles is to minimize common code: if we write it only once, we'll save time. If we test and debug it only once, we'll save more time.

Now that we know more about what the method invocation arrow actually does, we've got an easier way to do the same thing.

The Extra Parameter of Method Invocation

The invocation of:

```
Class->method(@args)
```

attempts to invoke the subroutine Class::method as:

```
Class::method('Class', @args);
```

(If it can't find the method, inheritance kicks in, but we'll show that later.) This means that we get the class name as the first parameter, or the only parameter, if no arguments are given. We can rewrite the Sheep speaking method as:

```
sub speak { # In lib/Sheep.pm
  my $class = shift;
  print "a $class goes baaaah!\n";
}
```

The other two animals come out similarly. We make the same change in *Cow.pm*:

```
sub speak { # In lib/Cow.pm
  my $class = shift;
  print "a $class goes moooo!\n";
}
```

and in *Horse.pm*:

```
sub speak { # In lib/Horse.pm
  my $class = shift;
  print "a $class goes neigh!\n";
}
```

In each case, $class gets the value appropriate for that method. But once again, we have a lot of similar structure. Can we factor out that commonality even further? Yes– by calling another method in the same class.

Calling a Second Method to Simplify Things

We can call out from speak to a helper method called sound. This method provides the constant text for the sound itself. In *Cow.pm*, we make a sound subroutine that returns a string for the noise a cow makes:

```
# In lib/Cow.pm
sub sound { 'moooo' }
sub speak {
  my $class = shift;
  print "a $class goes ", $class->sound, "!\n";
}
```

Now, when we call Cow->speak, we get a $class of Cow in speak. This, in turn, selects the Cow->sound method, which returns moooo. How different would this be for the *Horse.pm*? It's not that different:

```
# In lib/Horse.pm
sub sound { 'neigh' }
sub speak {
  my $class = shift;
  print "a $class goes ", $class->sound, "!\n";
}
```

Only the name of the package and the specific sound change. So can we share the definition for speak between the cow and the horse? Yes, with inheritance! It's the same thing for *Sheep.pm*:

```
# In lib/Sheep.pm
sub sound { 'baaaah' }
sub speak {
  my $class = shift;
  print "a $class goes ", $class->sound, "!\n";
}
```

Now we define a common method package called Animal with the definition for a common speak and a placeholder for sound:

```
# In lib/Animal.pm
sub speak {
  my $class = shift;
  print "a $class goes ", $class->sound, "!\n";
}

sub sound {
  die 'You have to define sound() in a subclass'
}
```

Although we don't want people to call the sound in Animal, since it just dies, we want to remind people that they need to define it themselves.

Then, for each animal, we can say it inherits from Animal, along with the animal-specific sound. In each of our animal modules we add an @ISA line to note the relationship (more on that in a moment):

```
use Animal;
our @ISA = qw(Animal);
sub sound { "moooo" }
```

What happens when we invoke Cow->speak now?

First, Perl constructs the argument list. Here, it's just Cow. Then Perl looks for Cow::speak. That's not there, so Perl checks for the inheritance array @Cow::ISA. It finds @Cow::ISA contains the single name Animal.

Perl next looks for speak inside Animal instead, as in Animal::speak. That found, Perl invokes that method with the already frozen argument list, as if we had said:

```
Animal::speak('Cow');
```

Inside the Animal::speak method, $class becomes Cow as the first argument is shifted off. We start with this statement in Animal::speak:

```
print "a $class goes ", $class->sound, "!\n";
```

We substitute Cow, which is the value of $class:

```
# but $class is Cow, so...
print 'a Cow goes ', Cow->sound, "!\n";
```

```
# which invokes Cow->sound, returning 'moooo', so
print 'a Cow goes ', 'moooo', "!\n";
```

and we get our desired output.

A Few Notes About @ISA

This magical @ISA variable (pronounced "is a" not "ice-uh") declares that Cow "is a" Animal. Note that it's an array, not a simple single value, because on rare occasions it makes sense to search for the missing methods in more than one parent class. We'll show more about that later.

If Animal does not have a speak but also had an @ISA, Perl would check that @ISA, too. The search is recursive, depth first, and left to right in each @ISA. Typically, each @ISA has only one element (multiple elements means multiple inheritance and multiple headaches), so we get a nice tree of inheritance.

 There is also inheritance through UNIVERSAL and AUTOLOAD; see *perlobj* or *Programming Perl* for the whole story.

When we turn on strict, we'll get complaints on @ISA because it's not a variable containing an explicit package name, nor is it a lexical (my or state) variable. We can't make it a lexical variable though: it has to belong to the package to be found by the inheritance mechanism.

There are a couple of straightforward ways to handle the declaration and setting of @ISA. The easiest is to spell out the package name:

```
@Cow::ISA = qw(Animal);
```

We can also allow it as an implicitly named package variable:

```
package Cow;
use vars qw(@ISA);
@ISA = qw(Animal);
```

We can also use the our declaration to shorten it to:

```
package Cow;
our @ISA = qw(Animal);
```

However, if we think our code might be used by people stuck with v5.5 or earlier, we should avoid our. However, we encourage everyone to use a Perl that came out within the last 10 years.[2]

---

2. Perl v5.6's first release was March 22, 2000. See *perlhist*.

To use the base class in our module, we not only need to declare the inheritance relationship with @ISA, but also load Animal, too:

```
package Cow;
use Animal;
our @ISA = qw(Animal);
```

To take care of all of those steps at once, we use the parent pragma:

```
use v5.10.1;
package Cow;
use parent qw(Animal);
```

That's pretty darn compact. Furthermore, use parent has the advantage that it's done at compile time, eliminating a few potential errors from setting @ISA at runtime, like some of the other solutions.

 If we have a Perl version prior to v5.10.1, we can use base instead, or install parent ourselves. We should declare it as a prerequisite since the earlier *perls* don't have it in the Standard Library.

Overriding the Methods

We add a mouse that we can barely hear. We create the Mouse package:

```
% module-starter --module=Mouse --dist=.
```

Once we have our *Mouse.pm*, we add its sound subroutine just like we did for the other animals. We change the speak subroutine to have a little bit extra in it:

```
package Mouse;
use parent qw(Animal);

sub sound { 'squeak' }

sub speak {
  my $class = shift;
  print "a $class goes ", $class->sound, "!\n";
  print "[but you can barely hear it!]\n";
}
```

Now we create a *scripts/mouse* program that uses the module and calls speak:

```
use Mouse;

Mouse->speak;
```

When we call this, we see:

```
a Mouse goes squeak!
[but you can barely hear it!]
```

Here, Mouse has its own speaking routine, so Mouse->speak doesn't immediately invoke Animal->speak. This is known as *overriding*. We override the method in the derived class (Mouse) when we need a specialized version of the routine. We didn't even need to initialize @Mouse::ISA to say that a Mouse was an Animal because all the methods needed for speak are defined completely with Mouse.

We've now duplicated some of the code from Animal->speak; this can be a maintenance headache. For example, suppose someone decides that the word goes in the output of the Animal class is a bug. Now the maintainer of that class changes goes to says. Our mice will still say goes, which means the code still has the bug. The problem is that we copied and pasted the code, and that's a sin. We should reuse code through inheritance, not by copy and paste.

How can we avoid that? Can we say somehow that a Mouse does everything any other Animal does, but add in the extra comment? Sure!

As our first attempt, we invoke the Animal::speak method directly. We change the speak in *Mouse.pm*:

```perl
package Mouse;
use parent qw(Animal);

sub sound { 'squeak' }

sub speak {
  my $class = shift;
  Animal::speak($class);          # MESSY!
  print "[but you can barely hear it!]\n";
}
```

Note that because we've stopped using the method arrow, we have to include the $class parameter (almost surely the value Mouse) as the first parameter to Animal::speak.

Why did we stop using the arrow? Well, if we invoke Animal->speak there, the first parameter to the method is "Animal", not "Mouse", and when the time comes for it to call for the sound, it won't have the right class to select the proper methods for this object.

Invoking Animal::speak directly is a mess, however. What if Animal::speak didn't exist before and it inherited from a class mentioned in @Animal::ISA? For example, we can create a LivingCreature module:

```
% module-starter --dist=LivingCreature
```

We add the speak subroutine to *LivingCreature.pm*:

```perl
package LivingCreature;

sub speak { ... }
```

We also remove the speak from *Animal.pm*:

```perl
package Animal;
use parent qw(LivingCreature);
```

Because we no longer use the method arrow in `Mouse::speak`, we get one and only one chance to hit the right method because we're treating it like a regular subroutine with no inheritance magic. We'll look for it in `Animal` and not find it, and the program aborts.

The `Animal` class name is now hardwired into the method selection. This is a mess if someone maintains the code, changing `@ISA` for `Mouse`, and didn't notice `Animal` there in `speak`. Thus, this is probably not the right way to go.

Starting the Search from a Different Place

A better solution is to tell Perl to search from a different place in the inheritance chain:

```
package Mouse;
use parent qw(Animal);

sub sound { 'squeak' }

sub speak {
  my $class = shift;
  $class->Animal::speak(@_);  # tell it where to start
  print "[but you can barely hear it!]\n";
}
```

Ahh. As ugly as this is, it works. Using this syntax, start with `Animal` to find `speak` and use all of `Animal`'s inheritance chain if not found immediately. The first parameter is `$class` (because we're using an arrow again), so the found `speak` method gets `Mouse` as its first entry and eventually works its way back to `Mouse::sound` for the details.

This isn't the best solution, however. We still have to keep the `@ISA` and the initial search package in sync (changes in one must be considered for changes in the other). Worse, if `Mouse` had multiple entries in `@ISA`, we wouldn't necessarily know which one had actually defined `speak`.

So, is there an even better way?

The SUPER Way of Doing Things

By changing the `Animal` class to the SUPER class in that invocation, we get a search of all our superclasses (classes listed in `@ISA`) automatically:

```
package Mouse;
use parent qw(Animal);

sub sound { 'squeak' }

sub speak {
  my $class = shift;
  $class->SUPER::speak;
  print "[but you can barely hear it!]\n";
}
```

Thus, SUPER::speak means to look in the current package's @ISA for speak, invoking the first one found if there's more than one. Here, we look in the one and only parent class, Animal, find Animal::speak, and pass it "Mouse" as its only parameter.

What to Do with @_

In that last example, had there been any additional parameters to the speak method (like how many times, or in what pitch for singing, for example), the parameters would be ignored by the Mouse::speak method. If we want them to be passed uninterpreted to the parent class, we can add it as a parameter:

```
$class->SUPER::speak(@_);
```

This invokes the speak method of the parent class, including all the parameters that we've not yet shifted off our parameter list.

Which one is correct? It depends. If we are writing a class that adds to the parent class behavior, it's best to pass along arguments we haven't dealt with. However, if we want precise control over the parent class's behavior, we should determine the argument list explicitly, and pass it.

Where We Are

So far, we've used the method arrow syntax to call a method on a class literal:

```
Class->method(@args);
```

We can do the same thing with a class name stored in a variable:

```
my $beast = 'Class';
$beast->method(@args);
```

In either case, Perl implicitly puts the class name on the front of the argument list:

```
('Class', @args)
```

If we wanted to do the same thing with a normal subroutine, we'd use the fully qualified package name and add the class name to the argument list ourself:

```
Class::method('Class', @args);
```

As long as we call it as a method, though, if Perl doesn't find Class::method, it examines @Class::ISA (recursively) to locate a package that does indeed contain method, and then invokes that version instead.

Chapter 15 shows how to distinguish the individual animals by giving them associated properties, called *instance variables*.

Our Barnyard Summary

Here is the code we put into our barnyard files after all of our changes.

The *lib/Animal.pm* file:

```
package Animal;

sub speak {
  my $class = shift;
  print "a $class goes ", $class->sound, "!\n";
}

sub sound {
  die 'You have to define sound() in a subclass'
}

1;
```

The *lib/Cow.pm* file:

```
package Cow;
use parent qw(Animal);

sub sound { 'moooo' }

1;
```

The *lib/Horse.pm* file:

```
package Horse;
use parent qw(Animal);

sub sound { 'neigh' }

1;
```

The *lib/Sheep.pm* file:

```
package Sheep;
use parent qw(Animal);

sub sound { 'baaaah' }

1;
```

The *lib/Mouse.pm* file:

```
package Mouse;
use parent qw(Animal);

sub sound { 'squeak' }

sub speak {
  my $class = shift;
  $class->SUPER::speak(@_); # tell it where to start
  print "[but you can barely hear it!]\n";
```

```
    }

    1;
```

Exercises

You can find the answers to these exercises in "Answers for Chapter 13" on page 336.

1. [20 minutes] Create the Animal, Cow, Horse, Sheep, and Mouse classes. Run the test target for your distribution to ensure that they all compile correctly (that is, your *t/00-load.t* test passes). Change what you need to get the tests to pass.

2. [20 minutes] Create a program to ask the user to enter the names of one or more barnyard animals. Create a barnyard with those animals, and have each animal speak once.

3. [40 minutes] Add a Person class at the same level as Animal, and have both of them inherit from a new class called LivingCreature. Also make the speak method take a parameter of what to say, falling back to the sound (humming for a Person) if no parameter is given. Since this isn't Dr. Doolittle, make sure the animals can't talk. (That is, don't let speak have any parameters for an animal.) Try not to duplicate any code, but be sure to catch likely errors of usage, such as forgetting to define a sound for an animal.

   Demonstrate the Person class in a program in *scripts/person.pl*. Make the person say "Hello, World!"

## CHAPTER 14

Introduction to Testing

In Chapter 13, we created a new Perl distribution, modified some modules, and added a program to our distribution. Since we have a full-fledged distribution at the start of our development, we can immediately start using Perl's extensive testing framework. Indeed, we already have some starter tests.

Now it's time to look morely closely at the tests already in the distribution and create some more of our own. As we continue to develop our modules, the tests will keep us on the right path.

Why Should We Test?

Why should we test during development? The short answer is that we find out about problems sooner and tests force us to program in much smaller chunks (since they are easier to test), which is generally good programming practice. Although we may think we have extra work to do, that's only short-term overhead because we win down the line when we spend less time debugging, both because we've fixed most of the problems before they were problems and because the tests usually point us right at the problem we need to fix.

Along with that, it's psychologically easier to modify code because the tests will tell us if we broke something. When we talk to our boss or coworkers, we also have the confidence in our code to answer their queries and questions. The tests tell us how healthy our code is.

We're never really done testing, either. Even when the module ships, we shouldn't abandon the test suite! Unless we code the mythical "bug-free module," our users will send us bug reports. We can turn each report into a test case. While fixing the bug, the remaining tests prevent our code from regressing to a less functional version of the code—hence the name *regression testing*.

If we report a bug in someone else's code, we can generally assume that the maintainers appreciate us sending them a test for the bug. They appreciate a patch even more!

Then there's always the future releases to think about. When we want to add new features, we start by adding tests. Because the existing tests ensure our upward compatibility, we can be confident that our new release does everything the old release did and then some.

As we show in Chapter 21, the CPAN Testers can use our tests to check how our code runs on systems and configurations that we don't have.

The Perl Testing Process

The Perl test conventions are built around a directory of Perl programs, which we call "tests files," or sometimes just "tests." Each of these programs runs code, decides if its tests pass or fail, and outputs the right stuff so a later step can tell what happened.

Test Anywhere Protocol

Perl has a simple way to note which tests pass and which fail. No one is quite sure who invented it (Tim Bunce and Andreas König credit each other), but it's become known as the Test Anywhere Protocol, or TAP. This simple text protocol started in Perl, but has made its way to other languages, too.

If the test passes, we output ok with a test number:

```
ok 1
```

We can attach a label to the test so we know what passed:

```
ok 1 - The boat motor works
```

If the test doesn't pass, we output not ok:

```
not ok 2 - The hull is intact
```

Besides the individual tests, we want to know that all of the tests we wanted to run actually ran. The *plan* gives the range of tests that we are going to run. The plan can come before the tests:

```
1..3
ok 1 - The boat motor works
ok 2 - The gas tank is full
not ok 3 - The hull is intact
```

Or the plan can come after the tests:

```
ok 1 - The boat motor works
ok 2 - The gas tank is full
```

```
not ok 3 - The hull is intact
1..3
```

In the early days of Perl, people took care of this test output directly:

```
print $motor_broken ? 'not ' : '', 'ok ', $test++, "\n";
```

When we did that, we had to keep track of the test number ourselves, at least until the Test::Simple module handled it for us. Although virtually no one uses this historical module, it still comes with Perl:

```
use Test::Simple tests => 3;

use Minnow::Diagnostics;

ok( try_motor(), 'The boat motor works' );
ok( check_gas() eq 'Full', 'The gas tank is full' );
ok( check_hull(), 'The hull is intact' );
```

We don't handle the plan or the output directly. The ok function's first argument is evaluated for truth. If it's true, it's ok, and not ok otherwise.

Testing has grown up quite a bit since then, and so has Perl's main testing module, Test::More, whose name plays off Test::Simple.[1] We have many more convenience subroutines to check values and output the right TAP. The rest of this section is about these subroutines.

 We can learn more about testing in the Test::Tutorial documentation.

The Test::More module handles the plan for use just like Test::Simple, and it has the ok subroutine that does the same thing:

```
use Test::More tests => 1;

ok( try_motor(), 'The boat motor works' );
```

In that example, we explicitly declared that we'd have one test, and that's how many test reports the test harness expects our program to report. If we don't know the number of tests, we can use done_testing at the end. If we reach that line, we can be reasonably sure that we made it to the end of the test program:

```
ok( try_motor(), 'The boat motor works' );

done_testing();
```

In our Test::Simple example, we had the single argument to decide the truth of whatever we want to test. We can still do that:

1. Both these modules come in the same distribution now.

```
ok( check_gas() eq 'Full', 'The gas tank is full' );
```

However, `Test::More` has `is`, which does the comparison for us. We tell it the value we have, the value we expect, and the test label:

```
is( check_gas(), 'Full', 'The gas tank is full' );
```

If this passes, we get the same output. It's more interesting when it fails, though, because `is` knows what it should have received. The TAP allows comments, which `is` supplies:

```
1..3
ok 1 - The boat motor works
not ok 2 - The gas tank is full
#   Failed test 'The gas tank is full'
#   in /Users/Gilligan/test.pl at line 9.
#          got: 'Empty'
#     expected: 'Full'
not ok 3 - The hull is intact
# Looks like you failed 1 test of 3 run.
```

There are more interesting subroutines. The `isnt` is the opposite of `is`. The value we get should *not* be the second argument:

```
isnt( check_hull(), 'Broken', 'The hull is intact' );
```

The `like` subroutine uses a regular expression:

```
like( 'Mary-Ann', qr/Mary[ -]Anne?/, 'Mary-Ann is a passenger' );
```

There's even an `unlike`, which is the pattern matching equivalent of `isnt`:

```
unlike( 'Ginger', qr/Mary[ -]Anne?/, 'Ginger is a passenger' );
```

We can test basic data structures:

```
is_deeply( \@this_array, \@that_array, 'The arrays are the same' );
```

That's it. Our test program is series of these sorts of subroutine calls. For the things that `Test::More` doesn't handle, we can use one of the CPAN `Test::` modules, such as `Test::Class`, `Test::File`, or one of the many other domain-specific modules. We show some of these in Chapter 20.

The Art of Testing

Good tests also give small examples of what we meant in our documentation. It's another way to express the same thing, and some people may like one way over the other. Good tests also give confidence to the user that our code (and all its dependencies) is portable enough to work on their system.

 Some modules are easier to learn from their test examples than by the documentation. Any really good example should be repeated in our module's documentation.

Testing is an art. People have written and read dozens of how-to-test books (and then ignore them, it seems). Mostly, it's important to remember everything we have ever done wrong while programming (or heard other people do), and then test that we didn't do it again for this project.

When we create tests, we try to think like a person using a module, not like the one writing a module. We know how we should use our module because we invented it and had a specific need for it. Other people will probably have different uses for it and they'll try to use it in all sorts of different ways. We probably already know that given the chance, users will find every other way to use our code. We need to think like that when we test.

We need to test things that should break as well as things that should work. We need to test the edges and the middle. We need to test one more or one less than the edge. We test things one at a time, and we test many things at once. If something should throw an exception, we make sure it doesn't also have bad side effects. We pass extra or junk parameters, or not enough parameters. We mess up the capitalization on named parameters. In short, we try to break our code until we can't figure out any other way to break it.

A Test Example

Suppose that we want to test Perl's `sqrt` function, which calculates square roots. It's obvious that we need to make sure it returns the right values when its parameter is a perfect square, such as 0, 1, 49, or 100. A call to `sqrt(0.25)` should come out to be 0.5. We should ensure that multiplying the value for `sqrt(7)` by itself gives something between 6.99999 and 7.00001.

Remember, floating-point numbers aren't always exact; there's usually a little roundoff. The `Test::Number::Delta` module can handle those situations.

We express that as code. This part tests things that should work when we give it good values:

```
use Test::More tests => 6;

is( sqrt(  0),  0, 'The square root of 0   is  0' );
is( sqrt(  1),  1, 'The square root of 1   is  1' );
is( sqrt( 49),  7, 'The square root of 49  is  7' );
is( sqrt(100), 10, 'The square root of 100 is 10' );

is( sqrt(0.25), 0.5, 'The square root of 0.25 is 0.5' );

my $product = sqrt(7) * sqrt(7);
```

```
ok( $product > 6.999 && $product < 7.001,
  "The product [$product] is around 7" );
```

That's boring. The fun is breaking things. What should sqrt(-1) do? That's a perfectly valid mathematical operation, but it's not something that Perl's version of sqrt does. Some programmer is going to do that, intentionally or otherwise, and our test should check that. We can catch it with eval:

```
{
$n = -1;
eval { sqrt($n) };
ok( $@, '$@ is set after sqrt(-1)' );
}
```

We can try to break it in other ways. We give it an undefined value:

```
eval { sqrt(undef) };
is( $@, '', '$@ is not set after sqrt(undef)' );
```

We give it no value:

```
is( sqrt, 0, 'sqrt() works on $_ (undefined) by default' );
```

We try it with its default variable, $_:

```
$_ = 100;
is( sqrt, 10, 'sqrt() works on $_ by default' );
```

What happens with really big numbers?

```
is( sqrt( 10**100 ), 10**50, 'sqrt() can handle a googol' );
```

The Test Harness

The test program outputs the TAP. The distribution we created in Chapter 12 came with several test programs in the *t* directory. When we run the **test** target, we invoke a thing we call the *test harness*, which finds all of our test programs (the files named with *.t*), runs each of them, captures their output, and provides an overall summary of the results. The test harness itself has several parts inside it to handle each of those parts, but we don't show those in this book.

 The Test::Harness module pulls together the parts to find our tests, runs our tests, and summarizes the results. We normally don't interact with it directly.

Our distribution tests are just collections of test programs similar to the ones we have shown so far.

The Standard Tests

When we created our distribution with *module-starter* (or *h2xs*), we got some starter tests along with the other files. By convention, the test files go in the *t* directory and have a *.t* extension:

```
% module-starter --module=Animal
...
Created Animal/t
Created Animal/t/pod-coverage.t
Created Animal/t/pod.t
Created Animal/t/boilerplate.t
Created Animal/t/00-load.t
...
```

When we run the `test` target, the build program runs each test file it finds in the *t* directory:

```
% perl Build.PL
...
% ./Build test
Copying lib/Animal.pm -> blib/lib/Animal.pm
t/00-load.........# Testing Animal 0.01, Perl 5.010000, /usr/bin/perl
t/00-load.........ok
t/boilerplate.....ok
t/manifest.......skipped
    all skipped: Author tests not required for installation
t/pod-coverage....skipped
    all skipped: Test::Pod::Coverage 1.08 required for testing POD coverage
t/pod.............ok
    all skipped: Test::Pod 1.22 required for testing POD coverage
All tests successful, 2 tests skipped.
Files=5, Tests=5,  0 wallclock secs ( 0.12 cusr +  0.04 csys =  0.16 CPU)
```

The *t/manifest.t* test did not run, saying "Author tests not required." Some tests are interesting to module maintainers so they can check the details of their distributions before they release them. By the time they get to the users, however, it's too late for those tests to do their job. Worse, if they fail for some reason, usually unrelated to the code, the CPAN clients will refuse to install the distribution and any distribution that depends on it. Because of this annoyance, test authors check the `RELEASE_TESTING` or `AUTOMATED_TESTING` environment variables to enable these tests only on their systems. Authors set `RELEASE_TESTING` in their environment and the CPAN Testers set `AUTOMATED_TESTING` when it runs to indicate that there isn't a person watching the tests. We can use these values to decide what to do.

 Some people put their author tests in the *xt* directory to separate them from the code tests in *t*.

This run also skipped the *t/pod-coverage.t* and *t/pod.t* tests because we haven't installed those modules. Before these tests try to do anything, they check for the special module that does the work. If it's not there, it skips the tests. We show test skipping in Chapter 20.

Checking that Modules Compile

We take a look at *t/00-load.t*, which is the first test file to run since the default test order is the lexigraphical order. Here's our test that tries to compile `Animal`:

```
#!perl -T

use Test::More tests => 1;

BEGIN {
  use_ok( 'Animal' ) || print "Bail out!\n";
}

diag( "Testing Animal $Animal::VERSION, Perl $], $^X" );
```

First, the test program loads the `Test::More` module and declares that there will be one test. Inside the `BEGIN` block, it uses `Test::More`'s `use_ok` subroutine. Given a module name, `use_ok` tries to load that module. If there's any problem, such as a syntax error, the test fails and `use_ok` returns false.

When `use_ok` returns false, it proceeds through the || operator to run the `print` statement. The testing framework stops immediately if it sees the string `Bail out!` on standard output. If we can't load the module, there's no sense going on with the rest of the tests. This is quite handy for discovering syntax errors without having to dig through screenfuls of failing test output to discover what went wrong.

 We have to use the -I to add to the module search path because these tests use taint checking, which ignores PERL5LIB.

To see what the test program is actually doing, we can run it ourselves. We can use -I to add the *blib/lib* build directory to `@INC`. Before we want to test from *blib*, though, we should rebuild the distribution to ensure we are using the latest code. We also have to specify -T on the command line because we have to turn on taint checking before:

```
% ./Build
% perl -Iblib/lib -T t/00-load.t
1..1
ok 1 - use Animal;
# Testing Animal 0.01, Perl 5.014002, perl
```

Every test outputs a single line that says either ok or not ok along with a test number. Test::More takes care of most of the details for us so we don't have to worry about most of the details.

Instead of that -Iblib/lib, we could use the blib module that searches the surrounding directories, including the parent directory, for a *blib* to add to @INC. We can load it on the command line with the -M switch:

```
% perl -Mblib -T t/00-load.t
```

 Before we run the tests, we rerun the build program to ensure we're testing the latest code.

Since we've added additional classes to our distribution, we want to test those too, so we'll rearrange the test program to handle more than one class:

```perl
#!perl -T

BEGIN {
  my @classes = qw(Animal Cow Sheep Horse Mouse);
  use Test::More;
  plan tests => scalar @classes;

  foreach my $class ( @classes ) {
    use_ok( $class ) or print "Bail out! $class did not load!\n"
  }
}
```

Now the output shows some more work that the test framework does for us. That first line is a test count: it tells the framework how many tests to expect. Each test line shows what test it is:

```
% ./Build
% perl -Iblib/lib -T t/00-load.t
1..5
ok 1 - use Animal;
ok 2 - use Cow;
ok 3 - use Sheep;
ok 4 - use Horse;
ok 5 - use Mouse;
```

The Boilerplate Tests

After *t/00-load.t*, we have the *t/boilerplate.t* file. When we created our module files, the tool added the text for us. There is some starter documentation in our stub modules:

```
=head1 SYNOPSIS

Quick summary of what the module does.
```

Perhaps a little code snippet.

```
use Horse;

my $foo = Horse->new();
...
```

There's some starter code:

```
sub function1 {
}
```

We should change that text to actually document our module and fill in the code. The stuff that is already there is the *boilerplate*. The *t/boilerplate.t* test looks for this place-holder text, and if it finds it, it complains that we didn't change it.

The start of this test file defines a not_in_file_ok subroutine:

```
#!perl -T

use 5.006;
use strict;
use warnings;
use Test::More tests => 7;

sub not_in_file_ok {
  my ($filename, %regex) = @_;
  open( my $fh, '<', $filename )
    or die "couldn't open $filename for reading: $!";

  my %violated;

  while (my $line = <$fh>) {
    while (my ($desc, $regex) = each %regex) {
      if ($line =~ $regex) {
        push @{$violated{$desc}||=[]}, $.;
      }
    }
  }

  if (%violated) {
    fail("$filename contains boilerplate text");
    diag "$_ appears on lines @{$violated{$_}}" for keys %violated;
  } else {
    pass("$filename contains no boilerplate text");
  }
}
```

This subroutine takes a filename and a hash of regular expressions as arguments. It reads the file and looks for lines that match those patterns. If if finds a line that matches, it remembers it in %violated. Once it has checked all of the files, it tests if(%violated) to see if it found any problems. If so, it calls fail, a Test::More subroutine that only takes a test label then outputs the not ok. If there were no violations, it calls pass.

The next part of *t/boilerplate.t* is another subroutine, `module_boilerplate_ok`. It takes a module filename and passes that to `not_in_file_ok` with a list of key-value pairs for the checks:

```
sub module_boilerplate_ok {
  my ($module) = @_;
  not_in_file_ok($module =>
    'the great new $MODULENAME'   => qr/ - The great new /,
    'boilerplate description'     => qr/Quick summary of what the module/,
    'stub function definition'    => qr/function[12]/,
  );
}
```

The next part of the file is interesting. There's a block labeled with TODO. This is a `Test::More` feature that lets us mark that we expect these tests to fail but we have deferred fixing them. Inside the block, it sets the value of `$TODO` as a label for test, which we'll show in a moment. After that, the rest of the block makes calls to `not_in_file_ok` and `module_boilerplate_ok`:

```
TODO: {
  local $TODO = "Need to replace the boilerplate text";

  not_in_file_ok(README =>
    "The README is used..."      => qr/The README is used/,
    "'version information here'"  => qr/to provide version information/,
  );

  not_in_file_ok(Changes =>
    "placeholder date/time"      => qr(Date/time)
  );

  module_boilerplate_ok('lib/Animal.pm');
  module_boilerplate_ok('lib/Cow.pm');
  module_boilerplate_ok('lib/Horse.pm');
  module_boilerplate_ok('lib/Mouse.pm');
  module_boilerplate_ok('lib/Sheep.pm');
}
```

These tests fail until we update our files, but when we run the tests, the tests appear to pass. That `$TODO` label attaches itself to the end of the test label. When the test harness sees this, it doesn't count it as a real failure:

```
%  ./Build
% perl -Iblib/lib -T t/boilerplate.t
1..7
not ok 1 - README contains boilerplate text # TODO Need to replace the boilerplate text
#   Failed (TODO) test 'README contains boilerplate text'
#   at t/boilerplate.t line 24.
# The README is used... appears on lines 3
# 'version information here' appears on lines 11
...
```

When we fix one of those boilerplate tests, the test now passes. Since the TODO denoted that we expected these tests to fail, the test harness adds a report that a TODO passed:

```
Test Summary Report
-------------------
t/boilerplate.t (Wstat: 0 Tests: 7 Failed: 0)
  TODO passed:   1
Files=5, Tests=20,  0 wallclock secs
Result: PASS
```

We don't keep the *t/boilerplate.t* file. Once we replace the placeholder text, we can get rid of this file.

The Pod Tests

module-starter already gave us some starting documentation, and it created some tests to check that documentation. The standard Pod tests are concerned with two things: that we haven't made any mistakes in our Pod format and that we documented every subroutine. Each test is optional and only runs if we have the `Test::Pod` and `Test::Pod::Coverage` modules. Both of these tests automatically find all of our module files and tests each one, so we don't need to adjust these tests.

If we haven't already documented the subroutines we added, the Pod coverage tests fail:

```
% ./Build test
t/00-load.t ....... 1/5
t/00-load.t ....... ok
t/boilerplate.t ... ok
t/manifest.t ...... skipped: Author tests not required for installation
t/pod-coverage.t .. 1/5
#   Failed test 'Pod coverage on Animal'
#   at .../Test/Pod/Coverage.pm line 126.
# Coverage for Animal is 0.0%, with 2 naked subroutines:
#       sound
#       speak

#   Failed test 'Pod coverage on Cow'
#   at .../Test/Pod/Coverage.pm line 126.
# Coverage for Cow is 0.0%, with 1 naked subroutine:
#       sound

...
Failed 5/5 subtests
t/pod.t ........... ok

Test Summary Report
-------------------
t/boilerplate.t (Wstat: 0 Tests: 7 Failed: 0)
  TODO passed:   3
t/pod-coverage.t (Wstat: 1280 Tests: 5 Failed: 5)
  Failed tests:  1-5
  Non-zero exit status: 5
Files=5, Tests=20,  1 wallclock secs ( 0.04 usr  0.02 sys +  0.19 cusr  0.03 csys = /
  0.28 CPU)
Result: FAIL
Failed 1/5 test programs. 5/21 subtests failed.
```

To fix the Pod tests, we need to replace the stub documentation with documentation for our methods. Once we do that, the Pod tests will pass.

Adding Our First Tests

We need to test our modules. We can add our own test files to the distribution. We build up one gradually.

First, we create a file named *t/Animal.t*, which we'll use to test the functions in *lib/Animal.pm*. To start, we use the special `pass` subroutine from `Test::More`, which is a test that always succeeds:

```
use strict;
use warnings;

use Test::More tests => 1;

pass();
```

Now we run our test suite again and we see that our *t/Animal.t* test runs and succeeds:

```
% ./Build test
t/00-load.t ....... ok
t/Animal.t ........ ok
t/boilerplate.t ... ok
t/manifest.t ...... skipped: Author tests not required
t/pod-coverage.t .. ok
t/pod.t ........... ok
All tests successful.
Files=6, Tests=11,  1 wallclock secs ( ... )
Result: PASS
```

Next we need to add some more interesting tests. Although we already tested that *lib/Animal.pm* compiles, we can test again in *t/Animal.t*. This is quite useful when we want to run this single test file by itself:

```
use strict;
use warnings;

use Test::More tests => 1;

BEGIN {
  require_ok( 'Animal' ) || print "Bail out!\n";
}

diag( "Testing Animal $Animal::VERSION, Perl $], $^X" );
```

If we have a recent enough version of `Test::More` (and we should because the minimum version is quite old), we can use the `BAIL_OUT` subroutine to handle the error:

```
use strict;
use warnings;

use Test::More 0.62 tests => 1;
```

```
BEGIN {
  require_ok( 'Animal' ) || BAIL_OUT();
}
diag( "Testing Animal $Animal::VERSION, Perl $], $^X" );
```

We run the tests again to ensure our tests still pass. There shouldn't be a problem. Now we want to test one of the methods in Animal. So far, we only have two methods, speak and sound. Although it's a bit overkill for our example, in more complex code we might want to check that we've defined the subroutines. That's an easy check: we use the ok function from Test::More:

```
use strict;
use warnings;

use Test::More tests => 3;

BEGIN {
  use_ok( 'Animal' ) || print "Bail out!\n";
}

diag( "Testing Animal $Animal::VERSION, Perl $], $^X" );

# they have to be defined in Animal.pm
ok( defined &Animal::speak, 'Animal::speak is defined' );
ok( defined &Animal::sound, 'Animal::sound is defined' );
```

In the case of Animal, we test for the methods with defined because we want to check that they were actually defined in that class and not inherited from another class, such as LivingCreature.

Once we're sure we've defined our methods, we test that our methods do what they are supposed to do. In this case, we have a bit of a twist because the job of Animal's sound is to merely die. We start testing at the lowest level and work our way up. Now we want to check that sound dies and that it gives us the right message. The like function from Test::More checks that its first argument matches a regular expression:

```
use strict;
use warnings;

use Test::More tests => 4;

# same as before
...

# check that sound() dies
eval { Animal->sound() } or my $at = $@;
like( $at, qr/You have/, 'sound() dies with a message' );
```

If the eval fails, we immediately store the value of $@ in a new variable. As with many Perl special (global) variables, the value might change the next time we do something. There are other ways that we can test for some of these failures, but that's not the point of this chapter.

Next we have to test speak. Since it calls sound, it's going to die too, so the test is almost the same:

```
use strict;
use warnings;

use Test::More tests => 5;

# same as before
...

# check that sound() dies
eval { Animal->sound() } or my $at = $@;
like( $at, qr/You have/, 'sound() dies with a message' );

# check that speak() dies too
eval { Animal->speak() } or my $at = $@;
like( $at, qr/You have/, 'speak() dies with a message' );
```

To fully test sound, however, we have to try it in a situation where it doesn't die. Most of sound's inner workings relies on a subclass, so we can make a small test subclass for that then use Test::More's is function to ensure that we get the right message. We'll create a Foofle subclass and wrap its definition and test in a bare block to limit its scope:

```
use strict;
use warnings;

use Test::More tests => 6;

# same as before
...

{
package Foofle;
use parent qw(Animal);
sub sound { 'foof' }
}

ok( Foofle->speak, 'An Animal subclass does the right thing' );
```

Putting that all together, we have a complete test for the Animal class:

```
use strict;
use warnings;

use Test::More tests => 6;

BEGIN {
  use_ok( 'Animal' ) || print "Bail out!\n";
}

diag( "Testing Animal $Animal::VERSION, Perl $], $^X" );

# they have to be defined in Animal.pm
ok( defined &Animal::speak, 'Animal::speak is defined' );
ok( defined &Animal::sound, 'Animal::sound is defined' );
```

```
{
# check that sound() dies
eval { Animal->sound() } or my $at = $@;
like( $at, qr/You have/, 'sound() dies with a message' );
}

{
# check that speak() dies too
eval { Animal->speak() } or my $at = $@;
like( $at, qr/You have/, 'speak() dies with a message' );
}

{
  package Foofle;
  use parent qw(Animal);
  sub sound { 'foof' }

  is(
    Foofle->speak,
    "A Foofle goes foof!\n",
    'An Animal subclass does the right thing'
  );
}
```

Measuring Our Test Coverage

Our goal is to always completely test all of our code. Although this might not always be practical or economical, it is still our goal. There are several coverage metrics, each of which looks at a different sort of test. We should keep in mind, however, that perfect metrics are not the goal. We want good code, and there's nothing that can represent that as a number.

We use the `Devel::Cover` module from CPAN to collect these metrics. If we are using `Module::Build`, we run the `testcover` target:

```
% ./Build testcover
```

If we're using `ExtUtils::Makemaker`, we can use the `HARNESS_PERL_SWITCHES` environment variable:

```
% HARNESS_PERL_SWITCHES=-MDevel::Cover make test
```

After we run our tests, we need to run the `cover` command to turn the collected statistics into human-readable reports. It prints a summary report:

```
% cover
```

The `cover` command creates a summary report that looks something like this:

```
Reading database from /Users/brian/Desktop/Animal/cover_db

-------------- ------ ------ ------ ------ ------ ------ ------
File            stmt   bran   cond   sub    pod    time   total
```

```
-------------  ------  ------  ------  ------  ------  ------  ------
Animal.pm       60.0    0.0    n/a    42.9   100.0    90.7   57.1
Cow.pm          85.7    n/a    n/a    66.7   100.0     0.9   81.8
Horse.pm        85.7    n/a    n/a    66.7   100.0     8.1   81.8
Sheep.pm        85.7    n/a    n/a    66.7   100.0     0.4   81.8
Total           78.9    0.0    n/a    60.0   100.0   100.0   74.5
-------------  ------  ------  ------  ------  ------  ------  ------
```

It also creates a *cover_db/coverage.html* file that provides much more detail for each file so we can look at the coverage for each line, as well as drill down into files and metrics to see exactly what we still need to test to improve our numbers.

Subroutine Coverage

This metric measures the percentage of subroutines that we test. We strive to test all subroutines, and this is probably the easiest metric to completely cover. We have to run every subroutine to get a perfect score. This is a dubious metric since we can have serious problems with our code even though we test every subroutine. As long as we run the subroutine, it counts, even if it does the wrong thing.

Statement Coverage

Running every subroutine isn't enough. We also want to test every statement, whether it's in a subroutine or not. This is a slightly better metric than subroutine coverage, but it doesn't guarantee correct code either. A statement is made up of expressions, and expressions are made up of terms. That we've executed the statement doesn't mean that we've tested all of the expressions or terms.

Branch Coverage

The if, unless, and given-when statements have several branches that program flow can follow:

```
if( )   { ... }
elsif() { ... }
else    { ... }

unless()
elsif() { ... }
else    { ... }

given( ... ) {
  when { ... }
  when { ... }
  when { ... }
  default { ... }
}
```

To get complete branch coverage, we need to test each branch of these structures, which means we need to make our tests trigger each of those blocks.

Conditional Coverage

Those conditionals inside the branch coverage might use more than one condition, but there are other places where a statement might have conditional behavior. We need to set up tests that exercise each of the conditions. For instance, these statements each have two parts:

```
my $foo = $n || $m;

if( $n && $m ) {
   ...
}

while( $n && $m ) {
   ...
}

open my($fh), '>', $file
   or die "Could not open file! $!\n";
```

To get full conditional coverage for these statements, we need to test each situation so each part of the conditional is followed. We need to test the statement for each combination of true or false for each logical operator.

Exercises

You can find the answers to these exercises in "Answers for Chapter 14" on page 340.

1. [35 minutes] Write a module distribution, starting from the tests first. Create a module My::List::Util that has two routines: sum and shuffle. The sum routine takes a list of values and returns the numeric sum. The shuffle routine takes a list of values and randomly shuffles the ordering, returning the list.

   Start with sum. Write the tests, and then add the code. You'll know you're done when the tests pass. Now include tests for shuffle, and then add the implementation for shuffle. You might peek in the *perlfaq4* or List::Util to find a shuffle implementation.

   Be sure to update the documentation and MANIFEST file as you go along.

   Save your distribution for the exercises in Chapter 17 and Chapter 20.

2. [25 minutes] Add the *t/Animal.t* test to your distribution and get it working. As you add parts of the tests, run the test suite before you add the next part of the tests.

3. [15 minutes] Create test files for the Cow, Horse, and Sheep classes. Add a test to ensure that each class compiles. Add tests to check the sound method for each class.

4. [5 minutes] Use `Devel::Cover` to measure your test suite coverage. Since you haven't fully tested the `Cow`, `Horse`, and `Sheep` classes, you should see that you have low numbers for the coverage metrics. That's okay, since you'll fix that in the next exercise.

5. [25 minutes] Finish your `Cow`, `Horse`, and `Sheep` tests so that you get perfect numbers for your test coverage (or close enough). Test the `sound` and `speak` methods for each animal and complete the documentation.

## CHAPTER 15

Objects with Data

Using the simple syntax introduced in Chapter 13, we have class methods, (multiple) inheritance, overriding, and extending. We've been able to factor out common code and to provide a way to reuse implementations with variations. This is at the core of what objects provide, but objects also provide *instance data*, which we cover in this chapter.

A Horse Is a Horse, of Course of Course—Or Is It?

We look at the code we used for the Animal classes and Horse classes. The Animal class provides the general speak subroutine:

```
package Animal;

sub speak {
  my $class = shift;
  print "a $class goes ", $class->sound, "!\n"
}
```

The Horse class inherits from Animal but provides its specific sound routine:

```
package Horse;
use parent qw(Animal);
sub sound { 'neigh' }
```

This lets us invoke Horse->speak to ripple upward to Animal::speak, calling back to Horse::sound to get the specific sound, and gives us this output:

```
a Horse goes neigh!
```

But all Horse objects would have to be absolutely identical. If we add a method, all horses automatically share it. That's great for making identical horses, but how do we capture the properties of an individual horse? For example, suppose we want to give our horse a name. There's got to be a way to keep its name separate from those of other horses.

We can do so by establishing an *instance*. An instance is generally created by a class, much like a car is created by a car factory. An instance will have associated properties, called *instance variables* (or member variables, if we come from a C++ or Java background). An instance has a unique identity (like the serial number of a registered horse), shared properties (the color and talents of the horse), and common behavior (e.g., pulling the reins back tells the horse to stop).

In Perl, an instance must be a reference to one of the built-in types. Start with the simplest reference that can hold a horse's name—a scalar reference.[1] We add a *scripts/horse.pl* to our distribution, which takes reference to our favorite horse's name, and "blesses" it into the Horse package (see Figure 15-1):

```perl
#!perl
# scripts/horse.pl
my $name = 'Mr. Ed';
my $tv_horse = \$name;

bless $tv_horse, 'Horse';
```

Now $tv_horse is a reference to what will be the instance-specific data (the name). The bless operator follows the reference to find what variable it points to—in this case the scalar $name. Then it "blesses" that variable by attaching a package name to it, turning $tv_horse into an object—a Horse object, of course. (Imagine that a little sticky-note that says Horse is now attached to $name.)

The PeGS structure for an object looks the same as that for the reference the object represents, but we put a "hat" on it to show the package name. For the basic object, we don't.

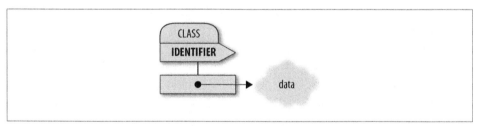

Figure 15-1. The PeGS for a generic object

We've blessed $tv_horse, which is a reference to a scalar. Its particular PeGS looks like Figure 15-2.

---

1. It's the simplest, but rarely used in real code for reasons we show later.

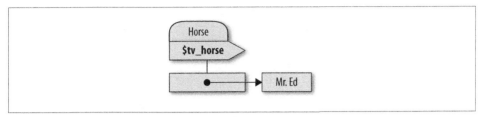

Figure 15-2. The PeGS for $tv_horse

At this point, $tv_horse is an instance of Horse.[2] That is, it's a specific horse. The reference is otherwise unchanged and can still be used with traditional dereferencing operators.[3]

Invoking an Instance Method

The method arrow can be used on instances, as well as on names of packages (classes). We expand *scripts/horse.pl* to get the sound that $tv_horse makes:

```
# scripts/horses.pl, as before
my $noise = $tv_horse->sound;
```

To invoke sound, Perl first notes that $tv_horse is a blessed reference, and thus an instance. Perl then constructs an argument list, similar to the way an argument list was constructed when we used the method arrow with a class name. Here, it'll be just ($tv_horse). Later, we'll show that arguments will take their place following the instance variable, just as with classes.

Now for the fun part: Perl takes the class in which we blessed the instance, in this case Horse, and uses it to locate and invoke the method as if we had said Horse->sound instead of $tv_horse->sound. The purpose of the original blessing is to associate a class with that reference to allow Perl to find the proper method.

Here, Perl finds Horse::sound directly (without using inheritance), yielding the final subroutine invocation:

```
Horse::sound($tv_horse)
```

The first parameter here is still the instance, not the name of the class as before. neigh is the return value, which ends up in the earlier $noise variable.

If Perl had not found Horse::sound, it would walk up the @Horse::ISA list to try to find the method in one of the superclasses, just as for a class method. The only difference between an instance method and a class method is whether the first parameter is an

---

2. Actually, $tv_horse points to the object, but in common terms, we nearly always deal with objects by references to those objects. Hence, it's simpler to say that $tv_horse is the horse, not "the thing that $tv_horse references."

3. Although doing so outside the class is a bad idea, as we'll show later.

instance (a blessed reference) or a class name (a string).[4] Otherwise, they are both just Perl subroutines.

Accessing the Instance Data

Because we get the instance as the first parameter, we can now access the instance-specific data. Here, we add a way to get at the name. In *lib/Horse.pm*, we add a name method:

```
sub name {
  my $self = shift;
  $$self;
}
```

Now we call for the name in *scripts/horse.pl*:

```
print $tv_horse->name, " says ", $tv_horse->sound, "\n";
```

Inside Horse::name, the @_ array contains just $tv_horse, which the shift stores into $self. It's traditional to shift the first parameter into a variable named $self for instance methods, so we stay with that unless we have strong reasons otherwise. Perl places no significance on the name $self, however.[5] Then we dereference $self as a scalar reference, yielding Mr. Ed. The result is:

```
Mr. Ed says neigh.
```

How to Build a Horse

If we constructed all our horses by hand, we'd most likely make mistakes from time to time. Making the "inside guts" of a Horse visible also violates one of the principles of OOP called *encapsulation*. Looking inside a horse is good if we're a veterinarian, but not if we just like horses. We let the Horse class build a new horse for us:

```
package Horse;
use parent qw(Animal);
sub sound { 'neigh' }
sub name {
  my $self = shift;
  $$self;
}
sub named {
  my $class = shift;
  my $name = shift;
  bless \$name, $class;
}
```

---

4. This is perhaps different from other OOP languages that you may know.

5. If we come from another OO language background, we might choose $this or $me for the variable name, but we'll probably confuse most other Perl OO hackers.

Now with the new named method, we build a Horse without making the reference directly:

```
# my $name = 'Mr. Ed';
# my $tv_horse = \$name;
my $tv_horse = Horse->named('Mr. Ed');
```

We're back to a class method, so the two arguments to Horse::named are "Horse" and "Mr. Ed". The bless operator not only blesses $name, it also returns the reference to $name, so that's fine as a return value. And that's how we build a horse.

We called the constructor named here so it denotes the constructor's argument as the name for this particular Horse. We can use different constructors with different names for different ways of "giving birth" to the object (such as recording its pedigree or date of birth). However, we'll find that most people use a single constructor named new, with various ways of interpreting the arguments to new. Either style is fine, as long as we document our particular way of giving birth to an object. Most core and CPAN modules use new, with notable exceptions, such as DBI's DBI->connect(). It's really up to the author, and any method can be a constructor.

Inheriting the Constructor

Was there anything specific to Horse in the named method? No. It's the same recipe for building anything else inherited from Animal, so we put it in the Animal class:

```
package Animal;

sub name {
  my $self = shift;
  $$self;
}

sub named {
  my $class = shift;
  my $name = shift;
  bless \$name, $class;
}
```

Ahh, but what happens if we invoke speak on an instance?

```
my $tv_horse = Horse->named('Mr. Ed');
$tv_horse->speak;
```

We get a debugging value:

```
a Horse=SCALAR(0xaca42ac) goes neigh!
```

Why? Because the Animal::speak method expects a class name as its first parameter, not an instance. When we pass in the instance instead, we use a blessed scalar reference as a string, which shows up as we just showed it now—similar to a stringified reference, but with the class name in front.

Making a Method Work with Either Classes or Instances

All we need to fix this is a way to detect whether the method is called on a class or an instance. The most straightforward way to find out is with the ref operator. This operator returns a string (the class name) when used on a blessed reference, and undef when used on a string (like a classname). We modify the name method first to notice the change:

```
# in lib/Animal.pm
sub name {
  my $either = shift;
  ref $either
    ? $$either              # it's an instance, return name
    : "an unnamed $either"; # it's a class, return generic
}
```

Here the ?: operator selects either the dereference or a derived string. Now we can use it with either an instance or a class. We changed the first parameter holder to $either to show that it is intentional:

```
print Horse->name, "\n";     # prints "an unnamed Horse\n"

my $tv_horse = Horse->named('Mr. Ed');
print $tv_horse->name, "\n";   # prints "Mr Ed.\n"
```

and now we'll fix speak to use this:

```
sub speak {
  my $either = shift;
  print $either->name, ' goes ', $either->sound, "\n";
}
```

Since sound already worked with either a class or an instance, we're done!

Adding Parameters to a Method

We want to allow our animals to eat. We add an eat method to Animal where we pass something for them to chew on:

```
package Animal;
sub named {
  my( $class, $name ) = @_;
  bless \$name, $class;
}
sub name {
  my $either = shift;
  ref $either
    ? $$either                # it's an instance, return name
    : "an unnamed $either"; # it's a class, return generic
}
sub speak {
  my $either = shift;
  print $either->name, ' goes ', $either->sound, "\n";
```

```
    }
    sub eat {
      my $either = shift;
      my $food = shift;
      print $either->name, " eats $food.\n";
    }
```

Now we try it out by giving our animals their favorite foods in a new program, *scripts/ horse-and-sheep.pl*:

```
    my $tv_horse = Horse->named('Mr. Ed');
    $tv_horse->eat('hay');
    Sheep->eat('grass');
```

It prints:

```
    Mr. Ed eats hay.
    an unnamed Sheep eats grass.
```

An instance method with parameters is invoked with the instance itself as the first argument, and then the list of parameters. That first invocation is like:

```
    Animal::eat($tv_horse, 'hay');
```

The instance methods form the *Application Programming Interface* (API) for an object. Most of the effort involved in designing a good object class goes into the API design because the API defines how reusable and maintainable the object and its subclasses will be. We don't want to rush to freeze an API design before we consider how we (or others) will use the object.

More Interesting Instances

What if an instance needs more data? Most interesting instances are made of many items, each of which can in turn be a reference or another object. The easiest way to store these items is often in a hash. The keys of the hash serve as the names of parts of the object (also called instance or member variables), and the corresponding values are, well, the values.

How do we turn the horse into a hash? Recall that an object is any blessed reference. We can easily make it a blessed hash reference as a blessed scalar reference, as long as everything that looks at the reference is changed accordingly.

We make a sheep that has a name and a color:

```
    my $lost = bless { Name => 'Bo', Color => 'white' }, 'Sheep';
```

$lost->{Name} has Bo, and $lost->{Color} has white. But we want to make $lost ->name access the name, and that's now messed up because it's expecting a scalar reference. Not to worry, because it's pretty easy to fix up:

```
    ## in Animal
    sub name {
      my $either = shift;
```

```
      ref $either
        ? $either->{Name}
        : "an unnamed $either";
    }
```

named still builds a scalar sheep, so we fix that as well:

```
## in Animal
sub named {
  my $class = shift;
  my $name = shift;
  my $self = { Name => $name, Color => $class->default_color };
  bless $self, $class;
}
```

What's this `default_color`? If named has only the name, we still need to set a color, so we'll have a class-specific initial color. For a sheep, we might define it as white:

```
## in Sheep
sub default_color { 'white' }
```

Then to keep from having to define one for each additional class, define a backstop method, which serves as the "default default," directly in Animal:

```
## in Animal
sub default_color { 'brown' }
```

Thus, all animals are brown (muddy, perhaps), unless a specific animal class gives a specific override to this method.

Now, because name and named were the only methods that reference the structure of the object, the remaining methods can stay the same, so speak still works as before. This supports another basic rule of OOP: if only the object accesses its internal data, there's less code to change when it's time to modify that structure.

A Horse of a Different Color

Having all horses be brown would be boring. We add a couple of methods to get and set the color:

```
## in Animal
sub color {
  my $self = shift;
  $self->{Color};
}


sub set_color {
  my $self = shift;
  $self->{Color} = shift;
}
```

Now we can fix that color for Mr. Ed:

```perl
my $tv_horse = Horse->named('Mr. Ed');
$tv_horse->set_color('black-and-white');
print $tv_horse->name, ' is colored ', $tv_horse->color, "\n";
```

which results in:

```
Mr. Ed is colored black-and-white
```

Getting Our Deposit Back

Because of the way we wrote the code, the setter also returns the updated value. We should think about this (and document it) when we write a setter. What should the setter return? Here are some common variations:

- The updated parameter (same as what was passed in)
- The previous value (similar to the way umask or the single-argument form of select works)
- The object itself
- A success/fail code

Each has advantages and disadvantages. For example, if we return the updated parameter, we can use it again for another object:

```perl
$tv_horse->set_color(
  $eating->set_color( color_from_user() )
);
```

Our earlier implementation returns the newly updated value. Frequently, this is the easiest code to write, and often the fastest to execute, too.

If we return the previous parameter, we can easily create "set this value temporarily to that" functions:

```perl
{
  my $old_color = $tv_horse->set_color('orange');
  ... do things with $tv_horse ...
  $tv_horse->set_color($old_color);
}
```

This is implemented as:

```perl
sub set_color {
  my $self = shift;
  my $old = $self->{Color};
  $self->{Color} = shift;
  $old;
}
```

For more efficiency, we can use the wantarray function to avoid stashing the previous value when we're called in void context:

```perl
sub set_color {
  my $self = shift;
```

```
      if (defined wantarray) {
        # this method call is not in void context, so
        # the return value matters
        my $old = $self->{Color};
        $self->{Color} = shift;
        $old;
      } else {
        # this method call is in void context
        $self->{Color} = shift;
      }
    }
```

If we return the object itself, we can chain settings:

```
my $tv_horse =
  Horse->named('Mr. Ed')
      ->set_color('grey')
      ->set_age(4)
      ->set_height('17 hands');
```

This works because the return value of each setter is the original object, becoming the object for the next method call. Implementing this is again relatively easy:

```
sub set_color {
  my $self = shift;
  $self->{Color} = shift;
  $self;
}
```

The void context trick can be used here too, although with questionable benefit because we've already established $self.

Finally, returning a success status is useful if it's fairly common for an update to fail, rather than an exceptional event. Other variations would have to indicate failure by throwing an exception with die.

 We can use what we want, be consistent if we can, but document it nonetheless (and don't change it after we've already released one version). There's not a single answer that covers every situation.

Don't Look Inside the Box

We might have obtained or set the color outside the class by following the hash reference: $tv_horse->{Color}. However, this violates the encapsulation of the object by exposing its internal structure. The object is supposed to be a black box, but we've pried off the hinges and looked inside.

One purpose of OOP is to enable the maintainer of Animal or Horse to make reasonably independent changes to the implementation of the methods and still have the exported interface work properly. To see why directly accessing the hash violates this, we say that Animal no longer uses a simple color name for the color, but instead changes to use a computed RGB triple to store the color (holding it as an arrayref). In this example, we use a fictional (at the time of this writing) Color::Conversions module to change the format of the color data behind-the-scenes:

```
use Color::Conversions qw(color_name_to_rgb rgb_to_color_name);

sub set_color {
  my $self = shift;
  my $new_color = shift;
  $self->{Color} = color_name_to_rgb($new_color);  # arrayref
}

sub color {
  my $self = shift;
  rgb_to_color_name($self->{Color});                # takes arrayref
}
```

We can still maintain the old interface if we use a setter and getter, because they can make the translations without the user knowing about it. We can also add new interfaces to enable the direct setting and getting of the RGB triple:

```
sub set_color_rgb {
  my $self = shift;
  $self->{Color} = [@_];                  # set colors to remaining parameters
}

sub get_color_rgb {
  my $self = shift;
  @{ $self->{Color} };                    # return RGB list
}
```

If we use code outside the class that looks at $tv_horse->{Color} directly, this change is no longer possible. It won't work to store a string (say, "blue") when it wants an arrayref ([0,0,255]), or to use an arrayref as a string. This is why OO programming encourages us to call getters and setters.

Faster Getters and Setters

Because we're going to play nice and always call the getters and setters instead of peeking into the data structure, getters and setters are called frequently. To save a teeny-tiny bit of time, we might see these getters and setters written as:

```
## in Animal
sub color     { $_[0]->{Color} }
sub set_color { $_[0]->{Color} = $_[1] }
```

We save a bit of typing when we do this, and the code is slightly faster, although probably not enough for us to notice with everything else that's going on in our program. The $_[0] is just the single element access to the @_ array. Instead of using shift to put the argument into another variable, we can use it directly.

Getters that Double as Setters

An alternative to creating two different methods for getting and setting a parameter is to create one method that notes whether it gets any additional arguments. Without arguments, it's a get operation; with arguments, it's a set operation. A simple version looks at the number of arguments to decide what to do:

```
sub color {
  my $self = shift;
  if (@_) {                   # are there any more parameters?
    # yes, it's a setter:
    $self->{Color} = shift;
  } else {
    # no, it's a getter:
    $self->{Color};
  }
}
```

Now we can use the same method to get or set the color:

```
my $tv_horse = Horse->named('Mr. Ed');
$tv_horse->color('black-and-white');
print $tv_horse->name, ' is colored ', $tv_horse->color, "\n";
```

The presence of the parameter in the second line denotes that we are setting the color, while its absence in the third line indicates we are getting the color.

This strategy is attractive because of its simplicity, but it also has disadvantages. It complicates the actions of the getter, which is called frequently. It also makes it difficult for us to search through our code to find the setters of a particular parameter, which are often more important than the getters. We've been burned in the past when a getter became a setter because another function returned more parameters than expected after an upgrade.

Restricting a Method to Class Only or Instance Only

Setting the name of an unnameable, generic Horse is probably not a good idea; neither is calling named on an instance. Nothing in the Perl method definition says "this is a class method" or "this is an instance method" because they are both just Perl subroutines. Fortunately, the ref operator lets us inspect the variable to know if we should throw an exception when our method is called incorrectly. As an example of instance- or class-only methods, consider the following where we check the argument to see what to do:

```
use Carp qw(croak);

sub instance_only {
  ref(my $self = shift) or croak "instance variable needed";
  ... use $self as the instance ...
}
```

```
sub class_only {
  ref(my $class = shift) and croak "class name needed";
  ... use $class as the class ...
}
```

The ref function returns true for an instance, which is just a blessed reference, or false for a class, which is just a string. If it returns an undesired value, we use the croak function from the Carp module (which comes in the standard distribution). The croak function places the blame on the caller by making the error message look like it came from the spot where we called the method instead of from the spot where we issued the error. The caller will get an error message like this, giving the line number in their code where they called the wrong method:

```
instance variable needed at their_code line 1234
```

Just like croak is an alternate form of die, Carp provides Carp as a replacement for warn. Each tells the user which line of code called the code that caused the problem. Instead of using die or warn in our modules, we use the Carp functions instead. Our users will thank us for it.

Exercise

You can find the answers to this exercise in "Answer for Chapter 15" on page 344.

1. [45 minutes] Give the Animal class the ability to get and set the name and color. Be sure that your result works under use strict. Also make sure your get methods work with both a generic animal and a specific animal instance. Test your work with:

```
my $tv_horse = Horse->named('Mr. Ed');
$tv_horse->set_name('Mister Ed');
$tv_horse->set_color('grey');
print $tv_horse->name, ' is ', $tv_horse->color, "\n";
print Sheep->name, ' colored ', Sheep->color, ' goes ', Sheep->sound, "\n";
```

What should you do if you're asked to set the name or color of a generic animal?

## CHAPTER 16

Some Advanced Object Topics

You might wonder, "Do all objects inherit from a common class?" "What if a method is missing?" "What about multiple inheritance?" or "How can I tell what sort of object I have?" Well, wonder no more. This chapter covers these subjects and more.

UNIVERSAL Methods

As we define classes, we create inheritance hierarchies through the global @ISA variables in each package. To search for a method, Perl wanders through the @ISA tree until it finds a match or fails.

After the search fails however, Perl always looks in one special class called UNIVERSAL and invokes a method from there, if found, just as if it had been located in any other class or superclass.

One way to look at this is that UNIVERSAL is the base class from which all objects derive. Any method we place here, such as:

```
sub UNIVERSAL::fandango {
  warn 'object ', shift, " can do the fandango!\n";
}
```

enables all objects of our program to be called as $some_object->fandango.

Generally, we should provide a fandango method for specific classes of interest, and then provide a definition in UNIVERSAL::fandango as a backstop, in case Perl can't find a more specific method. A practical example might be a data-dumping routine for debugging or maybe a marshaling strategy to dump all application objects to a file. We provide the general method in UNIVERSAL and override it in the specific classes for unusual objects.

Obviously, we should use UNIVERSAL sparingly because there's only one universe of objects, and our fandango might collide with some other included module's fandango. For this reason, UNIVERSAL is hardly used for anything except methods that must be completely, well, universal, like during debugging, or other Perl-internal behavior that ordinary programmers may blissfully ignore.

Testing Our Objects for Good Behavior

Besides providing a place for us to put universally available methods, the UNIVERSAL package comes preloaded with two very useful utility methods: DOES and can. Because UNIVERSAL defines these methods, they are available to all objects.

 The DOES method is available in v5.10 and later. Prior to that version, we can use isa to get much of the same thing, although isa tests only inheritance relationships.

The DOES method tests to see whether a given class or instance provides a certain *role*, which is a set of behaviors. For example, continuing on with the Animal family from the previous chapters:

```
use v5.10;

if (Horse->DOES('Animal')) {    # does Horse do Animal?
  print "A Horse is an Animal.\n";
}

my $tv_horse = Horse->named("Mr. Ed");
if ($tv_horse->DOES('Animal')) { # is it an Animal?
  print $tv_horse->name, " is an Animal.\n";
  if ($tv_horse->DOES('Horse')) { # is it a Horse?
    print 'In fact, ', $tv_horse->name, " is a Horse.\n";
  } else {
    print "...but it's not a Horse.\n";
  }
}
```

This is handy when we have a heterogeneous mix of objects in a data structure and want to distinguish particular categories of objects:

```
use v5.10;

my @horses = grep $_->DOES('Horse'), @all_animals;
```

The result will be only the horses (or race horses) from the array. We compare that with:

```
my @horses_only = grep ref $_ eq 'Horse', @all_animals;
```

which picks out *just* the horses because a RaceHorse won't return Horse for ref.

In general, we shouldn't use:

```
ref($some_object) eq 'SomeClass'
```

in our programs because it prevents future users from subclassing that class and using that class just like its more generic base class. Use the DOES construct as given earlier.

One downside of the DOES call here is that it works only on blessed references or scalars that look like class names. If we happen to pass it an unblessed reference, we get a fatal (but trappable) error of:

```
Can't call method "DOES" on unblessed reference at ...
```

To call DOES more robustly, we could call it as a subroutine:

```
if (UNIVERSAL::DOES($unknown_thing, 'Animal')) {
    ... it's an Animal! ...
}
```

This runs without error no matter what $unknown_thing contains. But it's subverting the OO mechanism, which has its own set of problems. This is a job for an exception mechanism, which is eval. If the value in $unknown_thing isn't a reference, then we can't call a method on it. The eval traps that error and returns undef, which is false, which is the right answer in that case:

```
if (eval { $unknown_thing->DOES('Animal') }) {
    ... it's an Animal ...
}
```

 If Animal has a custom DOES method (perhaps it rejects a mutant branch of talking animals in the family tree), calling UNIVERSAL::DOES skips past Animal::DOES and may give us the wrong answer.

As in the case of DOES, we can test for acceptable behaviors with the can method. Instead of broad checking like DOES, can looks for specific methods and doesn't care how they are defined. For example:

```
if ($tv_horse->can('eat')) {
    $tv_horse->eat('hay');
}
```

If the result of can is true, then somewhere in the inheritance hierarchy, a class claims it can handle the eat method. Again, the caveats about $tv_horse being only either a blessed reference or a class name as a scalar still apply, so the robust solution when we might deal with nearly anything uses eval:

```
if (eval { $tv_horse->can('eat') } ) { ... }
```

If we defined UNIVERSAL::fandango earlier, then a can check always returns true because all objects can do the fandango:

```
if( $object->can('fandango') ) { ... }  # true for all objects
```

can has the same traps as DOES; we can short circuit the path to UNIVERSAL by defining our own.

The Last Resort

After Perl searches the inheritance tree and UNIVERSAL for a method, it doesn't stop there if the search is unsuccessful. Perl repeats the search through the very same hierarchy (including UNIVERSAL), looking for a method named AUTOLOAD.

If an AUTOLOAD exists, the subroutine is called in place of the original method, passing it the normal predetermined argument list: the class name or instance reference, followed by any arguments provided to the method call. The original method name is passed in the package variable called $AUTOLOAD (in the package where the subroutine was compiled) and contains the fully qualified method name, so we should generally strip everything up to the final double colon if we want a simple method name.

The AUTOLOAD subroutine can execute the desired operation itself, install a subroutine and then jump into it, or perhaps just die if asked to call an unknown method.

One use of AUTOLOAD defers the compilation of a large subroutine until it is actually needed. For example, suppose the eat method for an animal is complex but unused in nearly every invocation of the program. We can defer its compilation until Perl calls AUTOLOAD:

```
## in Animal
use Carp qw(croak);

sub AUTOLOAD {
  our $AUTOLOAD;
  (my $method = $AUTOLOAD) =~ s/.*:://s; # remove package name
  if ($method eq "eat") {
    ## define eat:
    eval q{
      sub eat {
        ...
        long
        definition
        goes
        here
        ...
      }
    };                   # End of eval's q{} string
    die $@ if $@;        # if typo snuck in
    goto &eat;           # jump into it
  } else {               # unknown method
    croak "$_[0] does not know how to $method\n";
  }
}
```

If the method name is eat, we define the eat method, which we had previously stored in a string but had not compiled, and then jump into it with a special construct that replaces the current subroutine invocation of AUTOLOAD with an invocation of eat, just as if we invoked &eat instead of AUTOLOAD.[1] After the first AUTOLOAD hit, the eat subroutine is now defined, so we won't be coming back here. This is great for compile-as-you-go programs because it minimizes startup overhead.

For a more automated way of creating code to do this, which makes it easy to turn the autoloading off during development and debugging, see the AutoLoader and Self Loader core module documentation.

Using AUTOLOAD for Accessors

In Chapter 15, we showed how we can create color and set_color methods to get and set the color of an animal. If we had 20 attributes instead of 1 or 2, the code would be painfully repetitive. By using an AUTOLOAD method, we can construct the nearly identical accessors as needed, saving both compilation time and wear-and-tear on the developer's keyboard.

We use a code reference as a closure to do the job. First, we set up an AUTOLOAD for the object and define a list of hash keys for which we want trivial accessors:

```
use Carp qw(croak);
sub AUTOLOAD {
  my @elements = qw(color age weight height);
```

Next, we'll see if the method is a getter for one of these keys, and if so, we install a getter and jump to it:

```
our $AUTOLOAD;
if ($AUTOLOAD =~ /::(\w+)$/ and grep $1 eq $_, @elements) {
  my $field = ucfirst $1;
  {
    no strict 'refs';
    *$AUTOLOAD = sub { $_[0]->{$field} };
  }
  goto &$AUTOLOAD;
}
```

We use ucfirst because we named the method color to fetch the hash element called Color. The typeglob notation (*{$AUTOLOAD}) installs a wanted subroutine as defined by the coderef closure, which fetches the corresponding key from the object hash. Consider this part to be magic that we cut and paste into our program. Finally, the goto construct jumps into the newly defined subroutine.

---

1. Although goto is generally (and rightfully) considered evil, this form of goto, which gives a subroutine name as a target, is not really the evil goto; it's the good goto. In particular, this is the "magic goto." Its trick is that AUTOLOAD is completely invisible to the subroutine.

See *Mastering Perl* for more about typeglobs and symbol table manipulation.

Otherwise, perhaps it's a setter:

```
if ($AUTOLOAD =~ /::set_(\w+)$/ and grep $1 eq $_, @elements) {
  my $field = ucfirst $1;
  {
    no strict 'refs';
    *$AUTOLOAD = sub { $_[0]->{$field} = $_[1] };
  }
  goto &$AUTOLOAD;
}
```

If it is neither, death awaits:

```
(my $method = $AUTOLOAD) =~ s/.*:://s; # remove package name
croak "$_[0] does not understand $method\n";
```

Again, we pay the price for the AUTOLOAD only on the first hit of a particular getter or setter. After that, a subroutine is now already defined, and we can invoke it directly.

Creating Getters and Setters More Easily

If all that coding for creating accessors using AUTOLOAD looks messy, rest assured that we really don't need to tackle it, because there's a CPAN module that does it a bit more directly: Class::MethodMaker.[2]

For example, a simplified version of the Animal class might be defined as follows:

```
package Animal;
use Class::MethodMaker
  new_with_init => 'new',
  get_set       => [-eiffel => [qw(color height name age)]],
  abstract      => [qw(sound)],
;

sub init {
  my $self = shift;
  $self->set_color($self->default_color);
}

sub named {
  my $self = shift->new;
  $self->set_name(shift);
  $self;
}
```

---

2. Sometimes Class::MethodMaker can be a bit much. We can also check out the lighter Class::Accessor.

```
sub speak {
  my $self = shift;
  print $self->name, ' goes ', $self->sound, "\n";
}

sub eat {
  my $self = shift;
  my $food = shift;
  print $self->name, " eats $food\n";
}

sub default_color {
  'brown';
}
```

The getters and setters for the four instance attributes (name, height, color, and age) are defined automatically, using the method `color` to get the color and `set_color` to set the color. (The `eiffel` flag says "do it the way the Eiffel language does it," which is the way it should be done here.) The messy blessing step is now hidden behind a simple `new` method. We define the initial color as the default color, as before, because the generated `new` method calls the `init` method.

However, we can still call `Horse->named('Mr. Ed')` because it immediately calls the `new` routine as well.

`Class::MethodMaker` generated the `sound` method as an abstract method. *Abstract* methods are placeholders, meant to be defined in a subclass. If a subclass fails to define the method, the method `Class::MethodMaker` generated for `Animal`'s `sound` dies.

We lose the ability to call the getters (such as `name`) on the class itself, rather than an instance. In turn, this breaks our prior usage of calling `speak` and `eat` on generic animals, since they call the accessors. One way around this is to define a more general version of `name` to handle either a class or instance and then change the other routines to call it:

```
sub generic_name {
  my $either = shift;
  ref $either ? $either->name : "an unnamed $either";
}
sub speak {
  my $either = shift;
  print $either->generic_name, ' goes ', $either->sound, "\n";
}
sub eat {
  my $either = shift;
  my $food = shift;
  print $either->generic_name, " eats $food\n";
}
```

There. Now it's looking nearly drop-in compatible with the previous definition, except for those friend classes that referenced the attribute names directly in the hash as the initial-cap-keyed versions (such as `Color`) rather than through the accessors (`$self->color`).

This brings up the maintenance issue again. The more we can decouple our implementation (hash versus array, names of hash keys, or types of elements) from the interface (method names, parameter lists, or types of return values), the more flexible and maintainable our system becomes.

The flexibility isn't free, however. Since the execution cost of a method call is higher than that of a hash lookup, in some circumstances it may make sense to have a friend class peek inside.

Multiple Inheritance

How does Perl wander through the @ISA tree? The answer may be simple or complex. If we don't have multiple inheritance (that is, if no @ISA has more than one element), it is simple: Perl goes from one @ISA to the next until it finds the ultimate base class whose @ISA is empty.

Multiple inheritance is more complex. It occurs when a class's @ISA has more than one element. For example, suppose a class called Racer, which has the basic abilities for anything that can race, so that it's ready to be the base class for a runner, a fast car, or a racing turtle. With that, we could make the RaceHorse class as simply as this:

```
package RaceHorse;
use parent qw{ Horse Racer };
```

 If there is a conflict among the methods of Horse and Racer, or if their implementations aren't able to work together, they can become difficult. The various classes in @ISA may not play well together and may step on each other's data, for instance.

Now a RaceHorse can do anything a Horse can do, and anything a Racer can do as well. When Perl searches for a method that's not provided directly by RaceHorse, it first searches through all the capabilities of the Horse (including all its parent classes, such as Animal). When the Horse possibilities are exhausted, Perl turns to see whether Racer (or one of its parent classes) supplies the needed method. On the other hand, if we want Perl to search Racer before searching Horse, put them into @ISA in that order (see Figure 16-1).

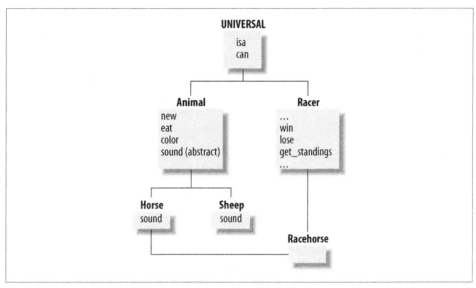

Figure 16-1. A class may not need to implement any methods of its own if it inherits everything it needs from its parent classes through multiple inheritance

Exercises

You can find the answers to these exercises in "Answers for Chapter 16" on page 345.

1. [20 minutes] Write a module named MyDate that has an AUTOLOAD method which handles the calls to the methods named date, month, and year, returning the appropriate value for each one. For any other method, the AUTOLOAD should Carp about the unknown method name. Write a script that uses your module and prints the values for the date, month, and year.

2. [20 minutes] Starting with the script you wrote for the previous exercise, add a UNIVERSAL::debug function that prints a timestamp before the message you pass to it. Call the debug method on the MyDate object. What happens? How does this get around the AUTOLOAD mechanism?

## CHAPTER 17

Exporter

In Chapter 2, we showed how to use modules, some of which pulled functions into the current namespace. Now we're going to show how to get our own modules to do that.

What use Is Doing

So, what does use do? How does the import list come into action? Perl interprets the use list as a particular form of BEGIN block wrapped around a require and a method call. The following two operations are equivalent:

```
use Island::Plotting::Maps qw( load_map scale_map draw_map );

BEGIN {
  require Island::Plotting::Maps;
  Island::Plotting::Maps->import( qw( load_map scale_map draw_map ) );
}
```

First, the require is a package-name require, rather than the string-expression require from Chapter 11. The colons are turned into the native directory separator (such as / for Unix-like systems), and the name is suffixed with *.pm* (for "perl module"). On a Unix-like system, we end up with:

```
require "Island/Plotting/Maps.pm";
```

 We can't use the *.pl* (for "perl library") extension that we used earlier since use won't find it. It only uses the *.pm* extension.

Recalling the operation of require from earlier, this means Perl looks in the current value of @INC, checks each directory in turn for a subdirectory named Island that contains a subdirectory named Plotting that contains the file named *Maps.pm*

If Perl doesn't find an appropriate file after looking at all of @INC, the program dies (which we can trap with an eval). Otherwise, Perl reads and evaluates the first file it finds. As always with `require`, the last expression evaluated must be true or the program dies thinking it encountered an error compiling the file. And, once Perl has read a file, it will not re-read it if we request it again. In the module interface, we expect the `require`'d file to define subroutines in the same-named package, not the caller's package. So, for example, a portion of the `File::Basename` file might look something like this, if we took out all the good stuff:

```
package File::Basename;
sub dirname { ... }
sub basename { ... }
sub fileparse { ... }
1;
```

These three subroutines are then defined in the `File::Basename` package, not the package in which our `use` occurs.

How do these subroutines get from the module's package into the calling package? That's the second step inside the `BEGIN` block: Perl automatically calls a routine called `import` in the module's package, passing along the entire import list. Typically, this routine aliases some of the names from the imported namespace (e.g., `File::Base name`) to the importing namespace (e.g., `main`). The module author is responsible for providing an appropriate `import` routine. It's easier than it sounds, as we'll show later in this chapter.

Finally, the whole thing is wrapped in a `BEGIN` block. This means that the `use` operation happens at compile time, rather than runtime, and indeed it does. Thus, subroutines are associated with those defined in the module, prototypes are properly defined, and so on.

Importing with Exporter

In Chapter 2, we skipped over that "and now magic happens" part where the `import` routine is supposed to take `File::Basename::fileparse` and somehow alias it into the caller's package so it's callable as `fileparse`.

Perl provides a lot of introspective capabilities. Specifically, we can look at the symbol table (where all subroutines and many variables are named), see what is defined, and alter those definitions. We showed a bit of that back in the `AUTOLOAD` mechanism earlier in Chapter 16. If we were the authors of `File::Basename` and we wanted to force `filename`, `basename`, and `fileparse` from the current package into the calling package, we can write `import` to make it happen:

```
sub import {
  for (qw(filename basename fileparse)) {
    no strict 'refs';
    *{"main::$_"} = \&$_;
  }
}
```

Boy, is that cryptic! And limited. What if the caller didn't want `fileparse`? What if the caller invoked `use` in a package other than `main`?

Thankfully, there's a standard `import` that's available in the `Exporter` module. As the module author, all we do is add `Exporter` as a parent class:

```
package Animal::Utils;
use parent qw(Exporter);
```

Now the `import` call to the package will inherit upward to the `Exporter` class, providing an `import` routine that knows how to take a list of subroutines[1] and export them to the caller's package. And, many people do it this way.

We don't really want to inherit from `Exporter`. Our class is usually not going to be a specialization of `Exporter`, so the ISA relationship isn't right. Instead, we can import the `import` subroutine without the inheritance, if we have v5.8.3 or later:

```
use v5.8.3;
package Animal::Utils;
use Exporter qw(import);
```

We prefer the latter, but we see both in existing code.

@EXPORT and @EXPORT_OK

The `import` provided by `Exporter` examines the `@EXPORT` variable in the module's package to determine which symbols it exports by default. `File::Basename` might do something like this:

```
package File::Basename;
use Exporter qw(import);
our @EXPORT = qw( basename dirname fileparse );
```

The `@EXPORT` list both defines which symbols are available for importing (the public interface) and provides a default list for Perl to use when we don't specify an import list. These two calls are equivalent:

```
use File::Basename;

BEGIN { require File::Basename; File::Basename->import }
```

We pass no list to `import` so the `Exporter->import` routine looks at `@EXPORT` and provides everything in the list. Remember, having no list is not the same as having an empty list. If the list is empty, the module's `import` method is not called at all.

What if we had subroutines we didn't want as part of the default import but would still be available if we asked for them? We can add those subroutines to the `@EXPORT_OK` list in the module's package. For example, suppose that Gilligan's module provides the `guess_direction_toward` routine by default but could also provide the

---

1. And variables, although far less common, and arguably the wrong thing to do.

ask_the_skipper_about and get_north_from_professor routines, if requested. We can start it like this:

```
package Navigate::SeatOfPants;
use Exporter qw(import);
our @EXPORT = qw(guess_direction_toward);
our @EXPORT_OK = qw(ask_the_skipper_about get_north_from_professor);
```

The following invocations would then be valid:

```
use Navigate::SeatOfPants;  # gets guess_direction_toward

use Navigate::SeatOfPants qw(guess_direction_toward); # same

use Navigate::SeatOfPants
  qw(guess_direction_toward ask_the_skipper_about);

use Navigate::SeatOfPants
  qw(ask_the_skipper_about get_north_from_professor);
  ## does NOT import guess_direction_toward!
```

If we specify any names, they must be in either @EXPORT or @EXPORT_OK, so this request is rejected by Exporter->import:

```
use Navigate::SeatOfPants qw(according_to_GPS);
```

because according_to_GPS is in neither @EXPORT nor @EXPORT_OK.[2] Thus, with those two arrays, we have control over our public interface. This does not stop someone from saying Navigate::SeatOfPants::according_to_GPS (if it existed), but at least now it's obvious that they're using something we didn't intend to offer them.

Grouping with %EXPORT_TAGS

We don't have to list every function or variable that we want to import, either. We can create shortcuts, or tags, to group them under a single name. In the import list, we precede the tag name with a colon. For example, the core Fcntl module makes the flock constants available as a group with the :flock tag:

```
use Fcntl qw( :flock );        # import all flock constants
```

As described in the Exporter documentation, a few shortcuts are available automatically. The DEFAULT tag pulls in the same things as if we had provided no import list:

```
use Navigate::SeatOfPants qw(:DEFAULT);
```

That isn't very useful on its own, but if we want to pull in the default symbols and more, we don't have to type everything out because we supply an import list:

```
use Navigate::SeatOfPants qw(:DEFAULT get_north_from_professor);
```

---

2. This check also catches misspellings and mistaken subroutine names, keeping us from wondering why the get_direction_from_professor routine isn't working.

These are rarely seen in practice. Why? The purpose of explicitly providing an import list generally means we want to control the subroutine names we use in our program. Those last examples do not insulate us from future changes to the module, which may import additional subroutines that could collide with our code.

 It is generally considered a bad idea for an update to a released module to introduce new default imports. If we know that our first release is still missing a function, though, there's no reason why we can't put in a placeholder: sub according_to_GPS { die "not implemented yet" }.

In a few cases, a module may supply dozens or hundreds of possible symbols. These modules can use advanced techniques (described in the Exporter documentation) to make it easy to import batches of related symbols.

In our modules, we use the %EXPORT_TAGS hash to define these tags. The hash key is the name of the tag (without the colon), and the value is an array reference of symbols:

```
package Navigate::SeatOfPants;
use Exporter qw(import);

our @EXPORT    = qw(guess_direction_toward);
our @EXPORT_OK = qw(
  get_north_from_professor
  according_to_GPS
  ask_the_skipper_about
);

our %EXPORT_TAGS = (
  all       => [ @EXPORT, @EXPORT_OK ],
  gps       => [ qw( according_to_GPS ) ],
  direction => [ qw(
    get_north_from_professor
    according_to_GPS
    guess_direction_toward
    ask_the_skipper_about
    ) ],
);
```

Our first tag, all, includes all the exportable symbols (everything in both @EXPORT and @EXPORT_OK). The gps tag comprises only the functions that deal with GPS, and the direction tag includes all the functions that deal with direction. The tags can contain overlaps too, and we'll notice that according_to_GPS shows up in each one of them. No matter how we define our tags, everything they include has to be either in @EXPORT or @EXPORT_OK.

Once we define our export tags, our users can use them in their import lists:

```
use Navigate::SeatOfPants qw(:direction);
```

Custom Import Routines

We'll use CGI.pm to show a custom import routine before we show how to write our own. Not satisfied with the incredible flexibility of the Exporter's import routine, CGI.pm author Lincoln Stein created a special import for the CGI module.[3] If you've ever gawked at the dizzying array of options that can appear after use CGI and wondered how it all worked, it's all a simple matter of programming. We can always look at the source ourselves.

We can use the CGI module as an object-oriented module:

```
use CGI;
my $q = CGI->new;          # create a query object
my $f = $q->param('foo'); # get the foo field
```

Through the magic of Lincoln's custom import, we can also treat CGI as a function-oriented module:[4]

```
use CGI qw(param);         # import the param function
my $f = param('foo');      # get the foo field
```

If we don't want to spell out every possible subfunction, we can bring them all in:

```
use CGI qw(:all);          # define 'param' and 800-gazillion others
my $f = param('foo');
```

And then there are pragmata available. For example, if we want to disable the normal sticky field handling, add -nosticky into the import list:

```
use CGI qw(-nosticky :all);
```

If we want to create the start_table and end_table routines in addition to the others, it's:

```
use CGI qw(-nosticky :all *table);
```

Not only that, we can invent new methods for HTML generation. The custom import turns imports it doesn't recognize into HTML convenience functions:

```
use CGI qw(foo bar);

print foo( 'Hello!' );     #   <foo>Hello!</foo>
```

Truly a dizzying array of options. How did Lincoln make it all work? We can look in the CGI.pm code to see for ourselves, but we show only the basics here.

The import method is a regular method, so we can make it do whatever we want. Earlier, we showed a simple (although hypothetical) example for File::Basename. In that case,

---

3. Some have dubbed this the "Lincoln Loader" out of a simultaneous deep respect for Lincoln and the sheer terror of having to deal with something that doesn't work like anything else they've encountered.

4. There's still an object behind the scenes, but we don't see it.

instead of using the `import` method from `Exporter` as the real module does, we wrote our own to force the symbols into the `main` package:

```
sub import {
  foreach my $name (qw(filename basename fileparse)) {
    no strict 'refs';
    *{"main::$name"}=\&$name;
  }
}
```

This only works for `main` since that's what we hardcoded into the routine. We can figure out the calling package on the fly, however, by using the built-in `caller`. In scalar context, `caller` returns the calling package:

```
sub import {
  my $package = caller;
  foreach my $name (qw(filename basename fileparse)) {
    no strict 'refs';
    *{$package."::$name"}=\&$name;
  }
}
```

We can get even more information from `caller` by calling it in list context:

```
sub import {
  my( $package, $file, $line ) = caller;
  warn "I was called by $package in $file\n";
  for (qw(filename basename fileparse)) {
    no strict 'refs';
    *{$package . "::$_"} = \&$_;
  }
}
```

Since `import` is a method, any arguments to it (that's the import list, remember) show up in `@_`. We can inspect the argument list and decide what to do. We turn on debugging output only if `debug` shows up in the import list. We're not going to import a subroutine named `debug`. We're only going to set `$debug` to a true value if it's there, then do the same stuff we did before. This time, we only print the warning if we've turned on debugging:

```
sub import {
  my $debug = grep { $_ eq 'debug' } @_;
  my( $package, $file, $line ) = caller;
  warn "I was called by $package in $file\n" if $debug;
  for (qw(filename basename fileparse)) {
    no strict 'refs';
    *{$package . "::$_"} = \&$_;
  }
}
```

These are the basic tricks that Lincoln used to work his CGI magic, and it's the same stuff that the `Test::More` module, which we showed in Chapter 14, uses in its own `import` to set the test plan.

Exercises

You can find the answers to these exercises in "Answers for Chapter 17" on page 347.

1. [15 minutes] Take the Oogaboogoo library you created in Chapter 11, Exercise 1, and turn it into a module you can bring in with use. Alter the invoking code so that it uses the imported routines (rather than the full package specification as you did before), and test it.

2. [15 minutes] Modify your answer to Exercise 1 to use an export tag named "all". When the user uses "all", your module should import all subroutine names:

   ```
   use Oogaboogoo::date qw(:all);
   ```

3. [10 minutes] Modify the My::List::Util module you created in Chapter 14 so it exports its sum and shuffle.

## CHAPTER 18

Object Destruction

In Chapters 13 and 15, we looked at basic object creation and manipulation. In this chapter, we'll look at an equally important topic: what happens when objects go away. In Perl, we call the process of cleaning up an object *destroying* it.

As we showed in Chapter 5, when the last reference to a Perl data structure goes away, Perl automatically reclaims the memory of that data structure, including destroying any links to other data. Of course, that in turn may cause Perl to destroy other ("contained") structures as well.

By default, objects work in this manner because objects use the same reference-count–based garbage collection to make more complex objects. Perl destroys an object built with a hash reference when the last reference to that hash goes away. If hash values are also references, they're similarly removed, possibly causing further destruction.

Cleaning Up After Ourselves

Suppose our object uses a temporary file to hold data that doesn't fit entirely in memory. The object can include a filehandle to a temporary file in its instance data. While the normal object destruction sequence will properly close the handle, we still have the temporary file on disk unless we take further action.

To do the proper cleanup operations when Perl destroys an object, we need to know when that happens. Thankfully, Perl provides such notification upon request. We can request this notification by giving the object a DESTROY method.

When the last reference to an object, say $bessie, disappears, Perl invokes that object's DESTROY method automatically, as if we had called it ourselves:

```
$bessie->DESTROY
```

This method call is like most other method calls: Perl starts at the class of the object and works its way up the inheritance hierarchy until it finds a suitable method. However, unlike most other method calls, there's no error if Perl doesn't find a suitable method.[1]

 Normally, our own method calls will cause an error if Perl doesn't find them. If we want to prevent that, we put a do-nothing method into the base class.

For example, going back to the Animal class defined in Chapter 13, we can add a DESTROY method to know when objects go away, purely for debugging purposes:

```
## in Animal
sub DESTROY {
  my $self = shift;
  print '[', $self->name, " has died.]\n";
}
```

Now when we create any Animals in the program, we get notification as they leave. For example:

```
## include animal classes from Chapter 15...

sub feed_a_cow_named {
  my $name = shift;
  my $cow = Cow->named($name);
  $cow->eat('grass');
  print "Returning from the subroutine.\n";    # $cow is destroyed here
}
print "Start of program.\n";
my $outer_cow = Cow->named('Bessie');
print "Now have a cow named ", $outer_cow->name, ".\n";
feed_a_cow_named('Gwen');
print "Returned from subroutine.\n";
```

This prints:

```
Start of program.
Now have a cow named Bessie.
Gwen eats grass.
Returning from the subroutine.
[Gwen has died.]
Returned from subroutine.
[Bessie has died.]
```

Note that Gwen is active inside the subroutine. However, as the subroutine exits, Perl notices there are no references to Gwen; it automatically invokes Gwen's DESTROY method, printing the Gwen has died message.

---

1. The import and unimport methods are also special in this way.

What happens at the end of the program? Since objects don't live beyond the end of the program, Perl makes one final pass over all remaining data and destroys it. This is true whether the data is held in lexical variables or package global variables. Because Bessie was still alive at the end of the program, she needed to be recycled, and so we get the message for Bessie after all other steps in the program are complete.

 Perl does its final cleanup right after the END blocks are executed and follows the same rules as END blocks: there must be a good exit of the program rather than an abrupt end. If Perl runs out of memory, all bets are off.

Nested Object Destruction

If an object holds another object (say, as an element of an array or the value of a hash element), Perl DESTROYs the containing object before any of the contained objects begin their discarding process. This is reasonable because the containing object may need to reference its contents in order to disappear gracefully. To illustrate this, we build a "barn" and tear it down. To be interesting, we'll make the barn a blessed array reference, not a hash reference:

```
{ package Barn;
  sub new { bless [  ], shift }
  sub add { push @{shift()}, shift }
  sub contents { @{shift()} }
  sub DESTROY {
    my $self = shift;
    print "$self is being destroyed...\n";
    for ($self->contents) {
      print '  ', $_->name, " goes homeless.\n";
    }
  }
}
```

Here, we're really being minimalistic in the object definition. To create a new barn, we bless an empty array reference into the class name passed as the first parameter. Adding an animal pushes it to the back of the barn. Asking for the barn's contents merely dereferences the object array reference to return the contents.

The fun part is the destructor. We take the reference to ourselves, display a debugging message about the particular barn being destroyed, and then ask for the name of each inhabitant in turn. In action, this would be:

```
my $barn = Barn->new;
$barn->add(Cow->named('Bessie'));
$barn->add(Cow->named('Gwen'));
print "Burn the barn:\n";
$barn = undef;
print "End of program.\n";
```

This prints:

```
Burn the barn:
Barn=ARRAY(0x541c) is being destroyed...
  Bessie goes homeless.
  Gwen goes homeless.
[Gwen has died.]
[Bessie has died.]
End of program.
```

Note that Perl first destroys the barn, letting us get the names of the inhabitants cleanly. Once the barn is gone, the inhabitants have no additional references, so they also go away because Perl invokes their destructors, too. Compare that with the cows having a life outside the barn:

```
my $barn = Barn->new;
my @cows = (Cow->named('Bessie'), Cow->named('Gwen'));
$barn->add($_) for @cows;
print "Burn the barn:\n";
$barn = undef;
print "Lose the cows:\n";
@cows = ( );
print "End of program.\n";
```

This produces:

```
Burn the barn:
Barn=ARRAY(0x541c) is being destroyed...
  Bessie goes homeless.
  Gwen goes homeless.
Lose the cows:
[Gwen has died.]
[Bessie has died.]
End of program.
```

The cows will now continue to live until the only other reference to the cows (from the @cows array) goes away.

The references to the cows disappear once the barn destructor completely finishes. Sometimes, we may wish instead to shoo the cows out of the barn as we notice them. Here, it's as simple as destructively altering the barn array, rather than iterating over it. We alter the Barn to Barn2 to illustrate this:

```
{ package Barn2;
  sub new { bless [  ], shift }
  sub add { push @{shift()}, shift }
  sub contents { @{shift()} }
  sub DESTROY {
    my $self = shift;
    print "$self is being destroyed...\n";
    while (@$self) {
      my $homeless = shift @$self;
      print '  ', $homeless->name, " goes homeless.\n";
    }
  }
}
```

If we're using a hash instead, we use delete on the elements we wish to process immediately.

Now use it in the previous scenarios:

```
my $barn = Barn2->new;
$barn->add(Cow->named('Bessie'));
$barn->add(Cow->named('Gwen'));
print "Burn the barn:\n";
$barn = undef;
print "End of program.\n";
```

This produces:

```
Burn the barn:
Barn2=ARRAY(0x541c) is being destroyed...
  Bessie goes homeless.
[Bessie has died.]
  Gwen goes homeless.
[Gwen has died.]
End of program.
```

Bessie has no home from having being booted out of the barn immediately, so she also died. (Poor Gwen suffers the same fate.) There were no references to her at that moment, even before the destructor for the barn was complete.

Thus, back to the temporary file problem: we modify our Animal class to use a temporary file by using the File::Temp module, which is part of the Standard Library. Its temp file routine knows how to make temporary files, including where to put them and so on, so we don't have to. The tempfile function returns a filehandle and a filename, and we store both because we need both in the destructor:

```
## in Animal
use File::Temp qw(tempfile);

sub named {
  my $class = shift;
  my $name = shift;
  my $self = { Name => $name, Color => $class->default_color };
  ## new code here...
  my ($fh, $filename) = tempfile();
  $self->{temp_fh} = $fh;
  $self->{temp_filename} = $filename;
  ## .. to here
  bless $self, $class;
}
```

We now have a filehandle and its filename stored as instance variables of Animal (or any class derived from Animal). In the destructor, we close it and unlink the file:

```
sub DESTROY {
  my $self = shift;
```

```
    my $fh = $self->{temp_fh};
    close $fh;
    unlink $self->{temp_filename};
    print '[', $self->name, " has died.]\n";
}
```

When Perl destroys the last reference to the Animal object (even if it's at the end of the program), it also automatically removes the temporary file to avoid a mess.

 As it turns out, we can tell File::Temp to do this automatically, but then we won't be able to illustrate doing it manually. Doing it manually lets us do extra processing, such as storing a summary of the information from the temporary file into a database.

Beating a Dead Horse

Because subclasses inherit the DESTROY method like any other method, we can also override and extend superclass methods. For example, we decide dead horses need a further use. In our Horse class, we override the DESTROY method inherited from Animal so we can do extra processing. However, since the Animal class might be doing things we aren't supposed to know about, we call its version of DESTROY using the SUPER:: pseudoclass we saw in Chapter 13:

```
## in Horse
sub DESTROY {
  my $self = shift;
  $self->SUPER::DESTROY if $self->can( 'SUPER::DESTROY' );
  print "[", $self->name, " has gone off to the glue factory.]\n";
}

my @tv_horses = map { Horse->named($_) } ('Trigger', 'Mr. Ed');
$_->eat('an apple') for @tv_horses;      # their last meal
print "End of program.\n";
```

This prints:

```
Trigger eats an apple.
Mr. Ed eats an apple.
End of program.
[Mr. Ed has died.]
[Mr. Ed has gone off to the glue factory.]
[Trigger has died.]
[Trigger has gone off to the glue factory.]
```

 Before calling SUPER::DESTROY, we check that we can call it. Although we haven't defined that method and Perl won't complain when it would call it implicitly, if we explicitly call DESTROY, it must be defined.

We'll feed each horse a last meal; at the end of the program, each horse's destructor is called.

The first step of this destructor is to call its parent destructor. Why is this important? Without calling the parent destructor, the cleanup steps needed in the superclasses do not properly execute. That's not much if it's a debugging statement as we've shown, but if it was the "delete the temporary file" cleanup method, we wouldn't delete that file!

So, the rule is that we should always include a call to `$self->SUPER::DESTROY` in our destructors (even if we don't yet have any base/parent classes).

Whether we call it at the beginning or the end of our own destructor is a matter of hotly contested debate. If our derived class needs some superclass instance variables, we should call the superclass destructor after we complete our operations because the superclass destructor will likely alter them in annoying ways. On the other hand, in the example, we called the superclass destructor before the added behavior, because we wanted the superclass behavior first.

Indirect Object Notation

The arrow syntax for invoking a method is sometimes called the *direct object* syntax[2] because there's also the *indirect object* syntax, also known as the "only works sometimes" syntax, for reasons we will explain in a moment. We can generally replace what we'd write with the arrow notation:

```
Class->class_method(@args);
$instance->instance_method(@other);
```

with the method name preceding the class name and the arguments at the end:

```
class_method Class @args;
instance_method $instance @other;
```

This idiom was more prevalent in the earlier days of v5, and we're still trying to eradicate it from the world. We wish that we didn't have to cover it here, because if you don't know about it you can't use it. Regardless, other people use it so you need to recognize it. The notation sticks around in otherwise good code and documentation so you need to know what is going on. We've encouraged you to always use the arrow notation:

```
my $obj = Some::Class->new(@constructor_params);
```

However, some Perlers put the new first to make the statement read more like English:

```
my $obj = new Some::Class @constructor_params;
```

This makes the C++ people feel right at home. In Perl, there's nothing special about the name new, but at least the syntax is hauntingly familiar.

---

2. We can also call is the *dative syntax*, although not many people use that term.

Why the "generally" caveat when we can replace the arrow syntax with indirect object syntax? Well, if the instance is something more complicated than a simple scalar variable:

```
$somehash->{$somekey}->[42]->instance_method(@parms);
```

then we can't swap it around to the indirect notation:

```
instance_method $somehash->{$somekey}->[42] @parms;
```

The only things acceptable to indirect object syntax are a bareword (e.g., a class name), a simple scalar variable, or braces denoting a block returning either a blessed reference or a class name.[3] This means we have to write it like we showed you for filehandle references in Chapter 8:

```
instance_method { $somehash->{$somekey}->[42] } @parms;
```

And that goes from simple to uglier in one step. There's another downside: ambiguous parsing. When we developed the classroom materials concerning indirect object references, we wrote:

```
my $cow = Cow->named('Bessie');
print name $cow, " eats.\n";
```

because we were thinking about the indirect object equivalents for:

```
my $cow = Cow->named('Bessie');
print $cow->name, " eats.\n";
```

However, the latter works; the former doesn't. We were getting no output. Finally, we enabled warnings and got this interesting series of messages:

```
Unquoted string "name" may clash with future reserved word at ./foo line 92.
Name "main::name" used only once: possible typo at ./foo line 92.
print( ) on unopened filehandle name at ./foo line 92.
```

 Using warnings should be the first step when Perl does something we don't understand. Or maybe it should be the zeroth because we should normally have warnings in effect whenever we're developing code.

Ahh, so that line was being parsed as:

```
print name ($cow, " eats.\n");
```

In other words, print the list of items to the filehandle named name. That's clearly not what we wanted, so we had to add additional syntax to disambiguate the call.

---

3. Astute readers will note that these are the same rules as for an indirect filehandle syntax, from which indirect object syntax directly mirrors, as well as the rules for specifying a reference to be dereferenced.

The ambiguity shows up because print itself is a method called on the filehandle. You're probably used to thinking of it as a function, but remember that missing comma after the filehandle. It looks like our indirect object calling syntax, because it is. This leads us to our next strong suggestion: use the arrow syntax at all times.

We realize, though, that some people write new Class ... rather than Class->new(...), and that most of us are fine with that. Older modules preferred that notation in their examples, and once you write it that way you tend to keep doing it that way. However, there are circumstances in which even that can lead to ambiguity (e.g., when a subroutine named new has been seen, and the class name itself has not been seen as a package). When in doubt, ignore indirect object syntax. Your maintenance programmer will thank you.

Additional Instance Variables in Subclasses

One of the nice things about using a hash for a data structure is that derived classes can add additional instance variables without the superclass knowing we added them. For example, we derive a RaceHorse class that is everything a Horse is but also tracks its race results. The first part of this is trivial. We create a RaceHorse subclass in *lib/RaceHorse.pm*:

```
package RaceHorse;
use parent qw(Horse);
```

We'll also want to initialize "no wins of no races" when we create a new RaceHorse. We do this by extending the named subroutine and adding four additional fields (wins, places, shows, and losses for first-, second-, and third-place finishes, and none of the above):

```
package RaceHorse;
use parent qw(Horse);
## extend parent constructor:
sub named {
  my $self = shift->SUPER::named(@_);
  $self->{$_} = 0 for qw(wins places shows losses);
  $self;
}
```

Here, we pass all parameters to the superclass, which should return a fully formed Horse. However, because we pass RaceHorse as the class, we bless it into the RaceHorse class. This is the same the way the Animal constructor created a Horse, not an Animal, when passed Horse as the class in Chapter 13. Next, we add the four instance variables that go beyond those defined in the superclass, setting their initial values to 0. Finally, return the modified RaceHorse to the caller.

It's important to note here that we've actually "opened the box" a bit while writing this derived class. We know that the superclass uses a hash reference and that the superclass hierarchy doesn't use the four names chosen for a derived class. This is because RaceHorse will be a "friend" class (in C++ or Java terminology), accessing the instance variables directly. If the maintainer of Horse or Animal ever changes representation or names of variables, there could be a collision, which might go undetected until that important day when we're showing off our code to the investors. Things get even more interesting if the hashref is changed to an arrayref as well.

One way to decouple this dependency is to use composition rather than inheritance as a way to create a derived class. In this example, we need to make a Horse object an instance variable of a RaceHorse and put the rest of the data in separate instance variables. You also need to pass any inherited method calls on the RaceHorse down to the Horse instance, through delegation. However, even though Perl can certainly support the needed operations, that approach is usually slower and more cumbersome. Enough on that for this book, however.

Next, we provide some accessor methods:

```
package RaceHorse;
use parent qw(Horse);
## extend parent constructor:
sub named {
  my $self = shift->SUPER::named(@_);
  $self->{$_} = 0 for qw(wins places shows losses);
  $self;
}
sub won { shift->{wins}++; }
sub placed { shift->{places}++; }
sub showed { shift->{shows}++; }
sub lost { shift->{losses}++; }
sub standings {
  my $self = shift;
  join ', ', map "$self->{$_} $_", qw(wins places shows losses);
}
```

In *scripts/racehorse.pl*, we create a program to try our new horse:

```
use RaceHorse;
my $racer = RaceHorse->named('Billy Boy');
# record the outcomes: 3 wins, 1 show, 1 loss
$racer->won;
$racer->won;
$racer->won;
$racer->showed;
$racer->lost;
print $racer->name, ' has standings of: ', $racer->standings, ".\n";
```

This prints:

```
Billy Boy has standings of: 3 wins, 0 places, 1 shows, 1 losses.
[Billy Boy has died.]
[Billy Boy has gone off to the glue factory.]
```

Note that we're still getting the `Animal` and `Horse` destructor. The superclasses are unaware that we've added four additional elements to the hash, so they still function as they always have.

Using Class Variables

What if we want to list all of the animals we've made so far? Animals may exist all over the program namespace but are lost once they're handed back from the `named` constructor method. They aren't really lost, but we haven't been keeping track of them.

We can record the created animal in a hash and iterate over that hash. The key to the hash can be the stringified form of the animal reference,[4] while the value can be the actual reference, allowing us to access its name or class.

For example, we extend `named` by recording each animal creation:

```
## in Animal
my %REGISTRY;
sub named {
  my $class = shift;
  my $name = shift;
  my $self = { Name => $name, Color => $class->default_color };
  bless $self, $class;
  $REGISTRY{$self} = $self;  # also returns $self
}
```

The uppercase name for `%REGISTRY` is a reminder that this variable is more global than most variables. Here, it's a metavariable that contains information about many instances. We can still use a lexical variable, but this time it is in the file scope.[5]

When we use `$self` as a key, Perl *stringifies* it, which means it turns into a string unique to the object.

We also need to add a new method:

```
sub registered {
  return map { 'a '.ref($_)." named ".$_->name } values %REGISTRY;
}
```

Now we can see all the animals we've made:

```
my @cows = map Cow->named($_), qw(Bessie Gwen);
my @horses = map Horse->named($_), ('Trigger', 'Mr. Ed');
my @racehorses = RaceHorse->named('Billy Boy');
print "We've seen:\n", map(" $_\n", Animal->registered);
print "End of program.\n";
```

---

4. Or any other convenient and unique string.

5. The file scope is as close as Perl gets to a private class variable without using other tricks.

This prints:

```
We've seen:
    a RaceHorse named Billy Boy
    a Horse named Mr. Ed
    a Horse named Trigger
    a Cow named Gwen
    a Cow named Bessie
End of program.
[Billy Boy has died.]
[Billy Boy has gone off to the glue factory.]
[Bessie has died.]
[Gwen has died.]
[Trigger has died.]
[Trigger has gone off to the glue factory.]
[Mr. Ed has died.]
[Mr. Ed has gone off to the glue factory.]
```

Note that the animals appear to die at their proper time because the variables holding the animals are all being destroyed at the final step. They really don't though, because we created an extra reference we have to clean up, and we'll handle that in the next section.

Weakening the Argument

The %REGISTRY variable also holds a reference to each animal, even if we toss away the containing variables, for instance, by letting them go out of scope:

```
{
  my @cows = map Cow->named($_), qw(Bessie Gwen);
  my @horses = map Horse->named($_), ('Trigger', 'Mr. Ed');
  my @racehorses = RaceHorse->named('Billy Boy');
}
print "We've seen:\n", map("  $_\n", Animal->registered);
print "End of program.\n";
```

The animals aren't destroyed even though none of the code is holding the animals. At first glance, it looks like we can fix this by altering the destructor:

```
## in Animal
sub DESTROY {
  my $self = shift;
  print '[', $self->name, " has died.]\n";
  delete $REGISTRY{$self};
}
## this code is bad (see text)
```

But this still results in the same output. Why? Because Perl doesn't call the destructor until the last reference is gone, but the last reference won't be destroyed until the destructor is called.[6]

---

6. We'd make a reference to chickens and eggs, but that would introduce yet another derived class to Animal.

One solution for Perl versions 5.8 and later (and we shouldn't be using anything earlier) is to use weak references. A *weak* reference doesn't count as far as the reference counting, um, counts. It's best illustrated by example.

The weak reference mechanism is built into the core of Perl v5.8. We need an external interface for the weaken routine though, which can be imported from the Scalar::Util module:[7]

```
## in Animal
use Scalar::Util qw(weaken); # in 5.8 and later

sub named {
  ref(my $class = shift) and croak 'class only';
  my $name = shift;
  my $self = { Name => $name, Color => $class->default_color };
  bless $self, $class;
  $REGISTRY{$self} = $self;
  weaken($REGISTRY{$self});
  $self;
}
```

When Perl counts the number of active references to a thingy,[8] it won't count any that have been converted to weak references by weaken. If all ordinary references are gone, Perl deletes the thingy and turns any weak references to undef.

Now we'll get the right behavior for:

```
my @horses = map Horse->named($_), ('Trigger', 'Mr. Ed');
print "alive before block:\n", map("  $_\n", Animal->registered);
{
  my @cows = map Cow->named($_), qw(Bessie Gwen);
  my @racehorses = RaceHorse->named('Billy Boy');
  print "alive inside block:\n", map("  $_\n", Animal->registered);
}
print "alive after block:\n", map("  $_\n", Animal->registered);
print "End of program.\n";
```

This prints:

```
alive before block:
  a Horse named Trigger
  a Horse named Mr. Ed
alive inside block:
  a RaceHorse named Billy Boy
  a Cow named Gwen
  a Horse named Trigger
  a Horse named Mr. Ed
  a Cow named Bessie
[Billy Boy has died.]
[Billy Boy has gone off to the glue factory.]
```

---

7. In v5.6, we can emulate the same function using the WeakRef CPAN module.

8. A *thingy*, as defined in *Programming Perl*, and then Perl's own documentation, is anything a reference points to, such as an object. If we were especially pedantic persons, we would call it a referent instead.

```
[Gwen has died.]
[Bessie has died.]
alive after block:
    a Horse named Trigger
    a Horse named Mr. Ed
End of program.
[Mr. Ed has died.]
[Mr. Ed has gone off to the glue factory.]
[Trigger has died.]
[Trigger has gone off to the glue factory.]
```

Notice that the racehorses and cows die at the end of the block, but the ordinary horses die at the end of the program. Success!

Weak references can also solve some memory leak issues. For example, suppose an animal wanted to record its pedigree. The parents might want to hold references to all their children while each child might want to hold references to each parent.

We can weaken one or the other (or even both) of these links. If we weaken the link to the child, Perl can destroy the child when all other references are lost, and the parent's link becomes undef (or we can set a destructor to completely remove it). However, a parent won't disappear as long as it still has offspring. Similarly, if the link to the parent is weakened, we'll get it as undef when the parent is no longer referenced by other data structures. It's really quite flexible.

 When using weak references, always ensure you don't dereference a weakened reference that has turned to undef.

Without weakening, as soon as we create any parent-child relationship, both the parent and the child remain in memory until the final global destruction phase regardless of the destruction of the other structures holding either the parent or the child.

Be aware though: use weak references carefully; don't throw them at a problem of circular references. If you destroy data that is held by a weak reference before its time, you may have some very confusing programming problems to solve and debug.

Exercise

You can find the answer to this exercise in "Answers for Chapter 18" on page 349.

1. [45 minutes] Modify the RaceHorse class to get the previous standings from persistent storage (e.g., DBM, Storable, JSON, and so on) when the horse is created, and update the standings when the horse is destroyed.

For example, running this program four times:

```
my $runner = RaceHorse->named('Billy Boy');
$runner->won;
print $runner->name, ' has standings ', $runner->standings, ".\n";
```

should show four additional wins. Make sure that a RaceHorse still does everything a normal Horse does otherwise.

## CHAPTER 19

Introduction to Moose

Moose is a relatively new object system for Perl and is available from CPAN.[1] It's become popular enough in the community that we think it deserves its own chapter in this book. We think everyone still needs to learn the basics of Perl, but when we get into the real world of programming, other people are going to tell us to use Moose.

The goal of Moose is to make OO Perl less tedious by making it easier for us to do the stuff we should do and probably normally skip. It also allows powerful code through its meta-object protocol, which we won't cover here.

In this chapter, we go through the classes we created in the previous chapters and redo them with basic Moose features. We can cover only the basics; Moose deserves its own book.

Making Animals with Moose

First, we'll create a horse class in *Horse.pm* that has a name and a color:

```
package Horse;
use Moose;

has 'name'  => ( is => 'rw' );
has 'color' => ( is => 'rw' );

no Moose;

__PACKAGE__->meta->make_immutable;

1;
```

Bringing in Moose defines has, which takes the name of an attribute along with its properties. Here, we're saying that the two attributes are "read/write," or rw. Moose sets up the accessors to set and fetch the values so we don't have to.

---

1. Moose has its own website, *http://moose.perl.org/*.

When we are done defining our class, we use `no Moose` to unimport the subroutines that Moose imported. We can also use `namespace::autoclean`, which works not only for Moose, but other, non-Moose modules we might write:

```
package Horse;
use Moose;
use namespace::autoclean;

has 'name'  => ( is => 'rw' );
has 'color' => ( is => 'rw' );

__PACKAGE__->meta->make_immutable;

1;
```

Finally, we call the meta object to tell it to make our class *immutable*, meaning that we don't plan on changing it. This makes things a bit faster since the Moose underpinnings don't have to constantly check its meta-object system for changes.

We can now use our Horse class in a program:

```
use Horse;
use v5.10;

my $talking = Horse->new( name => "Mr. Ed" );
$talking->color( "grey" ); # sets the color

say $talking->name, ' is colored ', $talking->color;
```

Note that we didn't have to define methods for new, color, or name: Moose does that for us.

As we wrote in previous chapters, these methods aren't special to a Horse, so we can define them in Animal. We can do that rather simply. In *Animal.pm*, we use the same thing we had previously in *Horse.pm*, although we change the package name:

```
package Animal;
use Moose;
use namespace::autoclean;

has 'name'  => ( is => 'rw' );
has 'color' => ( is => 'rw' );

__PACKAGE__->meta->make_immutable;

1;
```

 We don't have to define our own constructor in Animal because Moose does that for us. We *can* define our own if we need to. See Moose::Manual for more about Moose features we don't show.

To use Animal from Horse, we define the inheritance by using Moose's extends instead of parent:

```
package Horse;
use Moose;
use namespace::autoclean;

extends 'Animal';

__PACKAGE__->meta->make_immutable;

1;
```

With this, the Horse class is just Animal with a different package name. We need to add the sound method to make our horses go "neigh." We can add another attribute with a default:

```
package Horse;
use Moose;
use namespace::autoclean;

extends 'Animal';

has 'sound' => ( is => 'ro', default => 'neigh' );

__PACKAGE__->meta->make_immutable;

1;
```

To use sound, we need our speak method in Animal. We can define our own methods without using the Moose sugar. We also add a default sound dies with a message:

```
package Animal;
use Moose;
use namespace::autoclean;

has 'name'  => ( is => 'rw' );
has 'color' => ( is => 'rw' );
has 'sound' => ( is => 'ro', default => sub {
  confess shift, " needs to define sound!"
  } );

sub speak {
  my $self = shift;
  print $self->name, " goes ", $self->sound, "\n";
}

__PACKAGE__->meta->make_immutable;

1;
```

If the subclass does not define a sound, we use confess, which Moose gives us for free. Our program now looks like:

```
use Horse;

my $talking = Horse->new( name => "Mr. Ed" );
$talking->speak;
```

Roles Instead of Inheritance

So far, we have translated what we did previously to the same structure using Moose. There are many more features that we could use. Instead of inheriting from Animal, we could make it a *role*.

 A role is like a mix-in or a trait. Instead of inheriting the methods, they are added to our class without disturbing the inheritance tree.

Instead of using Moose, we use Moose::Role. When we do that, we don't need a default sound subroutine because we can use the role features to denote that all classes using this role need to define their own sound:

```
package Animal;
use Moose::Role;
use namespace::autoclean;

requires qw( sound );

has 'name'  => ( is => 'rw' );
has 'color' => ( is => 'rw' );

sub speak {
  my $self = shift;
  print $self->name, " goes ", $self->sound, "\n";
}

1;
```

To include a role in our class, we use with in place of extends:

```
package Horse;
use Moose;
use namespace::autoclean;

with 'Animal';

sub sound { 'neigh' }

__PACKAGE__->meta->make_immutable;
```

If we don't define sound, Moose::Role will give us a long backtrace noting our failure.

Default Values

Moose supports the notion of a default value. We add in the default color, and make that a class responsibility as well:

```
package Animal;
use Moose::Role;
use namespace::autoclean;

requires qw( sound default_color );

has 'name'  => ( is => 'rw' );
has 'color' => (
  is => 'rw',
  default => sub { shift->default_color }
);

sub speak {
  my $self = shift;
  print $self->name, " goes ", $self->sound, "\n";
}

1;
```

If the color isn't provided, the default color of the class will be consulted and ensures that the concrete class provides this default color. Our derived animal classes now look much simpler.

In *lib/Cow.pm*:

```
package Cow;
use Moose;
use namespace::autoclean;

with 'Animal';
sub default_color { 'spotted' }
sub sound { 'moooooo' }

__PACKAGE__->meta->make_immutable;

1;
```

In *lib/Horse.pm*:

```
package Horse;
use Moose;
use namespace::autoclean;

with 'Animal';
sub default_color { 'brown' }
sub sound { 'neigh' }

__PACKAGE__->meta->make_immutable;

1;
```

In *lib/Sheep.pm*:

```
package Sheep;
use Moose;
use namespace::autoclean;

with 'Animal';
sub default_color { 'black' }
sub sound { 'baaaah' }

__PACKAGE__->meta->make_immutable;

1;
```

Now we can count sheep as one of our implemented classes:

```
use Sheep;
my $baab = Sheep->new( color => 'white', name => 'Baab' );
$baab->speak; # prints "Baab goes baaaah"
```

In that example, we used a subroutine reference to set the color if we don't supply one. We could also just set the value directly by using a string (or other value):

```
has 'color' => (
  is => 'rw',
  default => 'white',
);
```

Constraining Values

If we set the color of an animal, we should probably check that the value is actually a color. Some of these calls shouldn't work:

```
$sheep->color( 'black' );
$sheep->color( 'Dolly' );    # oops, that's a name!
$sheep->color( 'Porkchop' ); # that's a name, too!
$sheep->color( 1/137 );      # what color is that?
$sheep->color( '#FFCCAA' );  # web safe sheep?
```

We didn't do anything in our earlier examples to limit the values that our methods would accept. Moose provides a way for us to reject some arguments with infinite flexibility. The has can take an isa argument:

```
has 'color' => ( is => 'rw', isa => 'Str' );
```

The Str type isn't particularly useful here because Perl still converts numbers to strings. None of the other default types listed in Moose::Util::TypeConstraints work for us either.

We can make our own type constraint by defining a subtype. In this example, we declare ColorStr as a subtype of Str, but we can also give it a validation subroutine as part of where. We check that the value, passed in as $_, exists in %colors. If it fails, we get the error string we supply in message:

```
{
  use Moose::Util::TypeConstraints;
  use namespace::autoclean;

  {
    my %colors = map { $_, 1 } qw( white brown black );
    subtype 'ColorStr'
      => as 'Str'
      => where { exists $colors{$_} }
      => message {
        "I don't think [$_] is a real color"
      };
  }
}
```

That might be too much work, though, to check merely for existence in a set. Instead, we can use enum to define a subtype:

```
{
  use Moose::Util::TypeConstraints;
  use namespace::autoclean;
  enum 'ColorStr' => [qw( white brown black )];
}
```

We only have to define these constraints once and they are available everywhere in our program. We're adding them to the Moose system, not just the class or file where we define them.

Now, although we've called these "type constraints" and Moose called them "type constraints," they aren't really the same thing that we see in other languages. Perl isn't going to tell us ahead of time that we've had a type violation. We don't find out until we try to call the method. That is, Moose isn't changing the dynamic nature of Perl. Think of these as parameter validation.

Wrapping Methods

Our Mouse class was special, because it extended speak with an another line of output. While we could use SUPER::-based method calls to call parent class behaviors, we can't do this with roles because they don't use inheritance. However, Moose lets us wrap existing methods. Using after, we can replace speak with a method that first calls the original speak then does our extra work (properly preserving the calling context):[2]

```
package Mouse;
use Moose;
use namespace::autoclean;

with 'Animal';

sub default_color { 'white' }
sub sound { 'squeak' }
```

---

2. We can wrap any subroutine with Hook::LexWrap, also available on CPAN.

```
after 'speak' => sub {
  print "[but you can barely hear it!]\n";
};

__PACKAGE__->meta->make_immutable;
1;
```

Now we have a speaking mouse:

```
use Mouse;
my $mickey = Mouse->new( name => 'Mickey' );
$mickey->speak;
```

Our output includes the extra line:

```
Mickey goes squeak
[but you can barely hear it!]
```

If we had wanted the extra behavior before we called the original method, we could have used before instead of after. Or, we could do stuff before *and* after the original method by using around. We can use that to handle both class and instance methods as we did earlier:

```
package Animal;
...
has 'name' => (is => 'rw');
around 'name' => sub {
  my $next = shift;
  my $self = shift;
  blessed $self ? $self->$next(@_) : "an unnamed $self";
};
```

We create the base behavior for name with has, but then surround it with around. The first argument to our new subroutine is the reference to the original method, followed by the usual arguments to a method. We check $self to see if it is a blessed reference. If it is, we call the method. If $self is not blessed, it must be a class name and we use an unnamed $self.

That around assumes that we gave our animal a name when we made our object. We don't have to specify a name. If we don't give new a name or specify one later, we can use a default name based on the class name:

```
has 'name' => (
  is => 'rw',
  default => sub { 'an unnamed ' . ref shift },
);
```

To force people to specify a name so we don't have to supply a default, we can make it a required attribute:

```
has 'name' => (
  is => 'rw',
  required => 1,
);
```

When we try to make an unnamed animal, we get an error:

```
Attribute (name) is required at constructor Sheep::new
```

Read-Only Attributes

If we don't want to let people change the color of their animals, we can make that attribute read-only with ro instead of rw:

```
has 'color' => (
  is => 'ro',
  default => sub { shift->default_color }
);
```

If we try to call color with an argument, we get an error:

```
Cannot assign a value to a read-only accessor
```

That doesn't mean we can never change the color. We can designate another method that can do the work:

```
has 'color' => (
  is => 'ro',
  writer => '_private_set_color',
  default => sub { shift->default_color },
);
```

Even though we can't change the color of a mouse directly:

```
my $m = Mouse->new;
my $color = $m->color;
$m->color('green');   # DIES
```

We can still use our private name instead:

```
$m->_private_set_color('green');
```

By convention, a leading underscore denotes a private method that we shouldn't use outside the class. This doesn't mean it's really a private method though.

Improving the Race Horse

We create a race horse by adding "racer features" to our Horse class.

We define the parts related to racing as a role. In our previous example, we had to inherit from Horse and RaceHorse. Now we can get rid of the multiple inheritance because we replace one of the parent classes with a role:

```
package Racer;
use Moose::Role;
use namespace::autoclean;
```

```
has $_ => (is => 'rw', default => 0)
  foreach qw(wins places shows losses);

1;
```

The has is just a subroutine, so we can call it as any other subroutine. We use a postfix foreach to make several methods that are all read/write and have a starting value of 0.

We add some methods to increment the values for each statistic and a standings method to create a summary:

```
package Racer;
...
sub won    { my $self = shift; $self->wins($self->wins + 1) }
sub placed { my $self = shift; $self->places($self->places + 1) }
sub showed { my $self = shift; $self->shows($self->shows + 1) }
sub lost   { my $self = shift; $self->losses($self->losses + 1) }

sub standings {
  my $self = shift;
  join ", ", map { $self->$_ . " $_" } qw(wins places shows losses);
}
...
```

Some people might think it would be easier just to access the hash directly, since this looks cleaner:

```
sub won { shift->{wins}++; }
```

However, we don't know what the wins method actually does. We showed before, after, and around. We subvert those when we break encapsulation. We should trust the interface.

To create a race horse, we extend a horse with the racer role:

```
package RaceHorse;
use Moose;
use namespace::autoclean;

extends 'Horse';
with 'Racer';

__PACKAGE__->meta->make_immutable;
1;
```

And now we can ride the ponies:

```
use RaceHorse;
my $s = RaceHorse->new( name => 'Seattle Slew' );
$s->won;
$s->won;
$s->won;
$s->placed;
$s->lost;
print $s->standings, "\n"; # 3 wins, 1 places, 0 shows, 1 losses
```

Further Study

We've only scratched the surface of what Moose provides. We can make powerful and flexible custom constructors (notice we don't have one anywhere in this chapter), coerce argument values to the right types, handle multiple roles and dispatch appropriately when roles conflict, and many other things you can read about in the Moose documentation.

Exercises

You can find the answers to these exercises in "Answers for Chapter 19" on page 349.

1. [45 minutes] Reimplement your Animal classes as Moose classes, making the subclasses extend Animal. Adjust your documentation and tests to handle the changes. Ensure you update your build file for any new dependencies.

2. [10 minutes] Adjust the distribution you created in Exercise 1 to use Animal as a role instead of a parent class.

## CHAPTER 20

Advanced Testing

In this chapter, we offer a taste of some of the more popular test modules, along with some advanced features of `Test::More`. Unless we say otherwise, these modules are not part of the Perl standard distribution (unlike `Test::More`) and we'll need to install them ourselves. You might feel a bit cheated by this chapter since we're going to say "See the module documentation" quite a bit, but we're gently nudging you out into the Perl world. For much more detail, you can also check out *Perl Testing: A Developer's Notebook*, which covers the subject further.

Skipping Tests

In some cases, we want to skip tests. For instance, some of our features may only work for a particular version of Perl, a particular operating system, or only work when optional modules are available. To skip tests, we do much the same thing we did for the `TODO` tests, but `Test::More` does something much different.

We again use a bare block to create a section of code to skip, and we label it with `SKIP`. While testing, `Test::More` will not execute these tests, unlike the `TODO` block where it ran them anyway. At the start of the block, we call the `skip` function to tell it why we want to skip the tests and how many tests we want to skip.

In this example, we check if the `Mac::Speech` module is installed before we try to test the `say_it_aloud` method. If it isn't, the `eval` block returns false and we execute the `skip` function:

```
SKIP: {
  skip 'Mac::Speech is not available', 1
    unless eval { require Mac::Speech };

  ok( $tv_horse->say_it_aloud( 'I am Mr. Ed' );
}
```

When `Test::More` skips tests, it outputs special ok messages to keep the test numbering right and to tell the test harness what happened. Later, the test harness can report how many tests we skipped.

We shouldn't skip tests because they aren't working right. We use the TODO block for that. We use SKIP when we want to make tests optional in certain circumstances.

Testing Object-Oriented Features

For OO modules, we want to ensure that we get back an object when we call the constructor. For this, Test::More's isa_ok and can_ok are good interface tests:

```
use Test::More;

BEGIN{ use_ok( 'Horse' ); }
my $trigger = Horse->named('Trigger');
isa_ok($trigger, 'Horse');
isa_ok($trigger, 'Animal');
can_ok($trigger, $_) for qw(eat color);
done_testing();
```

These tests have default test names, so our test output looks like this:

```
ok 1 - use Horse;
ok 2 - The object isa Horse
ok 3 - The object isa Animal
ok 4 - Horse->can('eat')
ok 5 - Horse->can('color')
1..5
```

Here we're testing that it's a horse, but also that it's an animal, and that it can both eat and return a color. We could further test to ensure that each horse has a unique name:

```
use Test::More;

BEGIN{ use_ok( 'Horse' ); }

my $trigger = Horse->named('Trigger');
isa_ok($trigger, 'Horse');

my $tv_horse = Horse->named('Mr. Ed');
isa_ok($tv_horse, 'Horse');

# Did making a second horse affect the name of the first horse?
is($trigger->name, 'Trigger', "Trigger's name is correct");
is($tv_horse->name, 'Mr. Ed', "Mr. Ed's name is correct");
is(Horse->name, 'a generic Horse');

done_testing();
```

The output of this shows us that the unnamed horse is not quite what we thought it was:

```
ok 1 - use Horse;
ok 2 - The object isa Horse
ok 3 - The object isa Horse
ok 4 - Trigger's name is correct
ok 5 - Mr. Ed's name is correct
not ok 6
```

```
#    Failed test at t/horse.t line 14.
#         got: 'an unnamed Horse'
#    expected: 'a generic Horse'
1..6
# Looks like you failed 1 test of 6.
```

Oops! Look at that. We wrote a generic Horse, but the string really is an unnamed Horse. That's an error in our test, not in the module, so we should correct that test error and retry. Unless the module's specification actually called for "a generic Horse."[1] We shouldn't be afraid to just write the tests and test the module. If we get either one wrong, the other will generally catch it.

Grouping Tests

Not every test represents a logical test of our code. We may actually want to test several things leading up to testing a single feature. We can group those tests into a unit that represents one test by using Test::More's subtest feature. We give it a label, this time as the *first* argument, and a code reference that groups our tests:

```
use Test::More;

subtest 'Major feature works' => sub {
    ok( defined &some_subroutine, 'Target sub is defined' );
    ok( -e $file, 'The necessary file is there' );
    is( some_subroutine(), $expected, 'Does the right thing' );
  };

done_testing();
```

At the top level, the three tests in the code reference count as a single test. TAP accomplishes this with nested tests. The output for the subtests is indented and has its own plan:

```
ok 1 - Target sub is defined
ok 2 - The necessary file is there
ok 3 - Does the right thing
1..3
  ok 1 - Major feature works
  1..1
```

If all of the subtests pass, the overall test passes. We could modify our *t/Animal.t* test to group the tests for the speak and sound subroutines, and adjust the plan to only count the top-level tests:

```
use strict;
use warnings;

use Test::More tests => 3;
```

1. And we'll find that the tests not only check the code, but they create the specification in code form.

```
BEGIN {
  use_ok( 'Animal' ) || print "Bail out!\n";
}


subtest 'sound() works' => sub {
  ok( defined &Animal::sound, 'Animal::sound is defined' );
  eval { Animal->sound() } or my $at = $@;
  like( $at, qr/You have/, 'sound() dies with a message' );
};

subtest 'speak() works' => sub {
  ok( defined &Animal::speak, 'Animal::speak is defined' );
  eval { Animal->speak() } or my $at = $@;
  like( $at, qr/You have/, 'speak() dies with a message' );
};
```

Testing Large Strings

We showed in Chapter 14 that when a test fails, Test::More can show us what we expected and what we actually got:

```
use Test::More;
is( "Hello Perl", "Hello perl" );
done_testing();
```

When we run this program, Test::More shows us what went wrong:

```
% perl test.pl
not ok 1
#      Failed test (test.pl at line 5)
#           got: 'Hello Perl'
#      expected: 'Hello perl'
1..1
# Looks like you failed 1 test of 1.
```

What if that string is really long? We don't want to see the whole string, which might be hundreds or thousands of characters long. We just want to see where they start to be different:

```
use Test::More;
use Test::LongString;

is_string(
  "The quick brown fox jumped over the lazy dog\n" x 10,

  "The quick brown fox jumped over the lazy dog\n" x 9 .
  "The quick brown fox jumped over the lazy camel",
  );

done_testing();
```

The error output doesn't have to show us the whole string to tell us where things went wrong. It shows us the relevant parts along with the string lengths. Although our

---

example is a bit contrived, imagine doing this with a web page, configuration file, or some other huge chunk of data that we don't want cluttering our testing output:

```
not ok 1
#   Failed test in long_string.pl at line 6.
#        got: ..." the lazy dog\x{0a}"...
#     length: 450
#   expected: ..." the lazy camel"...
#     length: 451
#   strings begin to differ at char 447
1..1
# Looks like you failed 1 test of 1.
```

Testing Files

The code to test things like file existence and file size is simple, but the more code we write, and the more parts each code statement has, the more likely we are to not only mess up, but also miscommunicate our intent to the maintenance programmer.

We could test for file existence very easily. We use the -e file test operator in the ok function from Test::More. That works just fine:

```
use Test::More;
ok( -e 'minnow.db' );

done_testing();
```

Well, that works just fine if that's what we meant to test, but nothing in that code tells anyone what we meant to do. What if we wanted to ensure the file did not exist before we started testing? The code for that is a difference of one character:

```
use Test::More;
ok( ! -e 'minnow.db' );

done_testing();
```

We could add a code comment, but most code comments seem to assume that we already know what's supposed to happen. Does this comment let us know which of the two situations we want? Should we pass the test if the file is there?

```
use Test::More;
# test if the file is there
ok( ! -e 'minnow.db' );

done_testing();
```

The Test::File module, written by brian, encapsulates intent in the name of the function. If we want the test to pass when the file is there, we use file_exists_ok:

```
use Test::More;
use Test::File;

file_exists_ok( 'minnow.db' );
```

```
done_testing();
```

If we want the test to pass when the file is not there, we use `file_not_exists_ok`:

```
use Test::More;
use Test::File;

file_not_exists_ok( 'minnow.db' );

done_testing();
```

That's a simple example, but the module has many other functions that follow the same naming scheme: the first part of the name tells us what the function checks, `file_exists`, and the last part tells us what happens if that's true, `_ok`. It's a lot harder to miscommunicate the intent when we have to type it out:

```
use Test::More;
use Test::File;

my $file = 'minnow.db';

file_exists_ok(    $file );
file_not_empty_ok( $file );
file_readable_ok(  $file );
file_min_size_ok(  $file, 500 );
file_mode_is(      $file, 0775 );

done_testing();
```

So, not only do the explicit function names communicate intent, but they also contribute to parallel structure in the code.

Testing STDOUT or STDERR

One advantage to using the `ok` functions (and friends) is that they don't write to STDOUT directly, but to a filehandle secretly duplicated from STDOUT when our test script begins. If we don't change STDOUT in our program, this is a moot point. But if we wanted to test a routine that writes something to STDOUT, such as making sure a horse eats properly, we need to be careful:

```
use Test::More;
use_ok 'Horse';
isa_ok(my $trigger = Horse->named('Trigger'), 'Horse');

open STDOUT, ">test.out" or die "Could not redirect STDOUT! $!";
$trigger->eat("hay");
close STDOUT;

open T, "test.out" or die "Could not read from test.out! $!";
my @contents = <T>;
close T;
is(join("", @contents), "Trigger eats hay.\n", "Trigger ate properly");
```

```
done_testing();

END { unlink "test.out" }  # clean up after the horses
```

Just before we start testing the eat method, we (re-)open STDOUT to our temporary output file. The output from this method ends up in the *test.out* file. We bring the contents of that file in and give it to the is function. Even though we've closed STDOUT, the is function can still access the original STDOUT, and thus the test harness sees the proper ok or not ok messages.

If we create temporary files like this, we need to remember that our current directory is the same as the build script, not the location of the test program. Also, we need to pick fairly safe cross-platform names if we want people to be able to use and test our module portably.

There is a better way to do this though. The Test::Output module can handle this for us. This module gives us several functions that automatically take care of all of the details:

 Older versions of Test::Output module have some problems reading some special cases of output. See *http://www.dagolden.com/wp-content/uploads/2009/04/how-not-to-capture-output-in-perl.pdf*.

```
use Test::More;
use Test::Output;

sub print_hello { print STDOUT "Welcome Aboard!\n" }
sub print_error { print STDERR "There's a hole in the ship!\n" }

stdout_is( \&print_hello, "Welcome Aboard!\n" );

stderr_like( \&print_error, qr/ship/ );

done_testing();
```

All of the functions take a code reference as their first argument, but that's not a problem because we told you all about those in Chapter 7. If we don't have a subroutine to test, we wrap the code we want to test in a subroutine and use that:

```
sub test_this {
  print_error();
  print STDERR "Some other output";
  ...;
}

stdout_is( \&test_this, ... );
```

If our code is short enough, we might want to skip the step where we define a named subroutine and use an anonymous one:

```
    stdout_is( sub { print "Welcome Aboard" }, "Welcome Aboard" );
```

We can even use an inline block of code, like we did with grep and map. As with those two list operators, notice that we don't have a comma after the inline code block:

```
    stdout_is { print "Welcome Aboard" } "Welcome Aboard";
```

Besides Test::Output, we can do something similar with Test::Warn, which specifically tests warning output. Its interface uses the inline block form exclusively:

```
    use Test::More;
    use Test::Warn;

    sub add_letters { "Skipper" + "Gilligan" }

    warnings_like { add_letters() } [qr/numeric/, qr/numeric/];

    done_testing();
```

We all strive to make our code warning free, and we can test for that, too. Perl warnings can change from version to version, and we want to know when the new warnings pop up, or if Perl will emit warnings on one of our customer's computers. The Test::NoWarnings module is a bit different from the ones we've already shown. It automatically adds a test just by loading the module and we just have to ensure we add the hidden test to the count we give to Test::More:

```
    use Test::More tests => 1;
    use Test::NoWarnings;

    my( $n, $m );
    # use an uninitialized value
    my $sum = $n + $m;
```

When we try to compute the sum, we use two variables to which we haven't given values. That triggers the annoying "use of uninitialized value" warning (ensure we have warnings turned on!). We don't want those sorts of things filling up our logfiles, now, do we? Test::NoWarnings tells us when that happens so we can fix it:

```
    1..1
    not ok 1 - no warnings
    #   Failed test 'no warnings'
    #   in /usr/local/lib/perl5/5.8.7/Test/NoWarnings.pm at line 45.
    # There were 2 warning(s)
    #       Previous test 0 ''
    #       Use of uninitialized value in addition (+) at nowarnings.pl line 6.
    #
    # ----------
    #       Previous test 0 ''
    #       Use of uninitialized value in addition (+) at nowarnings.pl line 6.
    #
    # Looks like you failed 1 test of 1 run.
```

Using Mock Objects

Sometimes we don't want to ramp up the entire system to test only parts of it. We can be fairly certain, or at least assume, that other parts of the system work. We don't need to open expensive database connections or instantiate objects with large memory footprints to test every part of the code.

The `Test::MockObject` module creates "pretend" objects. We give it information about the parts of the object's interface we want to use, and it pretends to be that part of the interface. Basically, the pretend method has to return the right thing when we call it, and it doesn't have to do any processing.

Instead of creating a real `Minnow` object, which would mean turning on all sorts of things on the boat, we can create a mock object for it instead. Once we create the mock object and store it in `$Minnow`, we tell it how to respond to the methods we need to call. In this case, we tell the mock object to return true for `engines_on` and to return false for `moored_to_dock`. We're not really testing the object for the ship, but we want to test our quartermaster object, which takes a ship as an argument. Rather than test the quartermaster with a real ship, we use our mock one:

```
use Test::More;
use Test::MockObject;

# my $Minnow = Real::Object::Class->new( ... );
my $Minnow = Test::MockObject->new();

$Minnow->set_true( 'engines_on' );
$Minnow->set_true( 'has_maps' );
$Minnow->set_false( 'moored_to_dock' );

ok( $Minnow->engines_on, "Engines are on" );
ok( ! $Minnow->moored_to_dock, "Not moored to the dock" );

my $Quartermaster = Island::Plotting->new(
  ship => $Minnow,
  # ...
  )

ok( $Quartermaster->has_maps, "We can find the maps" );

done_testing();
```

We can create more complex methods that do anything we like. Suppose, instead of methods that return true or false, we need one that returns a list. Perhaps we need to pretend to connect to a database and retrieve some records. As we're developing, we might try this several times and we'd rather not connect and disconnect from the real database every time we try to track down a bug.

In this example, we mock the database method `list_names`, which we know will return us three names. Since we already know this, and we're actually testing something else (which we don't show in this contrived example), it doesn't bother us to create the mock method that stands in place of the real database:

```
use Test::More;
use Test::MockObject;

my $db = Test::MockObject->new();

# $db = DBI->connect( ... );
$db->mock(
  list_names => sub { qw( Gilligan Skipper Professor ) }
  );

my @names = $db->list_names;

is( scalar @names, 3, 'Got the right number of results' );
is( $names[0], 'Gilligan', 'The first result is Gilligan' );

print "The names are @names\n";

done_testing();
```

Writing Our Own Test::* Modules

We don't have to wait for other people to write cool test modules. If we have a particular testing situation that we'd like to wrap up in a test function, we can write our own Test::* module using the Test::Builder module, which handles all of the tricky integration with Test::Harness and Test::More. If we look behind the scenes of many of the Test::* modules, we'll likely find Test::Builder.

Again, the advantage to test functions is that they wrap reusable code in a function name that describes the expected behavior. To test something, we use the function name rather than typing out a bunch of separate statements. It's easy for people to understand what we mean to test based on a single function name, but that gets harder as we write out several statements to do the same thing.

In Chapter 4, we wrote some code to check that the castaways had all of their required items. We turn that into a Test::* module. Here's the check_required_items subroutine as we left it in Chapter 4:

```
sub check_required_items {
  my $who = shift;
  my $items = shift;
  my %whose_items = map { $_, 1 } @$items;
  my @required = qw(preserver sunscreen water_bottle jacket);
  my @missing = ( );
  for my $item (@required) {
    unless ( $whose_items{$item} ) { # not found in list?
      print "$who is missing $item.\n";
      push @missing, $item;
    }
  }
}
```

```
  if (@missing) {
    print "Adding @missing to @$items for $who.\n";
    push @$items, @missing;
  }
}
```

We need to turn this into a `Test::*` module that simply checks the items (so it doesn't add the missing ones) and then outputs the right thing. The basics for any new testing module is the same. We call our new module `Test::Minnow::RequiredItems` and start with this stub:

```
package Test::Minnow::RequiredItems;
use strict;
use warnings;

use Exporter qw(import);
use vars qw(@EXPORT $VERSION);

use Test::Builder;

my $Test = Test::Builder->new();

$VERSION = '0.10';
@EXPORT  = qw(check_required_items_ok);

sub check_required_items_ok {
  # ....
  }

1;
```

We start by declaring the package, then turning on strictures and warnings because we want to be good programmers (even if this 3-hour tour is ultimately doomed, it won't be from one of our software errors). We pull in the `Exporter` module and add `check_required_items_ok` to `@EXPORT` since we want that function to show in the calling namespace, just as we showed in Chapter 17. We set `$VERSION` just like we showed in Chapter 12. The only stuff we haven't shown is `Test::Builder`. At the beginning of our test module we create a new `Test::Builder` object, which we assign to the lexical variable `$Test`, which is scoped to the entire file.[2]

The `$Test` object is going to handle all of the testing details for us. We remove all of the output parts from `check_required_items`, and we take out the parts to modify the input list. Once we go through the other logic, the only thing we need to do at the end is tell the test harness if the test is `ok` or `not_ok`:

```
sub check_required_items {
  my $who = shift;
  my $items = shift;
  my %whose_items = map { $_, 1 } @$items;
  my @required = qw(preserver sunscreen water_bottle jacket);
```

---

2. It's almost like a global variable, except it doesn't live in a package and can't be seen outside its file.

```
    my @missing = ( );
    for my $item (@required) {
      unless ( $whose_items{$item} ) { # not found in list?
        push @missing, $item;
      }
    }
    if (@missing) {
    ...
    }
    else {
    ...
    }
  }
```

Now we have to add the parts to turn our function into a testing one. We call methods on $Test to tell the test harness what happened. In each case, the last evaluated expression should be a call to $Test->ok so that becomes the return value of the entire function.

 We often don't use the return value since most people call most test functions in a void context, but we might as well return something that makes sense.

If we discover missing items, we want the test to fail so we pass a false value to $Test ->ok, but before we do that we use $Test->diag with a message to tell us what went wrong:

```
sub check_required_items_ok {
  my $who = shift;
  my $items = shift;
  my %whose_items = map { $_, 1 } @$items;
  my @required = qw(preserver sunscreen water_bottle jacket);
  my @missing = ( );
  for my $item (@required) {
    unless ( $whose_items{$item} ) { # not found in list?
      push @missing, $item;
    }
  }
  if (@missing) {
    $Test->diag( "$who needs @missing.\n" );
    $Test->ok(0);
  }
  else {
    $Test->ok(1);
  }
}
```

That's it. Although there are more things that we can do, there isn't more that we have to do. Once we save our Test::Minnow::RequiredItems, we can use it immediately in a test script. We still use Test::More to set the plan:

```
use Test::More;
use Test::Minnow::RequiredItems;

my @gilligan = (
  Gilligan => [ qw(red_shirt hat lucky_socks water_bottle) ]
  );

check_required_items_ok( @gilligan );

done_testing();
```

 We could set the plan from our module, but most likely the test script will use other modules, too. Only one of them can set the plan, so we let Test::More handle that.

Since Gilligan doesn't have all of his required items, the test fails. It prints the not_ok along with the diagnostic message:

```
not ok 1
1..1
# Gilligan needs preserver sunscreen jacket.
#     Failed test (/Users/Ginger/Desktop/package_test.pl at line 49)
# Looks like you failed 1 test of 1.
```

And, now that we've created Test::Minnow::RequiredItems module, how do we test the test? We can use the Test::Builder::Tester module. You'll have to investigate that one yourself, though.

Exercises

You can find the answers to these exercises in "Answers for Chapter 20" on page 352.

1. [30 minutes] Use the Test::File module to check for the existence and readability of the */etc/hosts* file on Unix and the *C:\windows\system32\drivers\etc\hosts* file on Windows (or, if you don't have those files, choose one you do have). Skip the test for the platform you are not on by inspecting the value of $^O (capital O) variable. You can add this test file to your distribution for My::List::Util or use it as a standalone program.

2. [30 minutes] Write your own test module (Test::My::List::Util), that has a single test function (sum_ok), which takes two arguments: the actual sum and the expected sum. Print a diagnostic message if the two do not match:

    ```
    my $sum = sum( 2, 2 );
    sum_ok( $sum, 4, 'The sums match' );
    ```

Besides the example in this chapter, you can also look at the source for Test::File (or most other Test::* modules) to get ideas for your module.

## CHAPTER 21

Contributing to CPAN

Besides allowing others in our organization to receive the benefits of these wonderful modules and distributions we've created, we can contribute to the Perl community at large. The mechanism for sharing your work is the Comprehensive Perl Archive Network (CPAN), which is almost 20 years old as we write this and has over 100,000 different modules.

The Comprehensive Perl Archive Network

We covered the basic CPAN mechanics in Chapter 2, but that was from a user's perspective. Now we want to contribute to CPAN, so we have to look at it from an author's perspective.

It's no accident that CPAN is so useful. The ethos of the project has been that anyone should be able to contribute and that it should be easy for people to share their work. The unofficial CPAN motto is "upload early, upload often." We don't have to finish our code to start sharing it with others.

Remember that CPAN is a big storage device. That's its magic. Everything else that revolves around it, such as MetaCPAN (*https://www.metacpan.org/*), CPAN.pm, and CPANPLUS, merely uses what's already there; there's no need for creation.

Getting Prepared

Since CPAN is a big file storage site, we need to upload our distribution. To contribute to CPAN, we need two things:

- Something to contribute, ideally already in the shape of a module
- A Perl Authors Upload Server (PAUSE) account

The PAUSE account is our passport to contributing to CPAN. We get a PAUSE account simply by asking.[1] We fill out a web form (linked from there) with a few basic details, such as our name, email address, and our preferred PAUSE account name. At the moment, PAUSE names must be between four and nine characters. (Some legacy PAUSE names are only three characters long.)[2] All accounts are human approved, mostly to protect against bots and duplicate accounts, so it may take a day or so for the request to be approved. It's rare that there is any problem with that. If you skipped the introduction of this book, or didn't set up a PAUSE account when we told you to, do it right now (or the next time you can get network access) so it's waiting for you to use when you need it later in this chapter.

Once we have our PAUSE account, we need to think globally about our contribution. Because our module will be used in programs along with other modules from other authors, we need to ensure that the package names for modules don't collide with existing modules or confuse the people who browse CPAN. Luckily for us, there is a loose collection of volunteers on the Perl Modules list (*modules@perl.org*) who've been working with CPAN and modules for quite a while and who can help you sort through most problems.

How PAUSE Works

PAUSE is the way we insert our modules and programs into CPAN. Each account gets its own directory. Randal's directory is *authors/id/M/ME/MERLYN*. You'll see these directories when you browse CPAN. When Randal uploads a distribution, it goes into his directory. He could upload almost anything he likes, too. It all ends up in his directory.

Randal doesn't have to work alone, though. Although he may upload code, he doesn't have to be the person who wrote it. Likewise, he can write code and someone else can upload it for him. Some distributions have more than one maintainer, and some projects specifically designate a release manager. PAUSE always puts the distribution in the uploader's directory. Some distributions rotate the release manager duties, so each new distribution shows up in a different author directory. As such, for the rest of this chapter, we talk about the *uploader*, and if we say "author," we really mean "uploader."

PAUSE does some work to index each distribution and produces a mapping from namespaces to distributions. In CPAN, that's the *modules/02packages.details.txt.gz*, which has lines with a namespace, version, and distribution path:

---

1. You should already have your PAUSE account if you did the exercises in Chapter 1, but if not, go to *http://www.cpan.org/modules/04pause.html*.

2. Originally, the PAUSE names had to be five characters or less, until Randal wanted the MERLYN name, and the appropriate accommodation was made.

```
File::Finder           0.53  M/ME/MERLYN/File-Finder-0.53.tar.gz
File::Finder::Steps    0.53  M/ME/MERLYN/File-Finder-0.53.tar.gz
File::Findgrep         0.02  S/SB/SBURKE/File-Findgrep-0.02.tar.gz
File::FindLib          0.001001  T/TY/TYEMQ/File-FindLib-0.001001.tar.gz
File::Flock            2008.01  M/MU/MUIR/modules/File-Flock-2008.01.tar.gz
```

The CPAN clients use these data to find the distribution they need to fetch to install a module. When we run the client:

```
% cpan File::Finder
```

The program looks in *modules/02packages.details.txt.gz* to find `File::Finder`. It gets the latest version number and compares it to what we have already installed. If the version number in the index is greater, the client knows it needs to fetch *M/ME/ MERLYN/File-Finder-0.53.tar.gz*. It appends that path to the CPAN mirror address to get the full URL, such as *http://www.cpan.org/authors/id/M/ME/MERLYN/File-Finder -0.53.tar.gz*.

The *02packages.details.txt.gz* file lists each namespace exactly once, and lists only the latest version it indexed.

The Indexer

Everything starts when we upload a distribution to PAUSE. Anything we upload goes into our author directory. The trick, though, is to upload something that people can install with a CPAN client.

Log into PAUSE and upload your distribution at *https://pause.perl.org/ pause/authenquery?ACTION=add_uri*.

When PAUSE notices a new distribution, it tries to index it by unpacking it and looking at the namespaces the distribution contains. It compares the namespaces it finds in the distribution to a list of namespaces it has previously indexed. A successful indexing adds the namespace and version to *02packages.details.txt.gz*.

If PAUSE has never seen the namespace, the uploader gets *first come* privileges for that name, and PAUSE indexes the namespace and the module version (looking for `$VERSION`). The uploader only gets permissions on that exact namespace, not every namespace below it. For instance, when Randal uploaded `File::Finder`, he got first-come permissions on that namespace, but not on `File::Finder::Enhanced`, a namespace under the hierarchy of `File::Finder` but not in his distribution. Anyone else can upload a module with a namespace under `File::Finder`, even if it has nothing to do with Randal's module.

If PAUSE has seen that namespace before and the uploader has maintainership privileges, PAUSE compares the version number of the module to the one it indexed previously. If the new version is larger, it indexes the namespace and updates the version. If the version is lower, it does not index the namespace and sends a failure report to the uploader. The distribution still goes into the uploader's directory.

If PAUSE has seen the namespace before but the uploader does not have maintainership privileges, PAUSE does not index that namespace. The distribution still goes into the uploader's directory, but that namespace won't show up in the metadata files. Other people can still download it from CPAN, but they have to fetch the file distribution file by its path.

Since PAUSE goes through this process for every namespace it finds in the distribution, it might index some of them and ignore others. When we run into this problem, PAUSE sends us an email. These completely or partially unindexed distributions may still show up in search results, but may be tagged as "Unauthorized."

 PAUSE uses the email address we configured in our account, so if we try to get around that with a bad address such as *gilligan@no.spam*, we'd never see PAUSE's helpful messages.

Module Maintainers

We mentioned the first-come maintainer in the previous section. There are two other sorts of maintainership.

- The *first-come maintainer* is the person who uploaded the namespace first. A *modulelist* maintainer has completed the additional step of optionally registering the namespace (*https://pause.perl.org/pause/authenquery?ACTION=apply_mod*).
- The *primary maintainer* is the person configured to be responsible for the namespace permissions. By default, this is the first-come person, but the primary maintainership can also be passed on to someone else. The primary maintainer can assign comaintainer permissions to other people, but, as the name denotes, there is only one primary maintainer.
- A *comaintainer* has the permissions to upload and index a namespace, but cannot give comaintainer permissions to other people.

A primary maintainer can pass on that role to another person, but they can also give it up without designating another primary maintainer, leaving the namespace with no one who can create new comaintainers.

Sometimes, all of the maintainers disappear. Some lose interest in the modules that they no longer use for their work, others move on in life, and some are too busy. When no one wants to hand over a module, the PAUSE admins can help. They have a process for transferring control of a namespace to new developers when the original authors have disappeared.

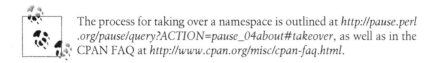

The process for taking over a namespace is outlined at *http://pause.perl .org/pause/query?ACTION=pause_04about#takeover*, as well as in the CPAN FAQ at *http://www.cpan.org/misc/cpan-faq.html*.

It's easy to find out who has which permissions on a namespace. The PAUSE website will let you search for modules or authors, then display the namespace, author, and permission.

Before We Start Work

Before we start to write our module, we should do a little research that might end up saving us a lot of time.

Is there a module that already does what we need? Are we reinventing a subset of something that already exists, or can we contribute our work as a patch to another module? We might find something that's really close but needs a little extra help. Instead of creating yet another mostly done module, collaborate on the existing one. If the original author has disappeared, the PAUSE admins can transfer maintainership.

We should figure out a good name for our module, and that name should make sense to the universe, just not our use of it. How does that name fit into the names already on CPAN? What name will help people find our work? Once we choose a name and release it to the public, we're virtually stuck with it because people have already used it in their code and are loathe to change it. The people who read the module-authors@perl.org and modules@perl.org mailing lists have experience helping people choose good module names, and the PAUSE admins have naming guidelines.

For the PAUSE naming guidelines, see *https://pause.perl.org/pause/au thenquery?ACTION=pause_namingmodules*.

If we tell the world what we are working on, the community of Perl developers might know about a module that already does what we were thinking of doing. With over 100,000 modules on CPAN, that's not such a bad bet. We don't have to know all of the modules ourselves. We have to know enough people who could collectively know them.

Preparing the Distribution

Once we settle on our module name and we've tested our module with its new name (if needed), we should ensure it is ready for distribution. Once it's out there, people can see it. If we used one of the module creation tools, we should already have these files. If we made our module by hand, we should ensure that we've included these files.

> *Writing Perl Modules for CPAN* by Sam Tregar (Apress) is an entire book about what we try to summarize in this tiny chapter. It's a bit old, but things haven't changed that much.

Create or Update the README

Create (or update) a *README* file. This file is automatically extracted to a separate file on the CPAN archives and lets someone view or download the key facts about your distribution before fetching or unpacking the rest.

Check the Build File

Make and test your *Makefile.PL* or *Build.PL*. Modules without a working build file, or without any build file, still go into the CPAN but usually are met with angry complaints from downloaders. One of the common complaints is missing prerequisites in the build file (see Chapter 12).

Update the Manifest

We need to ensure our *MANIFEST* is up to date. If we had added files that should be part of the distribution, those files also need to be in the *MANIFEST*. The distribution archive only includes the files we list in that file.

One quick trick is to clean things up as you would want them in the distribution, and then invoke `./Build manifest` (or `make manifest`), which updates the *MANIFEST* file to be exactly what is in the distribution directory.

> These are not the glob patterns we would put in *.gitignore* or use on the command line.

If `./Build manifest` adds too many files, we can create a *MANIFEST.SKIP* file that has a set of Perl regular expressions that tells `./Build manifest` which files to ignore. Here's a sample *MANIFEST.SKIP* that *module-starter* creates:

```
# Avoid configuration metadata file
^MYMETA\.

# Avoid Module::Build generated and utility files.
\bBuild$
\bBuild.bat$
```

```
\b_build
\bBuild.COM$
\bBUILD.COM$
\bbuild.com$
^MANIFEST\.SKIP

# Avoid archives of this distribution
\bAnimal-[\d\.\_]+
```

This is a text file. We can add anything we like to it. If we added *lib/Kangaroo.pm*, `./Build manifest` adds it for us because it's a new file in the distribution and it's not excluded by any of the patterns in *MANIFEST.SKIP*:

```
% ./Build manifest
File 'MANIFEST.SKIP' does not exist: Creating a temporary 'MANIFEST.SKIP'
Added to MANIFEST: lib/Kangaroo.pm
```

If we added some files, such as making the distribution a Git repository, `./Build manifest` will add them:

```
% ./Build manifest
File 'MANIFEST.SKIP' does not exist: Creating a temporary 'MANIFEST.SKIP'
Added to MANIFEST: .git/config
Added to MANIFEST: .git/description
Added to MANIFEST: .git/HEAD
Added to MANIFEST: .git/hooks/applypatch-msg.sample
Added to MANIFEST: .git/hooks/commit-msg.sample
Added to MANIFEST: .git/hooks/post-commit.sample
...
```

We can exclude those files by adding \.git.* to *MANIFEST.SKIP*. The next time we run `./Build manifest`, those entries disappear (but the files themselves are left alone):

```
% ./Build manifest
Removed from MANIFEST: .git/config
Removed from MANIFEST: .git/description
Removed from MANIFEST: .git/HEAD
Removed from MANIFEST: .git/hooks/applypatch-msg.sample
Removed from MANIFEST: .git/hooks/commit-msg.sample
Removed from MANIFEST: .git/hooks/post-commit.sample
Removed from MANIFEST: .git/hooks/post-receive.sample
Removed from MANIFEST: .git/hooks/post-update.sample
Removed from MANIFEST: .git/hooks/pre-applypatch.sample
Removed from MANIFEST: .git/hooks/pre-commit.sample
Removed from MANIFEST: .git/hooks/pre-rebase.sample
Removed from MANIFEST: .git/hooks/prepare-commit-msg.sample
Removed from MANIFEST: .git/hooks/update.sample
Removed from MANIFEST: .git/info/exclude
Removed from MANIFEST: .gitignore
```

We might go crazy if we had to add entries to *MANIFEST.SKIP* every time we did something. Fortunately, there's a default list of patterns that we can use by including this line in the file:

```
#!include_default
```

That will add the patterns from *ExtUtils/MANIFEST.SKIP* to our existing *MANIFEST.SKIP* (the file is different after we do this). We can see that default list with *perldoc*, although this seems to accidentally work:

```
% perldoc -m ExtUtils/MANIFEST.SKIP
```

Increase the Version String

We need to use a distribution version string that makes sense, and that string needs to be larger (numerically, not stringwise) than the previous version that PAUSE indexed. We can't stress enough: Version 1.9 is greater than version 1.10! It's even more complicated than that, but we don't want to tell the whole story because we're still not over it.

 "Unfortunately, version numbers in Perl aren't boring and easy," writes David Golden. See *http://www.dagolden.com/index.php/369/version -numbers-should-be-boring/*.

Our *Build.PL* file should specify either a `VERSION` value or a `VERSION_FROM` value. If we have a single module (such as a *.pm* file) in our distribution, it's usually best to grab the version number from there with `dist_version_from` (or `VERSION_FROM` in *Makefile.PL*). If we have multiple *.pm* files, we can designate one of them as the source for the version number:

```
my $builder = Module::Build->new(
  module_name       => 'Animal',
  dist_version_from => 'lib/Animal.pm',
  ...
);
```

We can put the version in *Build.PL* directly:

```
my $builder = Module::Build->new(
  module_name    => 'Animal',
  dist_version   => '1.023',
  ...
);
```

Test the Distribution

So far, we've tested our work with the `test` target:

```
% ./Build test
```

That uses our current working directory, including whatever files we've added to the directory. When we archive our distribution, we only include the files in *MANIFEST*. If we forget to update that file or use an overly exclusive pattern in *MANIFEST.SKIP*, some of the files we need for our tests might not make it into the distribution:

```
% ./Build disttest
```

This builds a distribution archive of everything in *MANIFEST*, unpacks the archive into a separate directory, then runs the tests on our distribution. If that doesn't work for us, we can't expect it to work for anyone else who downloads our distribution from the CPAN.

Uploading the Distribution

Once our distribution is ready to share (and maybe even before then), we can upload through the PAUSE page at *https://pause.perl.org/pause/authenquery?ACTION=add _uri*. Log in using your PAUSE name and password then choose one of the upload options. We can upload a file, specify a URL to fetch the distribution, or *claim* a file that we uploaded through an anonymous FTP.

Some online source control services will archive a directory given an appropriate URL.

No matter which way we upload the file, it should appear in the list of uploaded files at the bottom of that page. We might have to wait a bit for PAUSE to fetch remote files, but they usually show up within an hour. If we don't see our PAUSE name next to our distribution name, we can't claim it.

Since we upload to an anonymous, but public, FTP site, other Perl programmers may download directly from the *incoming* directory so they can use the code before PAUSE has even looked at it.

Once PAUSE has the file and knows who it belongs to, it indexes it. You should get an email from the PAUSE indexer telling you what happened. After that, your distribution is on its way to CPAN proper. Remember that the N in CPAN is "Network," so your distribution may take hours or days to reach all of the CPAN mirrors. It shouldn't take longer than a couple of days though, and it usually happens in minutes using some of the fast *rsync* stuff the PAUSE workers have developed.

If you have a problem or think something didn't happen the way it should have, you can ask the PAUSE administrators about it by sending an email to *modules@perl.org*.

Testing on Multiple Platforms

The CPAN Testers (*http://cpantesters.org/*) automatically test almost all distributions uploaded to CPAN. Volunteers around the world automatically download and test each distribution on whatever setup they have. Among them, they test our modules on about every platform, operating system, and *perl* version that matters (and many that we probably don't pay attention to). They send an email to the module authors telling them what happened, and they automatically update the Testers database. We can look at the results for any module through the Testers website (*http://www.cpantesters .org/*) or on MetaCPAN (*https://www.metacpan.org/*).

Often, testers can help us figure out problems for platforms for which we do not have access. Although failing test reports can be frustrating, we should remember to be nice to the testers themselves. It's (usually) not their fault that our distributions don't pass our tests.

Announcing the Module

We release a module partly so other people can use it and partly so other people will improve it. People need to know about our module for either of those to happen. Our module gets noticed automatically in many places, including:

- The "Recent modules" page of CPAN Search (*http://search.cpan.org/recent*)
- The "new modules" section of MetaCPAN (*https://www.metacpan.org/recent*)
- A daily announcement in the "Perl news" mailing list

Many of the short talks at Perl conferences involve the author of a distribution talking about his or her work. After all, who is better qualified to help others use our module than us? The more interested other people are in our module, the better it gets as they send in their bug reports, feature requests, and patches.

 If you want to become a speaker, though, one of us has encouraging words in "Nobody is a good speaker when they start" (*http://blog.yapcna .org/post/17253936133/nobody-is-a-good-speaker-when-they-start*).

If the idea of proposing a conference talk intimidates you a bit (it doesn't intimidate any of the authors anymore), or you don't want to wait that long, look to your local Perl user group. They're generally looking for speakers (usually for the meeting coming up in the next week or two), and the group size is usually small enough to be a nice casual setting. You can generally find a Perl user group near you by looking on the Perl Mongers website (*http://www.pm.org/*). If you can't find a local group, start one!

Exercises

You can find the answers to these exercises in "Answers for Chapter 21" on page 354.

---

1. [5 minutes] Register for your PAUSE account if you don't already have one. You won't get it immediately, but you don't need it to start working.

2. [10 minutes] Ensure your Animal distribution can pass its `disttest` checks. Check that it passes the `test` check first! Make any adjustments you may need to get a passing `disttest`.

3. [45 minutes] Create a new distribution named after your PAUSE name, using the `Acme::*` namespace. For instance, if your PAUSE name is "GILLIGAN," create the `Acme::GILLIGAN::Utils` module. Create a function, `sum`, to add numbers and create a test for that function. Prepare your distribution for upload then upload it to PAUSE.

4. [10 minutes] Add a *lib/Tie/Cycle.pm* to the distribution you created in Exercise 3, perhaps copying it from the `Tie::Cycle` distribution. Prepare your distribution for uploading to PAUSE, ensuring that *lib/Tie/Cycle.pm* shows up in *MANIFEST*. Upload your distribution. Wait for PAUSE to index it so you can see the failure you get for an unauthorized namespace.

5. [20 minutes] Take the `Acme::*` module you created in the previous exercise and change the `sum` function so that it multiplies numbers instead of adding them. The tests should now fail; let them fail so you can see what happens when you upload a broken distribution.

6. [5 minutes] View your distribution's page on MetaCPAN (*https://www.metacpan .org/*). This site updates very quickly from PAUSE, so you should be able to see your module within an hour.

7. [10 minutes] Install your `Acme::*` distribution from CPAN using one of the CPAN clients. You might have to wait until your distribution reaches your configured CPAN mirror.

Answers to Exercises

This appendix contains the answers to the exercises presented throughout the book. Some exercises have additional resources in the Downloads section at *http://www.in termediateperl.com/*.

Answers for Chapter 1

We promised answers to the exercises, but there's not much to do for the first section.

Exercise 1

To get a PAUSE account, which we explain in Chapter 21, we visit *http://pause.perl .org/* and follow the "Request PAUSE account" link. After filling in the information, our application goes to the PAUSE admins for human inspection. We don't have to prove our worthiness; we just have to appear to be human (instead of being a company or a role) and not already have an account. Our application should be approved in a day or two, just in time for us to use it later when we need it.

Once our account is approved, we'll have an *@cpan.org* address with our account name. Our next step is possibly to create a gravatar (*http://www.gravatar.com/*) with that address. The CPAN search interfaces looks for a gravatar attached to our *@cpan.org* address when it wants to display an author picture. See, for instance, *https: //metacpan.org/author/BDFOY*.

Exercise 2

The *http://www.intermediateperl.com/* website has additional material for this book and pictures of alpacas.

Answers for Chapter 2

Exercise 1

The trick in this exercise is to let the modules do all of the hard work. It's a good thing we've shown you how to use modules! The Cwd module ("cwd" is an initialism for "current working directory") automatically imports the getcwd function. We don't have to worry about how it does its magic, but we can be confident that it does it correctly for most major platforms.

Once we have the current path in $cwd, we can use that as the first argument to the catfile method from File::Spec. The second argument comes from the input list to our foreach and shows up in $file:

```
use Cwd;
use File::Spec;

my $cwd = getcwd;

foreach my $file ( glob( ".* *" ) ) {
  print "    ", File::Spec->catfile( $cwd, $file ), "\n";
}
```

If we wanted to use File::Spec::Functions, the code in foreach is a bit shorter:

```
use Cwd;
use File::Spec::Functions;

my $cwd = getcwd;

foreach my $file ( glob( ".* *" ) ) {
  print "    ", catfile( $cwd, $file ), "\n";
}
```

Exercise 2

To install with local::lib so we can install modules with local::lib, we have a chicken and egg problem. We want to install it in our own directories but we don't have local::lib yet. Fortunately, there's a bootstrap process in the documentation.

First, download the local::lib distribution (*https://www.metacpan.org/module/local:: lib*). Unpack the distribution and run the *Makefile.PL* with the --bootstrap option:

```
% perl Makefile.PL --bootstrap
% make install
```

Now we have it installed and we can use it with one of the CPAN tools:

```
% cpan -I Module::CoreList
% cpanm Module::CoreList
```

Inside our program, we load local::lib to pull in the same settings:

```
use local::lib;
use v5.14;
use Module::CoreList;

my @modules     = sort keys $Module::CoreList::version{5.014002};

my $max_length = 0;
foreach my $module ( @modules ) {
  $max_length = length $module if
    length $module > $max_length;
}

foreach my $module ( @modules ) {
  printf "%*s %s\n",
    - $max_length,
    $module,
    $Module::CoreList::released{
        Module::CoreList->first_release( $module )
        };
  }
```

The output looks like:

```
AnyDBM_File                        5
App::Cpan                          5.011003
App::Prove                         5.010001
App::Prove::State                  5.010001
App::Prove::State::Result          5.010001
App::Prove::State::Result::Test    5.010001
```

Although the point of this exercise is local::lib, there are some interesting things in this answer. The first column has the right width so that the numbers in the second column align.

Once we get the list of modules in v5.14.2, we get the length of the longest name by going through all of the module names. In the printf, we use the %*s format specifier. The * tells printf to get the length of the field from the next argument, which is - $max_length. The - left aligns the strings.

We haven't shown map yet (it's the next chapter). If we could use map, we could get rid of the first foreach as we feed all of the lengths to List::Util's max:

```
use List::Util qw(max);

my $max_length = max map { length } @modules;
```

Exercise 3

We install Business::ISBN using one of the CPAN clients:

```
% cpan -I Business::ISBN
% cpanm Business::ISBN
```

Once we have the `Business::ISBN` module, we just follow the example in the documentation. Our program takes the ISBN from the command line and creates the new ISBN object, which we store in `$isbn`. Once we have the object, we follow the examples in the documentation:

```
use Business::ISBN;

my $isbn = Business::ISBN->new( $ARGV[0] );

print "ISBN is "        . $isbn->as_string     . "\n";
print "Group code:    " . $isbn->group_code . "\n";
print "Publisher code: " . $isbn->publisher_code . "\n";
```

Answers for Chapter 3

Exercise 1

Here's one way to do it. The command line arguments show up in the special array `@ARGV` so we use that for our input list. The file test operator `-s` works on `$_` by default, and that's the current element that `grep` tests. All of the files with sizes in bytes smaller than 1,000 bytes end up in `@smaller_than_1000`. That array becomes the input for the map, which takes each element and returns it with spaces tacked on the front and a newline on the end:

```
my @smaller_than_1000 = grep { (-s) < 1000 } @ARGV;

print map { "    $_\n" } @smaller_than_1000;
```

Typically, we'll do that without the intermediate array though:

```
print map { "    $_\n" } grep { (-s) < 1000 } @ARGV;
```

Exercise 2

We chose to use our home directory as the hardcoded directory. When we call `chdir` without an argument, it goes to our home directory (so this is one of the few places where Perl doesn't use `$_` as the default).

After that, an infinite `while` loop keeps our code running, at least until we can't satisfy the condition to `last`, which breaks us out of the loop. Look at the condition carefully: we don't test for truth. What would happen if we wanted to find all the files with a `0` in them? We look for defined values with a nonzero length, so `undef` (end of input) and the empty string (hitting enter) stop the loop.

Once we have our regular expression, we do the same thing we did in the previous answer. This time, we use the result of `glob` as the input list and a pattern match inside the `grep`. We wrap an `eval {}` around the pattern match in case the pattern doesn't compile (for instance, it has an unmatched parenthesis or square bracket):

```
chdir; # go to our home directory

while( 1 ) {
  print "Please enter a regular expression> ";
  chomp( my $regex = <STDIN> );
  last unless( defined $regex && length $regex );

  print
    map { "    $_\n" }
    grep { eval{ /$regex/ } }
    glob( ".* *" );
}
```

Answers for Chapter 4

Exercise 1

We asked to distinguish between these four expressions:

```
$ginger->[2][1]      # 1
${$ginger[2]}[1]     # 2
$ginger->[2]->[1]    # 3
${$ginger->[2]}[1]   # 4
```

They're all referring to the same thing, except for the second one, `${$ginger[2]}[1]`. That one is the same as `$ginger[2][1]`, whose base is the array @ginger, rather than the scalar $ginger.

It's a bit easier to see those when we draw the PeGS. Figure A-1 is the diagram for the expressions with the `->` after `$ginger`, which is a reference (and a scalar because all references are scalars). Figure A-2 is the diagram for `${$ginger[2]}[1]`.

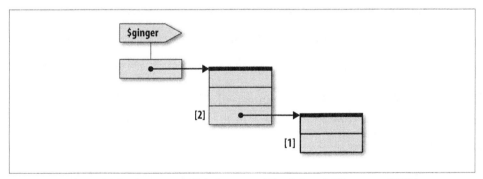

Figure A-1. The PeGS for $ginger->[2][1], $ginger->[2]->[1], and ${$ginger->[2]}[1]

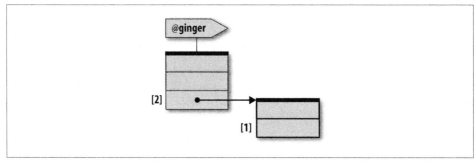

Figure A-2. The PeGS for ${$ginger[2]}}[1], a named array with an array reference element

Exercise 2

First, we construct the hash structure:

```
my @gilligan  = qw(red_shirt hat lucky_socks water_bottle);
my @professor = qw(sunscreen water_bottle slide_rule batteries radio);
my @skipper   = qw(blue_shirt hat jacket preserver sunscreen);
my %all = (
  "Gilligan"  => \@gilligan,
  "Skipper"   => \@skipper,
  "Professor" => \@professor,
);
```

Then we pass it to the first subroutine:

```
check_items_for_all(\%all);
```

In the subroutine, the first parameter is a hashref, so we dereference it to get the keys and the corresponding values:

```
sub check_items_for_all {
  my $all = shift;
  for my $person (sort keys %$all) {
    check_required_items($person, $all->{$person});
  }
}
```

From there, we call the original subroutine:

```
sub check_required_items {
  my $who = shift;
  my $items = shift;
  my @required = qw(preserver sunscreen water_bottle jacket);
  my @missing = (  );
  for my $item (@required) {
    unless (grep $item eq $_, @$items) { # not found in list?
      print "$who is missing $item.\n";
      push @missing, $item;
    }
  }
}
```

```
    if (@missing) {
      print "Adding @missing to @$items for $who.\n";
      push @$items, @missing;
    }
  }
```

Exercise 3

We start with the crew roster program, but we expand it to contain the rest of the castaways. We don't list all the castaways here, but we have a larger file in the Downloads section of *http://www.intermediateperl.com/*:

```
my %gilligan_info = (
  name     => 'Gilligan',
  hat      => 'White',
  shirt    => 'Red',
  position => 'First Mate',
);
my %skipper_info = (
  name     => 'Skipper',
  hat      => 'Black',
  shirt    => 'Blue',
  position => 'Captain',
);
my %mr_howell = (
  name     => 'Mr. Howell',
  hat      => undef,
  shirt    => 'White',
  position => 'Passenger',
);

my @castaways = (\%gilligan_info, \%skipper_info, \%mr_howell);
```

Once we have @castaways, we go through each element and add a hash key to it:

```
foreach my $person (@castaways) {
  $person->{location} = 'The Island';
}
```

After that, we go through @castaways again, skipping each element that is not for a Howell. For the elements that get by that, we change the location:

```
foreach my $person (@castaways) {
  next unless $person->{name} =~ /Howell/;
  $person->{location} = 'The Island Country Club';
}
```

Finally, we go through @castaways once more to make the report:

```
foreach my $person (@castaways) {
  print "$person->{name} at $person->{location}\n";
}
```

We don't have to go through @castaways three times though. We could do it all at once, changing the location then immediately reporting it:

```
foreach my $person (@castaways) {
  if( $person->{name} =~ /Howell/ ) {
    $person->{location} = 'The Island Country Club';
  }
  else {
    $person->{location} = 'The Island';
  }

  print "$person->{name} at $person->{location}\n";
}
```

That looks a bit better with the conditional operator:

```
foreach my $person (@castaways) {
  $person->{location} = ( $person->{name} =~ /Howell/ ) ?
    'The Island Country Club' : 'The Island';

  print "$person->{name} at $person->{location}\n";
}
```

Answers for Chapter 5

Exercise 1

The curly braces of the anonymous hash constructor make a reference to a hash. That's a scalar (as are all references), so it's not suitable to use alone as the value of a hash, which expects pairs of elements. Perhaps this code's author intended to assign to scalar variables (like $passenger_1 and $passenger_2) instead of hashes. But we can fix the problem by changing the two pairs of curly braces to parentheses.

If we tried running this, Perl may have given us a helpful diagnostic message as a warning. If we didn't get the warning, perhaps we didn't have warnings turned on, either with the -w switch or with the warnings pragma. Even if we don't usually use Perl's warnings, we should enable them during debugging. (How long would it take us to debug this without Perl's warnings to help us? How long would it take to enable Perl's warnings? 'Nuff said.)

What if we got the warning message but couldn't tell what it meant? That's what the *perldiag* is for. Warning texts need to be concise because they're compiled into the *perl* binary (the program that runs your Perl code). But *perldiag* lists all the messages we should ever get from Perl, along with a longer explanation of what each one means, why it's a problem, and how to fix it.

If we want to be lazy, we can add use diagnostics; at the beginning of our program, and any error message will look itself up in the documentation and display the entire detailed message. We don't leave this in production code, however, unless we like burning a lot of CPU cycles every time our program starts, whether or not an error occurs.

Exercise 2

We want a count of how much data have been sent to all machines, so at the start, we set the variable $all to a name that will stand in for all of them. It should be a name that will never be used for any real machine. Storing it in a variable is convenient for writing the program and makes it easy to change later:

```
my $all = "**all machines**";
```

The input loop is nearly the same as given in the chapter, but it skips comment lines. Also, it keeps a second running total, filed under $all:

```
my %total_bytes;
while (<>) {
  next if /^#/;
  my ($source, $destination, $bytes) = split;
  $total_bytes{$source}{$destination} += $bytes;
  $total_bytes{$source}{$all} += $bytes;
}
```

Next, we make a sorted list. This holds the names of the source machines in descending order of total transferred bytes. We use this list for the outer for loop. Rather than using a temporary array, @sources, we might have put the sort directly into the parens of the for loop:

```
my @sources =
  sort { $total_bytes{$b}{$all} <=> $total_bytes{$a}{$all} }
  keys %total_bytes;

for my $source (@sources) {
  my @destinations =
    sort { $total_bytes{$source}{$b} <=> $total_bytes{$source}{$a} }
    keys %{ $total_bytes{$source} };
  print "$source: $total_bytes{$source}{$all} total bytes sent\n";
  for my $destination (@destinations) {
    next if $destination eq $all;
    print "  $source => $destination:",
      " $total_bytes{$source}{$destination} bytes\n";
  }
  print "\n";
}
```

Inside the loop, we report the total number of bytes sent from that source machine, then make a sorted list of the destination files (similar to the list in @sources). As we step through that list, we use next to skip over the dummy $all item. Because that item will be at the head of the sorted list, why didn't we use shift to discard it, since that would avoid checking repeatedly for $all inside the inner loop?

Even though the dummy item will sort to the head of the sorted list, it won't necessarily be the first item in the list. If a machine sent data to just one other, that destination machine's total will be equal to the source machine's total output, so that list could sort in either order. You can simplify this program, perhaps. The subexpression $total_bytes{$source} is used many times in the large output for loop (and twice in the input loop as well). That can be replaced by a simple scalar, initialized at the top of the loop:

```
for my $source (@sources) {
  my $tb = $total_bytes{$source};
  my @destinations = sort { $tb->{$b} <=> $tb->{$a} } keys %$tb;
  print "$source: $tb->{$all} total bytes sent\n";
  for my $destination (@destinations) {
    next if $destination eq $all;
    print "  $source => $destination: $tb->{$destination} bytes\n";
  }
  print "\n";
}
```

This makes the code shorter and (likely) a bit faster as well. Give yourself extra credit if you thought to do this. Also give yourself extra credit if you thought that it might be too confusing and decided not to make the change.

Exercise 3

We start with the data aggregation code we had in the chapter:

```
my %total_bytes;
while (<>) {
  next if /\A\s*#/;  # skip comment lines
  my ($source, $destination, $bytes) = split;
  $total_bytes{$source}{$destination} += $bytes;
}
```

After we have filled out %total_bytes, we go through it to print each level. We sort the top-level keys and print each as we use them. After that, we get the second-level hash and put it in $dest_hash, which makes it a little easier to read. We have an inner foreach loop where we do much the same thing, but we report the destination machine and the byte count:

```
foreach my $source ( sort keys %total_bytes ) {
  print "$source\n";
  my $dest_hash = $total_bytes{$source};
  foreach my $dest ( sort keys %$dest_hash ) {
    print "  $dest $dest_hash->{$dest}\n";
  }
}
```

Answers for Chapter 6

Exercise 1

This is similar to what we showed in Chapter 5, but now it uses Storable:

```
use Storable;
```

```
my $all      = "**all machines**";
my $data_file = "total_bytes.data";

my %total_bytes;
if (-e $data_file) {
  my $data = retrieve $data_file;
  %total_bytes = %$data;
}

while (<>) {
  next if /\A\s+#/;   # skip comments
  my ($source, $destination, $bytes)  = split;

  $total_bytes{$source}{$destination} += $bytes;
  $total_bytes{$source}{$all}         += $bytes;
}

store \%total_bytes, $data_file;

### remainder of program is unchanged
```

Near the top, we put the filename into a variable. We can then retrieve the data but only if the data file already exists.

After reading the data, we use Storable again to write it back to the same disk file.

If we chose to write the hash's data to a file the hard way, by writing our own code and our own file format, we're working too hard. More to the point, unless we're extraordinarily talented or spend way too long on this exercise, we almost certainly have bugs in our serialization routines, or at least flaws in our file format.

We could have done much more. There should probably be some checks to ensure that Storable was successful. It will catch some errors (and die), but it will return undef for some. We should check the return values from store and retrieve.

Our program should save the old data file (if any) under a backup filename so that it's easy to revert the latest additions. In fact, it could even keep several backups, such as the last week's worth.

It might also be nice to be able to print the output without having any new input data. As we have it now, we can do this by giving an empty file (such as /dev/null) as the input. However, there should be an easier way. The output functionality could be separated entirely from the updating.

Exercise 2

If we want to use JSON instead of Storable, we have a little more work to do. We need to read the data from the file and reconstitute the data separately. Since JSON data are UTF-8, we have to read the data correctly by specifying the encoding. We covered this in *Learning Perl*, but we'll also say more about it in Chapter 8.

The decode_json takes a UTF-8 string, which is not the same thing as a character string. We need the raw data from the file, and we need it as a single string. The decode_json returns a hash reference, so we have a scalar where we had a hash before:

```perl
use JSON;

my $all       = "**all machines**";
my $data_file = "total_bytes.json";

my $total_bytes;  # need a reference now!
if (-e $data_file) {
  local $/;
  open my $fh, '<:raw', $data_file;
  $json_text   = <$fh>;
  $total_bytes = decode_json( $json_text );
}
```

The middle part of the program is almost the same, except for the reference instead of the hash:

```perl
while (<>) {
  next if /\A\s*#/;  # skip comments
  my ($source, $destination, $bytes)  = split;

  $total_bytes->{$source}{$destination} += $bytes;
  $total_bytes->{$source}{$all}         += $bytes;
}
```

When we are done, we write the data to the file, ensuring to encode it as UTF-8. We can add the pretty flag to to_json to make it easier for us to read:

```perl
{
  open my $fh, '>:utf8', $data_file;
  print $fh to_json( $total_bytes, { pretty => 1 } );
}
```

The rest of our program is the same:

```perl
foreach my $source ( sort keys %$total_bytes ) {
  print "$source\n";
  my $dest_hash = $total_bytes->{$source};
  foreach my $dest ( sort keys %$dest_hash ) {
    print "  $dest $dest_hash->{$dest}\n";
  }
}
```

The JSON output looks like this:

```
{
   "maryann.girl.hut" : {
      "maryann.girl.hut" : 185108,
      "gilligan.crew.hut" : 248228,
      "thurston.howell.hut" : 257710,
      "ginger.girl.hut" : 208854,
      "professor.hut" : 165854,
      "**all machines**" : 1512000,
```

```
        "laser3.copyroom.hut" : 251704,
        "lovey.howell.hut" : 194542
    },
    "gilligan.crew.hut" : {
        "maryann.girl.hut" : 247398,
        "thurston.howell.hut" : 207276,
        "gilligan.crew.hut" : 351378,
        "ginger.girl.hut" : 251480,
        "professor.hut" : 260128,
        "**all machines**" : 1718064,
        "laser3.copyroom.hut" : 224528,
        "lovey.howell.hut" : 175876
    },
    ...
}
```

Answer for Chapter 7

Exercise 1

We can start with the program skeleton from the Download section of *http://www
.intermediateperl.com/*. We have to add our gather_mtime_between subroutines:

```
sub gather_mtime_between {
  my($begin, $end) = @_;
  my @files;
  my $gatherer = sub {
    my $timestamp = (stat $_)[9];
    unless (defined $timestamp) {
      warn "Can't stat $File::Find::name: $!, skipping\n";
      return;
    }
    push @files, $File::Find::name
      if $timestamp >= $begin and $timestamp <= $end;
  };
  my $fetcher = sub { @files };
  ($gatherer, $fetcher);
}
```

The main challenge is getting the item names correct. When using stat inside the callback, the filename is $_, but when returning the filename (or reporting it to the user),
the name is $File::Find::name.

If the stat fails for some reason, the timestamp will be undef. That can happen, for
example, if it finds a dangling symbolic link. In that case, the callback warns the user
and returns early. If we omit that check, we can get warnings of an undefined value
during the comparison with $begin and $end.

When we run the completed program with this subroutine, our output should show
only file modification dates on the previous Monday (unless we changed the code to
use a different day of the week).

Answers for Chapter 8

Exercise 1

In this exercise, we have to use three different output methods: to a file, output to a scalar (and we'll need v5.8 for this), or to both at the same time. The trick is to store the output filehandles in the same variable that we'll use for the print statement. When the filehandle is a variable, we can put anything we like in it, and we can decide what to put in it at runtime:

```
use IO::Tee;
use v5.8;

my $fh;
my $scalar;

print 'Enter type of output [Scalar/File/Tee]> ';
my $type = <STDIN>;

if( $type =~ /^s/i ) {
  open $fh, '>', \$scalar;
}
elsif( $type =~ /^f/i ) {
  open $fh, '>', "$0.out";
}
elsif( $type =~ /^t/i ) {
  open my $file_fh,   '>', "$0.out"
    or die "Could not open $0.out: $!";
  open my $scalar_fh, '>', \$scalar;
  $fh = IO::Tee->new( $file_fh, $scalar_fh );
}

my $date        = localtime;
my $day_of_week = (localtime)[6];

print $fh <<"HERE";
This is run $$
The date is $date
The day of the week is $day_of_week
HERE

print STDOUT <<"HERE" if $type =~ m/^[st]/i;
Scalar contains:
$scalar
HERE
```

In this program, we prompt the user for the type of output, and we want them to type either "scalar," "file," or "tee." Once we read the input, we detect which one they typed by matching on the first character (using a case-insensitive match for more flexibility).

If the user chose "scalar," we open $fh to a scalar reference. If they chose "file," we open $fh to a file as you know from before. We name the file after the program name, stored in `$0`, and append `.out` to it. If the user chose "tee," we create filehandles for a file and a scalar, then combine both of those in an `IO::Tee` object, which we store in `$fh`. No matter which method the user chose, the output channels, whether sole or multiple, end up in the same variable.

From there, it's just a matter of programming, and it doesn't matter much what we actually print. For this exercise, we get the date string by using `localtime` in scalar context, then get the day of the week with a literal list slice.

In the string we print to `$fh`, we include the process ID (contained in the special variable `$$`) so we can tell the difference between separate runs of our program, and then the date and the day of the week.

Finally, if we choose to send the output to a scalar (either alone or with a file), we print the scalar value to STDOUT to ensure the right thing ended up there.

Exercise 2

For this problem, we need to maintain several open filehandles at the same time:

```
my %output_handles;

while (<>) {
  unless (/^([^:]+):/) {
    warn "ignoring the line with missing name: $_";
    next;
  }
  my $name = lc $1;
  unless( $output_handles{$name} ) {
    open my $fh, '>', "$name.info"
      or die "Cannot create $name.info: $!";
    $output_handles{$name} = $fh;
  }

  print { $output_handles{$name} } $_;
}
```

At the beginning of the `while` loop, we use a pattern to extract the person's name from the data line, issuing a warning if that's not found.

Once you have the name, force it to lowercase so that an entry for "Ginger" will get filed in the same place as one for "GINGER." This is also handy for naming the files, as the next statement shows.

Each time we encounter a name, we check for a filehandle stored in `%output_handles`. If we don't find one, we create it and store it in the hash.

After that, we print to the filehandle. Since we access the filehandle through its hash entry, we surround the filehandle argument with braces.

Exercise 3

Here's one way to do it. First, we go through the arguments in @ARGV to find out which ones don't represent directories, then print error messages for each of those.

After that, we go through @ARGV again to find which elements are valid directories. We take the list that comes out of that grep and send it into map where we use opendir to create the directory handle (although we skip the error checking parts). The file output list ends up in @dir_hs, which we go through with the foreach loop and send to print_contents.

There is nothing fancy about print_contents though. It takes its first argument and stores it in $dh, which it then uses to walk through the directory:

```
my @not_dirs = grep { ! -d } @ARGV;
foreach my $not_dir ( @not_dirs ) {
  print "$not_dir is not a directory!\n";
}

my @dirs = grep { -d } @ARGV;

my @dir_hs = map { opendir my $dh, $_; $dh } grep { -d } @ARGV;

foreach my $dh ( @dir_hs ) { print_contents( $dh ) };

sub print_contents {
  my $dh = shift;

  while( my $file = readdir $dh ) {
    next if( $file eq '.' or $file eq '..');
    print "$file\n";
  }
};
```

Answers for Chapter 9

Exercise 1

Most of our *rightmost* program is the same. We initialize the same hash of patterns:

```
my %patterns = (
  Gilligan    => qr/(?:Willie )?Gilligan/,
  'Mary-Ann'  => qr/Mary-Ann/,
  Ginger      => qr/Ginger/,
  Professor   => qr/(?:The )?Professor/,
  Skipper     => qr/Skipper/,
  'A Howell'  => qr/Mrs?. Howell/,
);
```

Instead of passing it patterns, though, we pass the entire hash as a reference, so the rightmost subroutine knows the keys and values:

```
my $key = rightmost(
  'There is Mrs. Howell, Ginger, and Gilligan, Skipper',
  \%patterns
);

say "Rightmost character is $key";
```

In rightmost, we use each to get key-value pairs. We needed v5.12 to do this with arrays, but we can relax that for hashes. As before, we find the matching position by using the value as the pattern. We still remember the greatest position, but we also remember the key that went with that. At the end, we return the key we stored instead of the position:

```
sub rightmost {
  my( $string, $patterns ) = @_;

  my( $rightmost_position, $rightmost_key ) = ( -1, undef );
  while( my( $key, $value ) = each %$patterns ) {
    my $position = $string =~ m/$value/ ? $-[0] : -1;
    if( $position > $rightmost_position ) {
      $rightmost_position = $position;
      $rightmost_key = $key;
    }
  }

  return $rightmost_key;
}
```

Exercise 2

This exercise has two parts. First, we read in a list of patterns from a file and make them into patterns. We read each line, chomp it to get rid of the newline, and use the qr// to precompile the pattern. We catch invalid patterns with eval:

```
open my $fh, '<', 'patterns.txt'
  or die "Could not open patterns.txt: $!";

my @patterns;
while( <$fh> ) {
  chomp;
  my $pattern = eval { qr/$_/ }
    or do { warn "Invalid pattern: $@"; next };
  push @patterns, $pattern;
}
```

We read each line, and test every pattern against it:

```
while( <> ) {
  foreach my $pattern ( @patterns ) {
    print "Match at line $. | $_" if /$pattern/;
```

```
    }
  }
```

If we are going to be that simple, though, merely reporting a match, we can stop once one pattern matches. We can skip to the next line when we find a match:

```
LINE: while( <> ) {
  foreach my $pattern ( @patterns ) {
    if( /$pattern/ ) {
      print "Match at line $. | $_";
      next LINE;
    }
  }
}
```

If we want to know which pattern matched, we could interpolate the pattern into the output:

```
while( <> ) {
  foreach my $pattern ( @patterns ) {
    print "Match of [$pattern] at line $. | $_" if /$pattern/;
  }
}
```

Exercise 3

For the first part, using Regexp::Assemble is much like using an array, just without the array variable. We read a line of input and add it to the $ra object:

```
use Regexp::Assemble;

open my $fh, '<', 'patterns.txt'
  or die "Could not open patterns.txt: $!";

my $ra = Regexp::Assemble->new;

while( <$fh> ) {
  chomp;
  $ra->add( $_ );
}
```

After we add all the patterns, we get the overall pattern. We can output that if we want to see what Regexp::Assemble created for us:

```
my $overall = $ra->re;
print "Regexp is: $overall\n";
```

When we read each line, we have only one check:

```
while( <> ) {
    print "Match at line $. | $_" if /$overall/;
}
```

Answers for Chapter 10

Exercise 1

The Schwartzian Transform saves the result of our -s computation to use later. The first map makes an anonymous array with the original filename and the size. The sort orders each anonymous array by comparing the size element. The last map extracts the filename as the only thing to output to @sorted:

```
use v5.10;

chdir;

my @sorted =
  map   $_->[0],
  sort { $a->[1] <=> $b->[1] }
  map   [$_, -s $_],
  glob '*';

say join "\n", @sorted;
```

Exercise 2

A basic Benchmark program using timethese looks like this, giving hash reference with labels for keys and code references for values:

```
use Benchmark qw(timethese);

timethese( -2, {
  LABEL => CODE_REF,
  LABEL => CODE_REF,
  ...
});
```

We want to compare two snippets that do the same thing, so we make two anonymous subroutines that sort the same list of files. We make the list of files first because we don't want the glob work to be part of the comparison:[1]

```
chdir;
my @files = glob '*';
print 'There are ' . @files . " files to compare\n";

my $ordinary = sub {
  my @sorted = sort { -s $a <=> -s $b } @files;
};
```

---

1. This turns out to be very important, as we explain in *http://www.perlmonks.com/?node_id=393128*. For more benchmarking wisdom, see the "Benchmarking" chapter in *Mastering Perl*.

```
my $transform = sub {
    my @sorted =
        map $_->[0],
        sort { $a->[1] <=> $b->[1] }
        map [$_, -s $_],
        @files;
};
```

Now we call timethese:

```
timethese( -2, {
    Ordinary    => $ordinary,
    Schwartzian => $transform,
});
```

The output shows us that even for a small number of files, the results are dramatic:

```
There are 21 files to compare
Benchmark: running Ordinary, Schwartzian for at least 2 CPU seconds...
   Ordinary:  2 wallclock secs ( 0.51 usr +  1.66 sys =  2.17 CPU) @ 3539.17/s (n=7680)
Schwartzian:  2 wallclock secs ( 1.28 usr +  0.79 sys =  2.07 CPU) @ 8618.36/s (n=17840)
```

Exercise 3

To make a "dictionary" sort, we remove nonletters and lowercase the comparison string while we use the normal Schwartzian Transform:

```
my @dictionary_sorted =
    map $_->[0],
    sort { $a->[1] cmp $b->[1] }
    map {
        my $string = $_;
        $string =~ tr/A-Z/a-z/;
        $string =~ tr/a-z//cd;
        [ $_, $string ];
    } @input_list;
```

Inside the second map, which executes first, we make a copy of $_. (If we don't, we'll mangle the original data.)

This isn't actually a good way to do this sort of thing, though, and we could write a whole book on sorting. First, we assumed ASCII letters, but the world is not ASCII. Instead, we can remove nonletters, which we match with negated Unicode property, \P{Letter}. After that, we use fc, from v5.16, to do a proper case fold:

```
use v5.16;

my @dictionary_sorted =
    map $_->[0],
    sort { $a->[1] cmp $b->[1] }
    map {
        my $string = $_;
        $string =~ s/\P{Letter}//g;  # remove nonletters
        $string = fc( $string );      # a proper case fold
```

```
    [ $_, $string ];
  } @input_list;
```

That's still usually not good enough, though, and when it's not, we reach for Unicode::Collate, which we'll skip in this book.

Exercise 4

In this exercise, we create a recursive subroutine to walk a directory structure using the data_from_path we created in this chapter. You can get that from the Downloads section at *http://www.intermediateperl.com/*. Our task is to take its data structure and report it, indenting each new level.

We want to call it like this, specifying the path, its hash value (either undef or another hash reference), and an indention level:

```
dump_data_for_path( $path, $data, $level );
```

The first part of the subroutine puts the arguments into named variables. We can immediately print the path, but we use the string replication operator, x, along with the indention level to add leading spaces:

```
sub dump_data_for_path {
  my $path  = shift;
  my $data  = shift;
  my $level = shift || 0;

  print '  ' x $level, $path;
```

After that, we look at $data. If it isn't a defined value, we print a newline and return:

```
if( not defined $data ) { # plain file
  print "\n";
  return;
}
```

If $data is a defined value, it should be a hash reference, so we'll check that it has keys. An empty directory will have an empty hash, but that's still a hash. For each key, we call dump_data_for_path again:

```
if( keys %$data ) {
  print ", with contents of:\n";
  foreach (sort keys %$data) {
    dump_data_for_path( $_, $data->{$_}, $level + 1 );
  }
} else {
  print ", an empty directory\n";
}
  }
```

Exercise 5

In the previous exercise, we used recursion. We don't need that though. We can do the task with an iterative solution that gives us more flexibility. The trick is to use a queue. This exercise wants us to allow the iterative `data_for_path` we created to use a breadth-first or depth-first search. This is, really, the decision to put new items to process on the front or the back of the queue (or to not even put them on the queue).

We can do this in many ways. The easiest for us, perhaps, is to have separate subroutines for each technique, but a higher level subroutine that chooses which one to call:

```perl
sub breadth_first {
    ...;
    push @queue, ...;
    ...;
}

sub depth_first {
    ...;
    unshift @queue, ...;
    ...;
}

sub data_for_path {
    my( $path, $threshold, $type ) = @_;
    if( $type eq 'depth-first'  ) { depth_first( $path ) }
    else                          { breadth_first( $path ) }
}
```

However, we have a lot of common code between `breadth_first` and `depth_first`. Instead of two separate subroutines, we can test the traversal type and choose the right one:

```perl
sub data_for_path {
    my( $path, $threshold, $type ) = @_;
    ...;
    if( $type eq 'depth-first' )   { unshift @queue, ... }
    else                           { push @queue, ... }
    ...;
}
```

A full implementation of that idea would look like:

```perl
sub data_for_path {
    my( $path, $type ) = @_;

    my $data = {};

    my @queue = ( [ $path, 0, $data ] );

    while( my $next = shift @queue ) {
        my( $path, $level, $ref ) = @$next;

        my $basename = basename( $path );
```

```
        $ref->{$basename} = do {
          if( -f $path or -l $path ) { undef }
          else {
            my $hash = {};
            opendir my $dh, $path;
            my @new_paths = map {
              catfile( $path, $_ )
              } grep { ! /^\.\.?\z/ } readdir $dh;
            if( $type eq 'depth-first' ) {
              unshift @queue, map { [ $_, $level + 1, $hash ] } @new_paths;
            }
            else {
              push @queue, map { [ $_, $level + 1, $hash ] } @new_paths;
            }
            $hash;
          }
        };
      }

      $data;
    }
```

There are some other tricks that we can use so we don't need this check every time. We can make a code reference that points to either a subroutine that adds to the front or one that adds to the back of an array:

```
sub data_for_path {
  my( $path, $threshold, $type ) = @_;
  my $coderef = $type eq 'depth-first' : \&add_to_front : \&add_to_front;
  ...;
    $coderef->( \@queue, ... );
  ...;
}
```

We'll leave the rest of that for you, though.

Answers for Chapter 11

Exercise 1

Here's one way we can do it. We start with the package directive and strict:

```
package Oogaboogoo::Date;
use strict;
```

We then define the constant arrays to hold the mappings for day-of-week and month names:

```
my @day = qw(ark dip wap sen pop sep kir);
my @mon = qw(diz pod bod rod sip wax lin sen kun fiz nap dep);
```

Next, we define the subroutine for day-of-week number to name. This subroutine will be accessible as Oogaboogoo::Date::day:

```
sub day {
  my $num = shift @_;
  die "$num is not a valid day number"
    unless $num >= 0 and $num <= 6;
  $day[$num];
}
```

Similarly, we have the subroutine for the month-of-year number to name:

```
sub mon {
  my $num = shift @_;
  die "$num is not a valid month number"
    unless $num >= 0 and $num <= 11;
  $mon[$num];
}
```

Finally, we have the mandatory true value at the end of the package:

```
1;
```

We name this file *Date.pm* in the *Oogaboogoo/* directory in one of the directories given in our @INC variable, such as the current directory.

Exercise 2

Here's one way we can do it. We pull in the *.pm* file from a place in our @INC path:

```
use strict;
require 'Oogaboogoo/Date.pm';
```

We get the information for the current time:

```
my($sec, $min, $hour, $mday, $mon, $year, $wday) = localtime;
```

Then we use the newly defined subroutines for the conversions:

```
my $day_name = Oogaboogoo::Date::day($wday);
my $mon_name = Oogaboogoo::Date::mon($mon);
```

The year number is offset by 1900 for historical reasons, so we need to fix that:

```
$year += 1900;
```

Finally, it's time for the output:

```
print "Today is $day_name, $mon_name $mday, $year.\n";
```

Answers for Chapter 12

Exercise 1

We start a new distribution with *module-starter*:

```
% module-starter --module=Animal --author=Gilligan --email="gilligan@example.net" --mb
```

We change into the *Animal* directory and run the build file:

```
% cd Animal
% perl Build.PL
Created MYMETA.yml and MYMETA.json
Creating new 'Build' script for 'Animal' version '0.01'
```

Before we do anything, we run the test target. It's a good idea to test your code before you work to ensure that you have a good starting point. Everything should pass since we haven't done anything yet:

```
% ./Build test
t/00-load.t ....... ok
t/boilerplate.t ... ok
t/manifest.t ...... skipped: Author tests not required
t/pod-coverage.t .. ok
t/pod.t ........... ok
All tests successful.
Files=5, Tests=6,  1 wallclock secs ( ... )
Result: PASS
```

We change *lib/Animal.pm* in some way to create a syntax error. For instance, we remove the semicolon after use strict:

```
use 5.006;
use strict  # syntax error
use warnings;
```

We run the tests again, and the *t/00–load.t* test catches the error:

```
% ./Build test
t/00-load.t ....... 1/1 Bailout called.  Further testing stopped:

#   Failed test 'use Animal;'
#   at t/00-load.t line 6.
#     Tried to use 'Animal'.
#     Error:  syntax error at lib/Animal.pm line 5, near "use strict
# use warnings"
# Compilation failed in require at (eval 4) line 2.
FAILED--Further testing stopped.
```

It's good to know that our tests will catch errors. We don't want tests that appear to work when they shouldn't.

Exercise 2

We create our *module-starter* configuration in our home directory in *.module-starter/config* (or the location we put in MODULE_STARTER_DIR):

```
author: Willie Gilligan
email: gilligan@island.example.com
builder: Module::Build
verbose: 1
```

Now our call to *module-starter* is less annoying:

```
% module-starter --module=Animal
```

Exercise 3

We install `Module::Starter::AddModule`, using any of the techniques we showed in Chapter 2:

```
% cpan -I Module::Starter::AddModule
```

Once we have that, we update our *.module-starter/config* to use the newly installed plug-in:

```
author: Willie Gilligan
email: gilligan@island.example.com
builder: Module::Build
verbose: 1
plugins: Module::Starter::AddModule
```

Now we can easily add another module. If we are in the distribution directory, the --dist argument is just .:

```
% module-starter --module=Cow --dist=.
```

Answers for Chapter 13

Exercise 1

We should already have our `Animal` distribution in place, but if we don't, we create a new distribution, declaring all the classes that we want to make:

```
% module-starter --module=Animal,Cow,Horse,Sheep,Mouse
```

If we already had the distribution with the `Animal` class, we can add modules:

```
% module-starter --module=Cow,Horse,Sheep,Mouse --dist=
```

Here's one way we can do it. We define the `Animal` class in *lib/Animal.pm*, with the speak method. For this answer, we only show you the code bits in abbreviated form, but we actually have the documentation around the code bits:

```
package Animal;
our $VERSION = '0.01';
sub speak {
  my $class = shift;
  print "a $class goes ", $class->sound, "!\n";
}
1;
```

We define each subclass with its specific sound method.

In the *lib/Cow.pm* file:

```
package Cow;
our $VERSION = '0.01';
use parent qw(Animal);
sub sound { 'moooo' }
1;
```

In the *lib/Horse.pm* file:

```perl
package Horse;
our $VERSION = '0.01';
use parent qw(Animal);
sub sound { 'neigh' }
1;
```

In the *lib/Sheep.pm* file:

```perl
package Sheep;
our $VERSION = '0.01';
use parent qw(Animal);
sub sound { 'baaaah' }
1;
```

The `Mouse` package is slightly different because of the extra quietness:

```perl
package Mouse;
our $VERSION = '0.01';
use parent qw(Animal);
sub sound { 'squeak' }
sub speak {
  my $class = shift;
  $class->SUPER::speak;
  print "[but you can barely hear it!]\n";
}
1;
```

We're not done, though. We want to ensure that we haven't made any syntax errors.
We use the *t/00-load.t* test for that. It checks merely that the modules compile correctly.
If we started with the `Animal` class, it only checks *lib/Animal.pm*:

```perl
#!perl -T

use Test::More tests => 1;

BEGIN {
  use_ok( 'Animal' ) || print "Bail out!\n";
}

diag( "Testing Animal $Animal::VERSION, Perl $], $^X" );
```

We update that to check our new classes:

```perl
#!perl -T

use Test::More tests => 5;

BEGIN {
  foreach my $class ( qw(Animal Cow Horse Sheep Mouse) ) {
    use_ok( $class )
      or print "Bail out! $class does not compile!\n";
  }
}
```

With our new test, we run the tests again:

```
% perl Build.PL
% ./Build test
t/00-load.t ....... 1/1
# Testing Animal , Perl 5.014002, /usr/local/perls/perl-5.14.2/bin/perl
t/00-load.t ....... ok
...
```

If our *t/00–load.t* test does not pass, we fix the failing module and try again. The other tests, such as *t/boilerplate.t* and *t/pod.t* probably fail, so we fix our modules until they pass, too.

Exercise 2

Now we need a program that makes our barnyard speak, which we put in *script/ barnyard.pl*. We load all of the modules that we need:

```
use Cow;
use Horse;
use Mouse;
use Sheep;

my @barnyard = ();
{
  print "enter an animal (empty to finish): ";
  chomp(my $animal = <STDIN>);
  $animal = ucfirst lc $animal;                 # canonicalize
  last unless $animal =~ /^(Cow|Horse|Sheep|Mouse)$/;
  push @barnyard, $animal;
  redo;
}

foreach my $beast (@barnyard) {
  $beast->speak;
}
```

This code uses a simple check, via a pattern match, to ensure that the user doesn't enter Alpaca or another unavailable animal, because doing so will crash the program.

Finally, we run our program, getting output such as:

```
% perl scripts/barnyard.pl
enter an animal (empty to finish): Cow
enter an animal (empty to finish): Cow
enter an animal (empty to finish): Sheep
enter an animal (empty to finish): Horse
enter an animal (empty to finish): Kangaroo
A Cow goes mooo!
A Cow goes mooo!
A Sheep goes baaaah!
A Horse goes neigh!
```

That final animal, Kangaroo, breaks out of the loop and never makes it into @barnyard, which is why we don't hear it speak.

Exercise 3

If we already had the distribution with the `Animal` class, we can add a `LivingCreature` and a `Person` module:

```
% module-starter --module=LivingCreature,Person --dist=.
```

We update *t/00–load.t*:

```perl
#!perl -T

use Test::More tests => 7;

BEGIN {
  my @classes = qw(Animal Cow Horse Sheep Mouse
    LivingCreature Person);
  foreach my $class ( @classes ) {
    use_ok( $class )
      or print "Bail out! $class does not compile!\n";
  }
}
```

Here's one way to do it. First, create the base class of `LivingCreature` with a single speak method:

```perl
package LivingCreature;
our $VERSION = '0.01';
sub speak {
  my $class = shift;
  if (@_) {           # something to say
    print "a $class goes '@_'\n";
  } else {
    print "a $class goes ", $class->sound, "\n";
  }
}
1;
```

A person is a living creature, so we inherit from `LivingCreature` and define a simple sound:

```perl
package Person;
use parent qw(LivingCreature);
sub sound { "hmmmm" }
```

The `Animal` class comes next, also inheriting from `LivingCreature`. The main `speak` routine has now moved into the `LivingCreature` class, which means we don't need to write it again to use it in `Person`. In `Animal`, though, you need to check that to ensure an `Animal` won't try to speak before calling `SUPER::speak`:

```perl
package Animal;
use parent qw(LivingCreature);
sub sound { die "all Animals should define a sound" }
sub speak {
  my $class = shift;
  die "animals can't talk!" if @_;
```

```
        $class->SUPER::speak;
    }
```

The other animal classes stay the same. They don't care how Animal does it as long as it happens.

Finally, we create *scripts/person.pl*. We load the new Person class and call its speak method:

```
use Person;

Person->speak;
Person->speak("Hello, World!");
```

When we run it, we see the person say their default sound and the line we gave them:

```
% perl scripts/person.pl
hmmmm
Hello, World!
```

Answers for Chapter 14

Exercise 1

We start by creating our distribution and change into our distribution directory:

```
% module-starter --module=My::List::Util
% cd My-List-Util
```

Instead of going right for the modules, we start with the tests. We want two subroutines, sum and shuffle, so we create *t/sum.t* and *t/shuffle.t*. In each file, we want to test good data, bad data, interface violations, and any other way we can think to break it. Here's a sample *t/sum.t*:

```
use Test::More;

BEGIN { use_ok( 'My::List::Util' ) }

ok( defined &My::List::Util::sum,
    'sum() is defined' );
is( My::List::Util::sum( 1, 2, 3 ), 6,
    '1+2+3 is six' );
is( My::List::Util::sum( qw(1 2 3) ), 6,
    '1+2+3 as strings is six' );
is( My::List::Util::sum( 4, -9, 37, 6 ), 38,
    '4-9+37+6 is six' );
is( My::List::Util::sum( 3.14, 2.2 ), 5.34,
    '3.14 + 2.2 is 5.34' );
is( My::List::Util::sum(), undef,
    'No arguments returns undef' );
is( My::List::Util::sum( qw(a b) ), undef,
    'All bad args gives undef' );
is( My::List::Util::sum( qw(a b 4 5) ), 9,
    'Some good args works' );
```

```
done_testing();
```

And here's a sample *t/shuffle.t*:

```
use Test::More;

BEGIN { use_ok( 'My::List::Util' ) }

ok( defined &My::List::Util::shuffle, 'shuffle() is defined' );

{
my @shuffled = My::List::Util::shuffle();
is( scalar @shuffled, 0, 'No args returns an empty list' );
}

{
my @array = 1 .. 10;
my @shuffled = My::List::Util::shuffle( @array );
is( scalar @array, scalar @shuffled,
  "The output list is the same size" );
isnt( "@array", "@shuffled", "The list is shuffled" );
}

done_testing();
```

We still haven't implemented these subroutines, so these tests fail. In particular, the ok tests fail because we haven't even defined the subroutines. We fix that in *lib/My/List/Util.pm*, along with their documentation stubs so the Pod tests pass:

```
=head2 sum

Returns the sum of the numbers passed to it, ignoring arguments
that don't look like numbers.

=cut

sub sum {
}

=head2 shuffle

Returns a shuffled version of the list.

=cut

sub shuffle {
}
```

We run the tests again, and the situation should be a little better because we've defined the subroutines. Now we need to do the hard bits. The particular implementation doesn't matter as much as the process and the tests. Here's what we might do for sum:

```
=head2 sum

=cut
```

```
sub sum {
  my $sum;
  foreach my $num ( grep {  /\A-?\d+\.*\d*\z/ } @_ ) {
  $sum += $num;
  }
  $sum;
}
```

We adapt the fisher_yates_shuffle from *perlfaq4*:

```
=head2 shuffle

=cut

sub shuffle {
  my @deck = @_;
  return unless @deck;

  my $i = @deck;
  while( --$i ) {
  my $j = int rand ($i+1);
  @deck[$i,$j] = @deck[$j,$i];
  }
  @deck;
}
```

Now all of our tests should pass. That doesn't mean that we are done or that the code is correct. It's a never-ending battle.

Exercise 2

This one was easy. We take the test we showed in the chapter and put it into *t/Animal.t*:

```
use strict;
use warnings;

use Test::More tests => 6;

BEGIN {
  use_ok( 'Animal' ) || print "Bail out!\n";
}

diag( "Testing Animal $Animal::VERSION, Perl $], $^X" );

# they have to be defined in Animal.pm
ok( defined &Animal::speak, 'Animal::speak is defined' );
ok( defined &Animal::sound, 'Animal::sound is defined' );

# check that sound() dies
eval { Animal->sound() } or my $at = $@;
like( $at, qr/You must/, 'sound() dies with a message' );

# check that speak() dies too
eval { Animal->speak() } or my $at = $@;
```

```
like( $at, qr/You must/, 'speak() dies with a message' );

{
  package Foofle;
  use parent qw(Animal);
  sub sound { 'foof' }
}

ok( Foofle->speak, 'An Animal subclass does the right thing' );
```

Exercise 3

We need to make test programs for Cow, Horse, and Sheep, but we start by testing only
the sound method. Here's what it looks like for *t/Horse.t*:

```
use Test::More;

BEGIN { use_ok( 'Horse' ) }

is( Horse->sound, 'neigh', 'The horse make the right sound' );

done_testing();
```

The other test files just swap out the animal and the sound it makes.

Exercise 4

In the previous exercises, we created the test files:

```
% ./Build testcover
```

After the tests, we get the results:

```
% cover
```

Exercise 5

We're not going to show you the code. The trick to this exercise is the HTML report
that *cover* creates. Use that to see what you need to test:

```
% ./Build testcover
% cover
% open cover_db/coverage.html
```

That *open* might not be available on our system (although it is because we use Mac
OS X). Our favorite browser might have installed another program, or we can open
that file through our web browser's GUI. When we update the code or tests, we rerun
the process:

```
% ./Build testcover
% cover
% open cover_db/coverage.html
```

Although it seems like this is a lot of work, we're really spending some time upfront to save much more time later.

Answer for Chapter 15

Exercise 1

First, we start the `Animal` package. Our named method checks that it got a string argument; we want to restrict that to a class method. We expect a name argument, and use `default_color` to set the initial color:

```
package Animal;
use Carp qw(croak);

sub named {
  ref(my $class = shift) and croak "class name needed";
  my $name = shift;
  my $self = { Name => $name, Color => $class->default_color };
  bless $self, $class;
}

## backstops (should be overridden)
sub default_color { "brown" }
sub sound { croak "subclass must define a sound" }
```

Next we define the methods that work with either a class or an instance:

```
sub speak {
  my $either = shift;
  print $either->name, " goes ", $either->sound, "\n";
}

sub name {
  my $either = shift;
  ref $either
    ? $either->{Name}
    : "an unnamed $either";
}

sub color {
  my $either = shift;
  ref $either
    ? $either->{Color}
    : $either->default_color;
}
```

Finally, we add some methods that work only for the particular instance. If the first argument isn't a reference, it's not an instance, so we croak:

```
sub set_name {
  ref(my $self = shift) or croak "instance variable needed";
  $self->{Name} = shift;
}
```

```
sub set_color {
  ref(my $self = shift) or croak "instance variable needed";
  $self->{Color} = shift;
}
```

Our concrete classes, including Horse, stay the same. We have hardly any code in them at all. We create *scripts/mr_ed.pl* to test our changes:

```
my $tv_horse = Horse->named("Mr. Ed");
$tv_horse->set_name("Mister Ed");
$tv_horse->set_color("grey");
print $tv_horse->name, " is ", $tv_horse->color, "\n";
print Sheep->name, " colored ", Sheep->color, " goes ", Sheep->sound, "\n";
```

Answers for Chapter 16

Exercise 1

There a couple of ways to tackle this problem. In our solution, we created a MyDate package in the same file as the script. The naked block defines the scope of the package MyDate statement. Later, in our script, we can't use the module because Perl won't find a file for it. We'll have to remember to call the import method to get the symbols into our main namespace.

To make the AUTOLOAD subroutine work only for the right subroutines, we defined %Allowed_methods to hold the names of the methods that will work. Their values are their offsets in the list we get back from localtime. That almost solves it, but localtime uses 0–based numbers for the month and year. In the @Offsets array, we store the number to add to the corresponding entry in the localtime list. It seems like a lot of work now since only two values have offsets, but doing it this way eliminates two special cases.

We need a new method (or some constructor) to give us an object. In this example, it doesn't really matter what the object actually looks like. We use an empty, anonymous hash blessed into the current package (that's the first thing in the argument list, so it's $_[0]). We also know that we'll need a DESTROY method since Perl will automatically look for it when it tries to clean up the object. If we don't have it, our AUTOLOAD will complain about an unknown method when it tries to handle DESTROY on its own (comment out the DESTROY to see what happens).

Inside the AUTOLOAD, we store the method name in $method so we can change it. We want to strip off the package information and get the unqualified method name. That's everything after the last ::, so we use the substitution operator to get rid of everything up to that point. Once we have the method name, we look for its key in %Allowed_methods. If it's not there, we print an error with carp. Try calling an unknown method. For which line does Perl report the error?

If we find the method name in %Allowed_methods, we get the value, which is the position of the value in the localtime list. We store that in $slice_index and use it to get the value from localtime as well as the offset for that value. We add those two values together and return the result.

That sounds like a lot of work, but how much work would we have to do to add new methods for the hour and minute? We simply add those names to %Allowed_methods. Everything else already works:

```
{
  package MyDate;
  use vars qw($AUTOLOAD);

  use Carp;

  my %Allowed_methods = qw( date 3 month 4 year 5 );
  my @Offsets         = qw(0 0 0 0 1 1900 0 0 0);

  sub new       { bless {}, $_[0] }
  sub DESTROY   {}

  sub AUTOLOAD {
    my $method = $AUTOLOAD;
    $method =~ s/.*:://;

    unless( exists $Allowed_methods{ $method } ) {
      carp "Unknown method: $AUTOLOAD";
      return;
    }

    my $slice_index = $Allowed_methods{ $method };

    return (localtime)[$slice_index] + $Offsets[$slice_index];
    }
  }

MyDate->import;  # we don't use it
my $date = MyDate->new();

print "The date is "  . $date->date  . "\n";
print "The month is " . $date->month . "\n";
print "The year is "  . $date->year  . "\n";
```

Exercise 2

Our script looks the same as the previous answer with the addition of the UNIVERSAL::debug routine. At the end of our script we call the debug method on our $date object. It works without changing the MyDate module:

```
use MyDate;
my $date = MyDate->new();

sub UNIVERSAL::debug {
```

```
      my $self = shift;
      my $when = localtime;
      my $message = join '|', @_;
      print "[$when] $message\n";
    }

    print "The date is "  . $date->date  . "\n";
    print "The month is " . $date->month . "\n";
    print "The year is "  . $date->year  . "\n";

    $date->debug( "I'm all done" );
```

Why didn't the debug method make the AUTOLOAD carp? Remember that Perl searches through all of @ISA and UNIVERSAL before it starts looking in any AUTOLOAD method. So, Perl finds UNIVERSAL::debug before it has to use our AUTOLOAD magic.

Answers for Chapter 17

Exercise 1

The module *Oogaboogoo/Date.pm* looks like this:

```
    package Oogaboogoo::Date;
    use strict;
    use Exporter qw(import);
    our @EXPORT = qw(day mon);

    my @day = qw(ark dip wap sen pop sep kir);
    my @mon = qw(diz pod bod rod sip wax lin sen kun fiz nap dep);

    sub day {
      my $num = shift @_;
      die "$num is not a valid day number"
        unless $num >= 0 and $num <= 6;
      $day[$num];
    }

    sub mon {
      my $num = shift @_;
      die "$num is not a valid month number"
        unless $num >= 0 and $num <= 11;
      $mon[$num];
    }

    1;
```

Our program now looks like this:

```
    use strict;
    use Oogaboogoo::Date qw(day mon);

    my($sec, $min, $hour, $mday, $mon, $year, $wday) = localtime;
    my $day_name = day($wday);
```

```
my $mon_name = mon($mon);
$year += 1900;
print "Today is $day_name, $mon_name $mday, $year.\n";
```

Exercise 2

Most of this answer is the same as the previous answer. We just need to add the parts for the export tag "all":

```
our @EXPORT = qw(day mon);
our %EXPORT_TAGS = ( all => \@EXPORT );
```

Everything that we put in %EXPORT_TAGS has to also be in either @EXPORT or @EXPORT_OK. For the all tag, we use a reference to @EXPORT directly. If we don't like that, we can make a fresh copy so the two do not reference each other:

```
our @EXPORT = qw(day mon);
our %EXPORT_TAGS = ( all => [ @EXPORT ] );
```

We modify the program from the previous exercise to use the import tag all by prefacing it with a colon in the import list. The main program now looks like this:

```
use strict;
use Oogaboogoo::Date qw(:all);
```

Exercise 3

Our changes to My::List::Util are easy. To export the subroutines, we add these two lines:

```
use Exporter qw(import);
our @EXPORT = qw(sum shuffle);
```

In our t/sum.t test, we don't need to put My::List::Util in front of every call to sum, so our code is easier to read:

```
use Test::More;

BEGIN { use_ok( 'My::List::Util' ) }

ok( defined &sum, 'sum() is exported' );
is( sum( 1, 2, 3 ), 6, '1+2+3 is six' );
is( sum( qw(1 2 3) ), 6, '1+2+3 as strings is six' );
is( sum( 4, -9, 37, 6 ), 38, '4-9+37+6 is 38' );
is( sum( 3.14, 2.2 ), 5.34, '3.14 + 2.2 is 5.34' );
is( sum(), undef, 'No arguments returns undef' );
is( sum( qw(a b) ), undef, 'All bad args gives undef' );
is( sum( qw(a b 4 5) ), 9, 'Some good args works' );

done_testing();
```

Answers for Chapter 18

Exercise 1

First, we start our RaceHorse class by inheriting from Horse:

```
package RaceHorse;
use parent qw(Horse);
```

Next, we use a simple dbmopen to associate %STANDINGS with permanent storage:

```
dbmopen (our %STANDINGS, "standings", 0666)
  or die "Cannot access standings dbm: $!";
```

When we name a new RaceHorse, we either pull the existing standings from the database or invent zeroes for everything:

```
sub named { # class method
  my $self = shift->SUPER::named(@_);
  my $name = $self->name;
  my @standings = split ' ', $STANDINGS{$name} || "0 0 0 0";
  @$self{qw(wins places shows losses)} = @standings;
  $self;
}
```

When we destroy the RaceHorse, we update the standings to flush to disk the stuff we stored in memory in the object:

```
sub DESTROY { # instance method, automatically invoked
  my $self = shift;
  $STANDINGS{$self->name} = "@$self{qw(wins places shows losses)}";
  $self->SUPER::DESTROY if $self->can( 'SUPER::DESTROY' );
}
```

Finally, we define the instance methods to increment the values:

```
## instance methods:
sub won { shift->{wins}++; }
sub placed { shift->{places}++; }
sub showed { shift->{shows}++; }
sub lost { shift->{losses}++; }
sub standings {
  my $self = shift;
  join ", ", map "$self->{$_} $_", qw(wins places shows losses);
}
```

Answers for Chapter 19

Exercise 1

We're not going to show the entire distribution, but you can get the whole thing from the Downloads section at *http://www.intermediateperl.com/*.

We start by creating our distribution with the modules that we need:

```
% module-starter --module=Animal,Horse,Cow,Sheep,Mouse
```

When we have our module stubs, we transplant the code from Chapter 19 into the module files. Our base Animal class looks like this, after we remove the Pod (which we did update):

```
package Animal;
use strict;
use warnings;

use Moose;
use namespace::autoclean;

our $VERSION = '0.01';

has 'name'  => ( is => 'rw' );
has 'color' => ( is => 'rw' );
has 'sound' => ( is => 'ro', default => sub { 'Grrrr!' } );

sub speak {
  my $self = shift;
  print $self->name, " goes ", $self->sound, "\n";
}

__PACKAGE__->meta->make_immutable;

1;
```

The Horse class uses extends to inherit from Animal:

```
package Horse;
use strict;
use warnings;

use Moose;
use namespace::autoclean;

extends 'Animal';

has 'sound' => ( is => 'ro', default => 'neigh' );

__PACKAGE__->meta->make_immutable;

1;
```

The Cow and Sheep classes do the same thing, but with their particular sounds. The Mouse class is slightly different:

```
package Mouse;
use strict;
use warnings;

use Moose;
use namespace::autoclean;
```

```
extends 'Animal';

has 'sound' => ( is => 'ro', default => 'squeak' );

after 'speak' => sub {
  print "[but you can barely hear it!]\n";
};

__PACKAGE__->meta->make_immutable;

1;
```

The tests for each class look similar. Here's one for Horse that we put in *t/horse.t*:

```
use Test::More;
use strict;
use warnings;

BEGIN { use_ok( 'Horse' ) }

can_ok( 'Horse', qw(new sound color name speak) );

my $horse = Horse->new( name => 'Mr. Ed' );
isa_ok( $horse, 'Horse' );
is( $horse->name, 'Mr. Ed', 'Got the name right' );

done_testing();
```

We perform similar tests for *t/cow.t*, *t/sheep.t*, and *t/mouse.t*.

Exercise 2

In the previous exercise, our animals inherited from Animal. Now we want to make Animal a role instead. This is the same code we had in Chapter 19. It's shorter than our nonrole class because we don't supply a sound and don't have to define a default:

```
package Animal;
use Moose::Role;

requires qw( sound );

has 'name'  => ( is => 'rw' );
has 'color' => ( is => 'rw' );


sub speak {
  my $self = shift;
  print $self->name, " goes ", $self->sound, "\n";
}

1;
```

Our Horse class uses with instead of extends:

```
package Horse;
use strict;
use warnings;

use Moose;
use namespace::autoclean;

with 'Animal';

sub sound { 'neigh' }

__PACKAGE__->meta->make_immutable;

1;
```

Our *t/animal.t* test has to change a little because we can't create a new Animal; it's just a role. We'll just get rid of *t/animal.t* for now since we haven't shown how to test roles.

Answers for Chapter 20

Exercise 1

We install the Test::File if we don't already have it:

```
% cpan -I Test::File
```

We check the documentation to see what subroutines it offers and find file_exists_ok and file_readable_ok. We want to check for one of two files, so we put SKIP blocks around the two groups, and skip them if they are or are not Windows:

```
use Test::More;
use Test::File;

my $unix_file    = '/etc/hosts';
my $windows_file = 'C:\\windows\\system32\\drivers\\etc\\hosts';

SKIP: {
  skip q(We're not on Windows), 1 unless $^O eq 'MSWin32';
  file_exists_ok( $windows_file );
  file_readable_ok( $windows_file );
}


SKIP: {
  skip q(We're not on Unix), 1 unless $^O ne 'MSWin32';
  file_exists_ok( $unix_file );
  file_readable_ok( $unix_file );
}

done_testing();
```

If we weren't demonstrating the SKIP block, we would only run the tests once but use $^0 to choose the file to test:

```
use Test::More;
use Test::File;

my $file = $^0 eq 'MSWin32' ?
  'C:\\windows\\system32\\drivers\\etc\\hosts'
    :
  '/etc/hosts.txt';

file_exists_ok( $file );
file_readable_ok( $file );

done_testing();
```

Exercise 2

Using the example for the Test::Minnow::RequiredItems in Chapter 20, we create a sum_ok subroutine that uses a Test::Builder object to handle the test result. Without its documentation, Test::My::List::Util looks like this:

```
package Test::My::List::Util;
use strict;
use warnings;

use v5.10;

use Exporter qw(import);
use Test::Builder;

my $Test = Test::Builder->new();

our $VERSION = '0.10';
our @EXPORT  = qw(sum_ok);

sub sum_ok {
  my( $got, $expected, $label ) = @_;
  $label //=  "The sum is $expected";

  if( $got eq $expected ) {
    $Test->ok( 1, $label );
  }
  else {
    $Test->diag("The sums do not match. Got $got, expected $expected");
    $Test->ok( 0, $label );
  }
}

1;
```

Now we use our new module in a test program:

```
use Test::More;
```

```
BEGIN { use_ok( 'Test::My::List::Util' ) }
BEGIN { use_ok( 'My::List::Util' ) }

ok( defined &sum, 'sum() is exported' );
ok( defined &sum_ok, 'sum_ok() is exported' );

sum_ok( sum( 1, 2, 3 ), 6, '1+2+3 is 6' );

done_testing();
```

Answers for Chapter 21

Exercise 1

Go to *https://pause.perl.org/* and follow the "Request PAUSE account" link. Fill out the info, send off the form, and wait. That last part, the waiting, is why we told you to do this in the exercises for Chapter 1.

Exercise 2

Once we have our Animal distribution, we test it:

```
% ./Build disttest
```

If all of that passes, we should build the distribution:

```
% ./Build dist
```

That's it. We're not doing anything else with Animal after this exercise.

Exercise 3

We start by creating a new distribution based on our PAUSE name:

```
% module-starter --module=Acme::GILLIGAN::Utils
```

We change into that directory to begin our work:

```
% cd Acme-GILLIGAN-Utils
```

We check that all of our tests pass. We haven't done anything yet, but we want to start from a good place:

```
% ./Build test
t/00-load.t ....... ok
t/boilerplate.t ... ok
t/manifest.t ...... skipped: Author tests not required
t/pod-coverage.t .. ok
t/pod.t ........... ok
All tests successful.
Files=5, Tests=6,  0 wallclock secs ( ... )
Result: PASS
```

In our new distribution, we have a *lib/Acme/GILLIGAN/Utils.pm*. We need to add our sum subroutine to that. It doesn't matter how we actually implement that, but whatever we do gets documentation:

```
=head2 sum( LIST )

Numerically sums the argument list and returns the result.

=cut

sub sum {
  my $sum;
  foreach ( @_ ) { $sum += $_ }
  return $sum;
}
```

We test again, and everything should pass. If we skipped the documentation, our *t/pod-coverage.t* test would fail.

Now that we have a new subroutine in our module, we should test it. Here's a simple test that we put in *t/sum.t*. We test that we can load the module and that our subroutine is defined. It would be really annoying to keep fixing our code to find out later we had the wrong subroutine name (it's happened more than we want to admit). After that, we test the sum of the numbers from 1 to 10. That's a test that takes good input and expects good output. We also test bad input in `@weird_list`, in which we have non-numbers in the list. What happens then?

```
use Test::More tests => 4;

use_ok( 'Acme::GILLIGAN::Utils' );
ok( defined &Acme::GILLIGAN::Utils::sum, 'sum() is defined' );

my @good_list = 1 .. 10;
is( Acme::GILLIGAN::Utils::sum( @good_list), 55,
  'The sum of 1 to 10 is 55' );

my @weird_list = qw( a b c 1 2 3 123abc );
is( Acme::GILLIGAN::Utils::sum( @weird_list), 129,
  'The weird sum is 129' );
```

When we run the tests, we get warnings about the weird elements:

```
% ./Build test
t/00-load.t ....... ok
t/boilerplate.t ... ok
t/manifest.t ...... skipped: Author tests not required
t/pod-coverage.t .. ok
t/pod.t ........... ok
t/sum.t ........... 1/2 Argument "a" isn't numeric ...
Argument "b" isn't numeric ...
Argument "c" isn't numeric ...
Argument "123abc" isn't numeric ...
t/sum.t ........... Dubious, test returned 255 (wstat 65280, 0xff00)
All 2 subtests passed
```

```
Test Summary Report
-------------------
t/sum.t          (Wstat: 65280 Tests: 4 Failed: 2)
  Failed tests:  3-4
  Non-zero exit status: 255
Files=6, Tests=10,  1 wallclock secs ( ... )
Result: FAIL
Failed 1/6 test programs. 2/10 subtests failed.
```

How do we want to handle those? We could leave them there so the programmer knows that he or she did something wrong. We could also ignore them:

```
sub sum {
  no warnings 'numeric';
  my $sum;
  foreach ( @_ ) { $sum += $_ }
  return $sum;
}
```

If we want to ensure that we've squashed all the warnings, we could use Test::NoWarnings (although we did not expect that in your answer):

```
use Test::More tests => 5;
use Test::NoWarnings;

use_ok( 'Acme::GILLIGAN::Utils' );
ok( defined &Acme::GILLIGAN::Utils::sum, 'sum() is defined' );

my @good_list = 1 .. 10;
is( Acme::GILLIGAN::Utils::sum( @good_list), 55,
  'The sum of 1 to 10 is 55' );

my @weird_list = qw( a b c 1 2 3 123abc );
is( Acme::GILLIGAN::Utils::sum( @weird_list), 129,
  'The weird sum is 129' );
```

Now when we run the tests, nothing seems amiss:

```
% ./Build test
t/00-load.t ....... ok
t/boilerplate.t ... ok
t/manifest.t ...... skipped: Author tests not required
t/pod-coverage.t .. ok
t/pod.t ........... ok
t/sum.t ........... ok
All tests successful.
Files=6, Tests=11,  0 wallclock secs ( ... )
Result: PASS
```

Everything works. It's time to upload it to PAUSE. We update our manifest to include our *t/sum.t*:

```
% ./Build manifest
Added to MANIFEST: t/sum.t
```

We test the distribution, and when it passes, we create the archive:

```
% ./Build disttest
% ./Build dist
```

It's ready to upload. We log into our PAUSE account and follow the link for "Upload a file to CPAN." From there, we follow the instructions and release our code. In less than an hour, and most likely much faster, we should be able to find our new distribution on *https://www.metacpan.org/*.

If that was your first CPAN release, congratulations!

Exercise 4

For this exercise, we are going to break our distribution. First, we update the version number in *lib/Acme/GILLIGAN/Utils.pm* so we can upload and index a new distribution archive:

```
our $VERSION = '0.02';
```

We're going to break our distribution by adding a namespace that's controlled by someone else. We suggested `Tie::Cycle`, controlled by `BDFOY` (one of the authors of this book, so it's okay!). We add a module:

```
% module-starter --module=Tie::Cycle --dist=
```

We now have a *lib/Tie/Cycle.pm* file. Although *module-starter* already updated *MANIFEST* for us, we can double check:

```
% ./Build manifest
```

From there, we create a new archive as we did before:

```
% ./Build disttest
% ./Build dist
```

We upload the file to PAUSE. When PAUSE tries to index, our new archive, it will fail on `Tie::Cycle`. Our module will still go into CPAN, but it won't be indexed and PAUSE will send us an email explaining what went wrong.

Exercise 5

This exercise is another sort of failure, but this time with CPAN Testers. We need to remove the *lib/Tie/Cycle.pm* file if it is still there.

We change the code in `sum` to multiply instead:

```
sub sum {
  my $sum;
  foreach ( @_ ) { $sum *= $_ }
  return $sum;
}
```

We want the tests to fail, so we should ensure they do:

```
% ./Build test
```

We won't show you the failure output. We build a new archive and upload it to PAUSE.

When our distribution reaches CPAN, the CPAN Testers volunteers will start downloading and testing it. Since it fails, we should get an email about that.

Exercise 6

When we look at the distribution page in MetaCPAN, we should see the Testers's results. Looking at CPAN Testers Matrix, we should also now see a matrix report that shows that we have one version that passes and one that doesn't. There's not much to this answer. Go to *https://www.metacpan.org/* to find our page. Explore.

You can also explore the pages for other modules you like.

Exercise 7

With our distribution on CPAN, we should be able to install it with a CPAN client:

```
% cpan -I Acme::GILLIGAN::Utils
```

If we follow the procedure in these examples, we left off with a failing distribution. We should fix the distribution, reupload, and try again later.

Having successfully installed the module, we have gone through the entire process. Congratulations again!

Index of Modules in this Book

We'd like to hear your suggestions for improving our indexes. Send email to *index@oreilly.com*.

Index

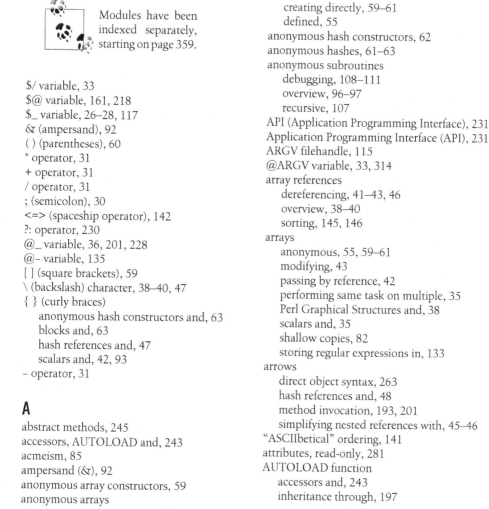

Modules have been indexed separately, starting on page 359.

We'd like to hear your suggestions for improving our indexes. Send email to *index@oreilly.com*.

About the Authors

Randal L. Schwartz is a renowned expert on the Perl programming language. In addition to writing *Learning Perl* and the first two editions of *Programming Perl*, he has been the Perl columnist for *UNIX Review*, *Web Techniques*, *Sys Admin*, and *Linux Magazine*. He has contributed to a dozen Perl books and over 200 magazine articles. Randal runs a Perl training and consulting company (Stonehenge Consulting Services) and is highly sought after as a speaker for his combination of technical skill, comedic timing, and crowd rapport. He's also a pretty good karaoke singer.

brian d foy has been an instructor for Stonehenge Consulting Services since 1998, a Perl user since he was a physics graduate student, and a die-hard Mac user since he first owned a computer. He founded the first Perl user group, the New York Perl Mongers, as well as the Perl advocacy nonprofit Perl Mongers, Inc., which helped form more than 200 Perl user groups across the globe. He maintains the perlfaq portions of the core Perl documentation, several modules on CPAN, and some standalone scripts. He's the publisher of *The Perl Review*, a magazine devoted to Perl, and is a frequent speaker at conferences including the Perl Conference, Perl University, MarcusEvans BioInformatics '02, and YAPC. His writings on Perl appear in *The O'Reilly Network*, *The Perl Journal*, *Dr. Dobbs*, and *The Perl Review*, on *use.perl.org*, and in several Perl usenet groups.

Tom Phoenix has been working in the field of education since 1982. After more than 13 years of dissections, explosions, working with interesting animals, and high-voltage sparks during his work at a science museum, he started teaching Perl classes for Stonehenge Consulting Services, where he's worked since 1996. Since then, he has traveled to many interesting locations, so you might see him soon at a Perl Mongers' meeting. When he has time, he answers questions on Usenet's comp.lang.perl.misc and comp.lang.perl.moderated newsgroups, and contributes to the development and usefulness of Perl. Besides his work with Perl, Perl hackers, and related topics, Tom spends his time on amateur cryptography and speaking Esperanto. His home is in Portland, Oregon.

Colophon

The animal on the cover of *Intermediate Perl* is an alpaca (*Lama pacos*). The alpaca is a member of the South American camelid family, which is closely related to the more familiar Asian and African camels. South American camelids also include the llama, the vicuna, and the guanaco. The alpaca is smaller (36 inches at the withers) than a llama, but larger than its other relations. Ninety-nine percent of the world's approximately 3 million alpacas are found in Peru, Bolivia, and Chile.

The evolution of the wild vicuna into the domestic alpaca began between 6,000 and 7,000 years ago. The specialized breeding of alpacas for fiber production wasn't developed until around 500 B.C. The Incas developed the alpaca into the two distinct fleece types, the Huacaya (pronounced wa-kai-ya) and the less common Suri. The main difference between the two types of alpacas is the fiber they produce. The Huacaya fleece has crimp or wave; the Suri fleece is silky and lustrous, and has no crimp. Alpacas are prized for their fleece, which is as soft as cashmere and warmer, lighter, and stronger than wool. Alpaca fleece comes in more colors than that of any other fiber-producing animal (approximately 22 basic colors with many variations and blends).

The lifespan of the alpaca is about 20 years. Gestation is 11.5 months, producing one offspring, or cria, every 14 to 15 months. The alpaca is a modified ruminant, not only eating less grass than most other animals but converting it to energy very efficiently. Unlike true ruminants, they have three compartments in their stomach, not four, and can thus survive in areas unsuitable to other domesticated animals. Alpacas are gentle and don't bite or butt. Even if they did, without incisors, horns, hoofs, or claws, they would do little damage.

The cover image is a 19th-century engraving from *Animate Creations*, Volume II. The cover font is Adobe ITC Garamond. The text font is Linotype Birka, the heading font is Adobe Myriad Condensed, and the code font is LucasFont's TheSansMonoCondensed.